CASEBOOK SERI[ES]

GENERAL EDITOR: A.

PUBLISHED

Shakespeare: *Othello* JOHN WAIN
Shakespeare: *Richard II* NICHOLAS BROOKE
Shakespeare: *The Tempest* D. J. PALMER
Shakespeare: *Troilus and Cressida* PRISCILLA MARTIN
Shakespeare: *Twelfth Night* D. J. PALMER
Shakespeare: *The Winter's Tale* KENNETH MUIR
Shelley: *Shorter Poems and Lyrics* PATRICK SWINDEN
Spenser: *The Faerie Queene* PETER BAYLEY
Swift: *Gulliver's Travels* RICHARD GRAVIL
Tennyson: *In Memoriam* JOHN DIXON HUNT
Webster: *'The White Devil' and 'The Duchess of Malfi'*
R. V. HOLDSWORTH
Virginia Woolf: *To the Lighthouse* MORRIS BEJA
Wordsworth: *Lyrical Ballads* ALUN R. JONES AND WILLIAM
TYDEMAN
Wordsworth: *The Prelude* W. J. HARVEY AND RICHARD GRAVIL
Yeats: *Last Poems* JON STALLWORTHY

TITLES IN PREPARATION INCLUDE

George Eliot: *'The Mill on the Floss' and 'Silas Marner'* R. P. DRAPER
T. S. Eliot: *'Prufrock', 'Gerontion', 'Ash Wednesday' and Other Shorter Poems*
B. C. SOUTHAM
Farquhar: *'The Beaux' Stratagem' and 'The Recruiting Officer'* RAY
ANSELMENT
Jonson: *'Every Man in His Humour' and 'The Alchemist'*
R. V. HOLDSWORTH
Shakespeare: *Coriolanus* B. A. BROCKMAN
Shakespeare: *'Much Ado about Nothing' and 'As You Like It'*
JENNIFER SEARLE
Shakespeare: *Sonnets* PETER JONES
Sheridan: *'The Rivals', 'The School for Scandal' and 'The Critic'*
WILLIAM RUDDICK
Thackeray: *Vanity Fair* ARTHUR POLLARD

*The Evolution of Novel Criticism* STEPHEN HAZELL
*The Romantic Imagination* JOHN S. HILL

# Peacock

## *The Satirical Novels*

### A CASEBOOK

### EDITED BY

### LORNA SAGE

*First published 1976 by*
THE MACMILLAN PRESS LTD
*London and Basingstoke*
*Associated companies in New York Dublin*
*Melbourne Johannesburg and Madras*

ISBN 0 333 18410 6 (hard cover)
     0 333 18411 4 (paper cover)

*Printed in Great Britain by*
THE ANCHOR PRESS LTD
*Tiptree, Essex*

# CONTENTS

Part Three: *Twentieth-century Interpretations*

# ACKNOWLEDGEMENTS

The editor and publishers wish to thank the following who have kindly given permission for the use of copyright material: Carl Dawson, extract from *His Fine Wit*, 1970, by permission of Routledge & Kegan Paul Ltd. John W. Draper, 'The Social Satires of Thomas Love Peacock', from *Modern Language Notes*, Vol. xxiii (December 1918), by permission of the author and The Johns Hopkins University Press. A. E. Dyson, extract from *The Crazy Fabric*, 1965, by permission of the author. Northrop Frye, extract from *The Anatomy of Criticism: Four Essays*; copyright 1957 by Princeton University Press (Princeton Paperback 1971), reprinted by permission of the publisher. Aldous Huxley, extract from *Point Counter Point*, 1928, by permission of Mrs Laura Huxley and Chatto and Windus Ltd. Lionel Madden, extract from *Thomas Love Peacock*, 1967, by permission of Evans Brothers (Books) Limited. Jean-Jacques Mayoux, extracts from *Un Epicurien Anglais: Thomas Love Peacock*, 1932, by permission of the author. Howard Mills, extract from *Peacock, His Circle and His Age*, 1968, by permission of the author and Cambridge University Press. Mario Praz, extract from *The Hero in Eclipse in Victorian Fiction*, 1956, by permission of Oxford University Press. J. B. Priestley, extracts from *Thomas Love Peacock*, 1927, by permission of A. D. Peters & Co. Carl Van Doren, extracts from *The Life of Thomas Love Peacock*, 1911, by permission of J. M. Dent & Sons Ltd. Virginia Woolf, extract from *Granite and Rainbow* by permission of the author's Literary Estate and The Hogarth Press. The publishers have made every effort to trace the copyright-holders but if they have inadvertently overlooked any they will be pleased to make the necessary arrangement at the first opportunity.

# GENERAL EDITOR'S PREFACE

Each of this series of Casebooks concerns either one well-known and influential work of literature or two or three closely linked works. The main section consists of critical readings, mostly modern, brought together from journals and books. A selection of reviews and comments by the author's contemporaries is also included, and sometimes comments from the author himself. The Editor's Introduction charts the reputation of the work from its first appearance until the present time.

The critical forum is a place of vigorous conflict and disagreement, but there is nothing in this to cause dismay. What is attested is the complexity of human experience and the richness of literature, not any chaos or relativity of taste. A critic is better seen, no doubt, as an explorer than as an 'authority', but explorers ought to be, and usually are, well equipped. The effect of good criticism is to convince us of what C. S. Lewis called 'the enormous extension of our being which we owe to authors'. A Casebook will be justified if it helps to promote the same end.

A single volume can represent no more than a small selection of critical opinions. Some critics have been excluded for reasons of space, and it is hoped that readers will follow up the further suggestions in the Select Bibliography. Other contributions have been severed from their original context, to which some readers may wish to return. Indeed, if they take a hint from the critics represented here, they certainly will.

A. E. DYSON

# INTRODUCTION

The kind of satirical fiction Peacock writes presents a special challenge to criticism because, as well as creating a shorthand (and, to that degree, cryptic) portrait of an age, it is further designed to put the reader himself on the spot. His whole fictional method partakes of the restless and risky mental life of the period of revolution and counter-revolution from 1789 to 1830 – a time of unprecedented intellectual free-enterprise when schemes of all kinds, from vegetarianism to phrenology to rights for women, were briefly and simultaneously on the market. In that 'age of transition' (John Stuart Mill's phrase) feelings and thoughts were precipitated into talk, and talk into print, with a new rapidity and impatience, and Peacock's characters reflect the change of pace. We see them in one or two aspects only, as conscious, overarticulate beings; they are roles, in fact, rather than characters, like parts in a script waiting to be given three dimensions by the actor who takes them on. We, as readers, must supply them in imagination with most of those parts of life that are *not* translatable into speeches; public postures and arguments.

From this point of view (and looking at Peacock from the perspective of the present) our first need is to identify the cast in each novel with their flesh-and-blood originals amongst his contemporaries. A great deal of the pleasure and profit of studying his fiction lies in the sharp, humorous focus he gives to the many forms of the spirit of the age – not by eavesdropping on private lives (except perhaps in the case of Shelley) but by anatomising public images. He is not at all esoteric or sly, and there has never been any significant critical disagreement about who his targets are, though there has been much anxious discussion of his right to be so irreverent about them. Thus, though he needs footnotes, they are footnotes that lead back to the excitement and insecurity of a generation that experimented with life, and are very much

worth pursuing. What makes him a truly difficult writer is not
his material, but his attitude to it, his mischievous refusal to
guide his readers through this maze of conflicting styles of
thought : his refusal to contain, judge or place his people's ob-
sessive, incompatible ideas. He pays them all the dubious compliment of mockery, and makes mediation or synthesis amongst them
seem impossible. And the result is that we are forced, for the
moment, into a very uncomfortable state of scepticism, an awareness of the ease with which Reason becomes the tool of Prejudice, and 'dialogue' serves to isolate each participant even further
in his own lonely conviction.

Peacock's irony (unlike Jane Austen's, at least in the conventional account of her) is open-ended. You can never be sure of
getting on the right side of it, since, as he says, in his one reluctant
Preface to his novels, 'I left them to speak for themselves.' This
makes him an anomaly in a climate of vociferous commitment :
a literary personality at once highly individual and yet somehow
anonymous. In his case the contemporary practice of reticence
about authorship which made him the nameless 'Author of
*Headlong Hall*' (as it made Scott 'the Author of *Waverley*')
was peculiarly apt. And his contemporaries found him as dis-
concerting and elusive as we do, in this respect. For although,
to take up Mill's phrase again, they were aware of living in 'an
age of transition', most of them thought of it as an interval between one period of consensus and another, and looked earnestly
for resolution, some new form of synthesis. Peacock attacked that
earnestness; he seemed bent on undermining his readers' confidence in their capacity to arrive at new truths, or even to choose
sensibly amongst the old. His lightness of touch by itself did real
damage to solemnity; 'his fine wit', as Shelley wrote, 'Makes such
a wound, the knife is lost in it'. From the earliest reviews onwards,
his critics have argued over the meaning and direction of his
mockery, seeing him as a secret Utilitarian, a disappointed
idealist, a reactionary, a prophet, an impossibly impersonal
joker. Only to the complacent has he seemed obvious.

Peacock's friendship with Shelley, which lasted from 1812 until
Shelley was drowned in Italy in 1822, was the most important

influence in shaping his sense of his role as a writer. When they met, Peacock was a cool, mildly meditative 'gentleman' poet without means, unserious and unfunny, self-educated and fashionably drifting. Swept into Shelley's hectic orbit, in the five years that followed he probably did more, met more people, thought more than in the whole of the rest of his long life. In 1813, for example, he visited Shelley at Bracknell and revelled in the numerous circle of cranks gathered there, insulated from the world, canvassing their opinions 'as matters of the greatest importance to mankind' over vegetarian dinners. These eager, absurd people, and especially their Zodiacal star J. F. Newton, seem to have coalesced with his reading in classical and French satire (of which he had made scant use in his writings before then) to issue two years later in his own special formula for comic fiction in *Headlong Hall.* In 1814, again, he was a fascinated but fairminded witness to Shelley's doomed, libertarian attempts to somehow combine his marriage to Harriet with his passionate new attachment to Mary Wollstonecraft Godwin – who so magically (and so suspiciously, to Peacock's ear) united the names of two of Shelley's philosophic mentors : the defender of the *Rights of Women* and the author of *Political Justice.* That episode, retold so many years later in his 'Memoirs of Shelley', was put to much more immediate use, as the germ of Scythrop's gloriously wretched dilemma in *Nightmare Abbey* (1818).

Even more telling than these ready-made events, however (and one should note that Peacock would have had to be super-humanly objective *not* to touch them up a little in his 'Memoirs'), was his experience of intermittent but intense dialogue with Shelley during the period from 1815 to 1817. The novel which reflects this interchange most directly is *Melincourt* (published in 1817, and omitted from the collection of his novels issued in 1837). In this book the areas of sympathy and near-agreement between Peacock and Shelley are in the foreground, represented (parodically but recognisably) in the unlikely, unstable alliance of Mr Fax and Mr Forester. In so far as these two are united, it is against abuses; each has his own very different schemes for what should replace them. However, on the slave trade, the subjection and trivialisation of woman, and reform of the franchise, they agree. And, notably, they also concur in the critical analysis of the political disillusionment of the earlier generation of Romantic writers (Wordsworth, Coleridge, Southey) and their retreat into mystificatory and repressive forms of imaginative toryism. Peacock makes Moly Mystic say (jumbling together quotations from Coleridge's *Lay Sermons*) :

The materials of political gloom will build the steadfast frame of hope. The main point is to get rid of analytical reason, which is experimental and practical, and live only by faith, which is synthetical and oracular. . . . But the spirit of Antichrist is abroad : – the people read ! – nay, they think ! !

At the same time, *Melincourt* shows signs of the danger of Shelley's influence for Peacock : the temptation into an enthusiasm and a high tone of outrage and self-righteousness he could not sustain. As James Spedding wryly observed in his *Edinburgh Review* article (page 72 below) : 'He began in joke, but he seems to have narrowly escaped ending in earnest.' In the event, the talk, the reading, the mutual education of 1815–17, were to prove most productive in helping both writers to sort out their vocations, not to blend them.

Their own dialogue was informed by a study of Greek literature, and especially Plato (of whom Peacock, seven years older and much better read, knew more than Shelley). But, while Shelley was to be profoundly persuaded by Plato's use of dialogue as a means of discriminating truth, Peacock cast himself in the role of the comic dramatist Aristophanes, whose parodic dialogue was a means of revealing bigotry and of destroying illusion. Something of the character and tone of their exchanges is still there in the confrontation of Peacock's 'Four Ages of Poetry' (1820) and Shelley's *In Defence of Poetry* (written in 1821), though of course on a grander scale, premeditated for print. The 'Four Ages' was clearly meant to elicit a response from Shelley in Italy; and it succeeded in this. Its ironic technique, as much as its argument, proved an irresistible challenge to Shelley.

What Peacock does is to impersonate a bigoted Utilitarian (revealed by catchphrases about 'the march of intellect' and 'the progress of reason') engaged in attacking the (equally bigoted) subjectivism and primitivism of contemporary Romantic poetry. In other words, he uses one prestigious intellectual position as a satiric norm against which to measure another, without committing himself to either. The advantage of this ploy is that it enables him to juggle several attitudes, and keep them all in the air. He can continue, and consolidate, his attack on the reactionary Romantics (the Lake Poets, for example, who shut themselves away to solve humanity's problems – not unlike Shelley's Bracknell circle). He can gleefully blaspheme against the sanctity of Poetry (already on its way to replacing religion in minds shaken by empirical science). He can point up the family resemblances among different forms of mystification and prejudice : the sort he is overtly attacking, and the sort he is exploding by impersonation. And, perhaps most important, he can demonstrate, by the pitfalls his irony creates for the reader, exactly how iconoclasts of the Utilitarian type run out of scepticism when it comes to analysing their own claims, and busily set about building new, improved castles in the air. This is the race of men that is to save the world from literature : 'mathematicians, historians, politicians, and political economists, who have built into the upper air of intelligence a pyramid, from the summit of which they see the modern Parnassus far beneath them . . .'.

With wicked precision, Peacock has caught the note of enthusiasm for progress just at the point where it modulates into insane arrogance. This mock-heroic climax should be compared with the list of his butts in his Preface of 1837 to the collected novels (see page 35 below), where 'political economists' and 'romantic enthusiasts' are lumped together as examples of the endemic egotism of the spirit of the age.

Shelley's *Defence* is equally in character : evocative, defiantly and most undefensively idealistic, treating 'imagination' not as a specialised faculty for producing works of art but as the creative principle that directs, or should direct, all merely technological or empirical skills. Where Peacock had used and parodied Utilitarian language, Shelley (typically) rescues and ennobles it, as he argues for a theory of Utility that will study the needs of the human psyche – 'true utility', 'the poetry of life'. For him

the use of poetry lies in discovering and symbolising the structure
of human thought, and thus providing the blueprints, as it were,
for social and political institutions. Against Gibbon, Voltaire,
Rousseau and Peacock's other favoured iconoclasts, Shelley sets
the great dramatists and myth-makers (Dante, Shakespeare,
Milton, Michelangelo) who outlined the potentialities of human
nature – constructive agents against destructive art. However,
for all this, he would agree with Peacock more than is at first
apparent. They both deplore the multiplication of specialised
sciences and sub-sciences, arts and sub-arts. They share the same
contempt for the notion that poetry should enshrine primitive,
superstitious responses or advocate a 'return' to nature. Where
they part company, decisively, is with Shelley's remark: 'But
whilst the sceptic destroys gross superstitions, let him spare to
deface, as some of the French writers have defaced, the eternal
truths charactered upon the imaginations of men.' Not that
Shelley believed in official Christianity any more than Peacock,
but he trusted man-made mythologies; whereas for Peacock the
distinctive function of art was to liberate men into scepticism
even about their own works.

His clearest statement of this view came years after Shelley's
death, in the essay on 'French Comic Romances', where he suggests that the long French literary tradition of robust mockery
(with which he feels at least as much at home as with Swift or
Fielding) played a significant part in preparing people's minds
for revolution, by tutoring them in doubt and irreverence.
Peacock takes care not to sound enthusiastic or assertive ('It
would be . . . an interesting and amusing inquiry'), and produces
an impressively long list of the new horrors and absurdities that
have succeeded the revolution in France (see page 33 below).
Nonetheless, it is a statement of faith, as near as he ever got to
claiming real value and power for his kind of writing. And even
here a final irony remains, for this is a statement of faith in *doubt*.
His last word on Shelley, in the 'Memoirs', strikes a similar note.
He says (as many of Shelley's critics say) that, if the poet had
lived longer, he would have become disillusioned. From most
quarters that would be a condescending observation, a judgement
on the immaturity of Shelley's ideals. But from Peacock it has a

different stress: for him *désillusionné* means, not humiliation, but achievement.

The first two substantial appraisals of Peacock appeared in the *Westminster Review* and the *Edinburgh Review*. This was not by coincidence for, as Hazlitt wrote in 1829,

There is a controversy at present raging with all the fury of ancient polemics between these two critical and philosophical journals respecting the *useful* and the *agreeable*. The *Westminster* contends that there is nothing useful but what is disagreeable, and exemplifies its doctrine in its mode of proving it . . . the *Edinburgh*, with better taste and manners, maintains that the agreeable forms part of the useful. . . .

In this context Peacock was eagerly read, and he provoked complicated responses – though for readers who relished novelistic realism, such as Henry Crabb Robinson (page 53 below), he seemed merely 'dull'. Hazlitt, being himself involved in the Utilitarian controversy, should have been well qualified to understand Peacock, but his description of the battle of the reviews suggests why he was not. For him, clearly, there is nothing to be said on one side, and everything on the other. And his own attempts at writing dialogues bear this out. He is incapable of impersonating a Rationalist with any conviction; and his irony is of the self-righteous kind, which is never turned on his own allies. Thus, misunderstanding the 'Four Ages of Poetry', and no doubt aware that Peacock by this time worked at East India House (and therefore associated with Bentham, James Mill and John Stuart Mill), Hazlitt assumes that he must be a thoroughgoing Utilitarian, and abuses him accordingly. Hazlitt's rather bland approval of the notion that 'the agreeable forms part of the useful' is a mere evasion compared with the quality of the argument between Peacock and Shelley, and his attitude foreshadows that depressing Victorian compromise whereby the real world was consigned to political economy, while art became a leisure-time activity. Leigh Hunt, though more appreciative of Peacock's capacity for 'the agreeable', assumes the same simple dichotomy.

The *Westminster* itself, however, in its 1831 review of *Crotchet Castle*, was more sensitive and more worried about its supposed ally. The basic embarrassment – and one which shows that Peacock has struck home – is that the reviewer *knows* that Peacock has 'liberal' opinions, and so finds the book not far removed from an act of treachery: 'It is a pity, that men are most inclined to satirise that of which they know the most. Juvenal, hot from the stews, Petronius Arbiter, fresh from the garden of Epicurus, in the first moments of re-action employed their genius upon the exposure of their partners in vice. . . .' He has got Peacock's classical antecedents more or less right, and thus places him in a literary sense. But he is still extremely uncomfortable: 'Political economy has enemies enough in the ranks of those who are ignorant of it; . . . weapons are now supplied from its own arsenal.' Though the *Westminster* reviewer does not take the next step, to argue that because political economy is ultimately good for us we should not question its logic or its local workings, he is clearly tempted to do so.

What has caused the trouble is Peacock's unravelling of Utilitarian thought, through the agency of Dr Folliott (himself addicted to quite other vices, and so clear-headed on this):

You have given the name of a science to what is yet an imperfect inquiry. . . . The greater the quantity of labour that has gone to the production of the quantity of things in a community, the richer is the community. That is your doctrine. . . . I say, the nation is best off . . . which has the greatest quantity of the common necessaries of life distributed among the greatest number of persons.

There is a further barb, of course, in giving a mere 'gormandiser' such a command of the language of Bentham. Peacock, one would think, could hardly have wished for a more revealing response than the *Westminster*'s complaint: 'he is a liberal in all his political opinions, and he attacks liberals only'. The reviewer feels so threatened here that he forgets the attacks on toryism and reaction, and with a curious twist of egotism takes his own school of thought as the sole victim. Later 'liberals', like George Barnett Smith in the *Fortnightly Review* (1873), became wadded in complacency and refused to see that Peacock was attacking *them*. Instead, they assumed that he must be aiming at a separate race of pseudo-utilitarians. But, as the *Westminster* reviewer recognised, the disturbing thing about Peacock was the way he showed the cant intimately entwined with the sense.

James Spedding, in the *Edinburgh Review* article of 1839, surveyed Peacock's whole achievement to date (that is, everything of note except *Gryll Grange*), and focused on what Hazlitt would have called 'the agreeable': the sheer fun and stylishness of the writing. He was, however, a much subtler critic (of Peacock, at least) than Hazlitt, and his essay remains one of the most perceptive, detailed and coherent accounts of the quality of Peacock's art. He sees him as a 'Court Jester' in modern dress: a self-appointed satirist whose technique was exactly adapted to the individualism of nineteenth-century culture, when 'Every man's peculiar set, creed, system, or party becomes a kind of court, in which he might live surrounded by the echoes of his own thoughts . . . as secure as kings were once from the intrusion of unwelcome censures.' Peacock uses that most private, individualistic and modern of literary forms, the novel, to enter the mental kingdom of each one of his readers, there to play the fool – in earnest. The specialised kind of fiction that results, Spedding points out, does not seek to *create* attitudes: 'The feast is ample and various, but every man must help and digest for himself. Indeed the very aim and idea . . . requires that it should be so. That the author should come before us, not as a teacher, but as a questioner of what others teach, is of the essence of his privilege.'

That 'privilege', the role of the licensed jester which Peacock plays so expertly, carries with it, for Spedding, equally clear limitations: there is something parasitical, something perverse, in the mind of a man who can be so disengaged. And he finds evidence for this view in his observation that Peacock delights to attack those values that are most widely and deeply held, and to defend those which are most remote and implausible. Peacock, in Spedding's careful assessment, is both the wielder and the victim of 'a scepticism truly impartial and insatiable'. The novels, certainly, show an internal development towards richer and more organic treatment of their targets, and exhibit a 'triumph of the

gentler nature' in the characterisation of their heroines. But
Peacock remains delightfully defined – and trapped – by his
chosen role: 'He dwells more habitually among doubts and
negations than we believe to be good for any man.'

This is an important and influential view of Peacock – the
more persuasive because Spedding obviously enjoys the novels
immensely. The central problem it raises concerns the quality of
Peacock's scepticism. Does it necessarily follow that he holds none
of the values he calls in question? Is 'the philosophy of incredulity
and irreverence' an anti-philosophy that is bound to erode the
mental integrity of its disciple? It is arguable that Peacock thought
that when even true opinions turn into assumptions, 'facts',
they become as dangerous as if they were false, and their pos-
sessors heretics in the truth. Put that way, the trap he was in –
his self-imposed limitation – looks rather different; he becomes
less of an outsider, an impartial mocker, more of a self-doubter.
Spedding's view of him, however, was supported by Peacock's
own style of life in the following years at East India House, and
in his retirement, when he seemed more and more the 'white-
headed, jolly old worldling' Thackeray met in 1850. This is the
image that the twentieth century inherited from the nineteenth,
based often less on his writing than on his character.

The conviviality that punctuates his books with dinner-parties
(so that they almost seem extended 'deliberative dinners') was
very much a feature of his life – though one might guess that
the diners agreed with each other as little as do the characters
in the novels. Grant Duff, who knew him in the 1850s, relates
an anecdote (page 76 below) which suggests that his humour in
later life was, if anything, tougher and nastier than ever. The
pleasures of food, wine and song (sometimes love comes into
this category too: in another century it certainly would have)
bring people together *without* resolving their obstinate intellectual obsessions, as he neatly demonstrates in *Crotchet Castle* :

SEVERAL VOICES : That is my scheme. I have not heard a
scheme but my own that has a grain of common sense.
MR TRILLO : Gentlemen, you inspire me. Your last exclama-
tion runs itself into a chorus, and sets itself to music. Allow me to
lead, and to hope for your voices in harmony.

After careful meditation,
And profound deliberation,
On the various pretty projects which have just been shown
Not a scheme in agitation,
For the world's amelioration,
Has a grain of common sense in it, except my own.

Mr Trillo fails, in fact, on this occasion, and the arguments go on. However, in the last novel, *Gryll Grange* (1860), the company is unmistakably more congenial, and the delights of living have ousted the fascination with ideas. Peacock's satire is now more generalised, though his Victorian targets are as wittily chosen as ever: spiritualism, automatic optimism about progress (better machines), prudery, competitive examinations. A measure of his relative mellowness, though, is that the company come together to put on their own comedy, 'Aristophanes in London' (in which the mighty dead are called up by spirit-rapping, only to be failed in competitive examinations). In no earlier novel would the cast have conspired together against 'the world' like this, and mocked it from outside. Peacock, as is observed in the 'Biographical Note' by his granddaughter Edith Nicolls, seemed at last to have found a philosophy to his taste. He had become an Epicurean, a deliberate connoisseur of the innocent, available pleasures of his garden, his library and his dining-room. As she describes his chosen way of life, it seems one of rational selfishness: the avoidance of pain, the cultivation of happiness. He never succumbed to the mystique of either progress or regress, and the small myths he played with (like the May-day celebration) were pleasing, pagan fictions.

This image of Peacock in his old age has its charm, but as taken up by Robert Buchanan or Gosse it acquires a rather spurious, nostalgic texture which is very much at odds with what is best in the novels. Thus, for example, Gosse sees him as the antithesis to 'the activity and energy of this age', whereas the earlier novels in many ways suggest an age of even greater *mental* activity than Gosse's own. Perhaps the best portrait is Meredith's fictional one, which turns Peacockian irony on Peacock. Meredith's disastrous marriage to Peacock's daughter Mary Ellen (who seems to have been as attractive, clever, enlightened and irreverent as his

heroines) may have sharpened his vision – at any rate, the
criticism sticks. Like Meredith's Dr Middleton, Peacock in
retirement became expert at excluding from his consciousness
anything that might pose a threat to his peace of mind or his
digestion. As a final comment on the world of earnest truth-
seekers, it makes sense. However, it was not this mood that
created *Nightmare Abbey* or *Crotchet Castle*.

If Peacock had not lived to be eighty – although he wrote only
*Gryll Grange* in his last thirty-five years – the twentieth-century
interpretations of his writing would have started on a very
different tack. Somehow that dry, knowing, pagan old escapist
attracted attention away from the novels, and coloured his
critics' reading of them. The 'Peacock' people looked back to was
much more vivid, believable and interesting when seen as an
eccentric Victorian – a natural focus for leisurely anecdote – than
as a satirist in the thick of debate. Thus, the most sophisticated
of the early pieces are biographical : criticism (see John W.
Draper's essay here) lags behind, and has to start from scratch.
J. B. Priestley's book of 1927 is still really a literary portrait, with
its humorous and eloquent description of Peacock's carefully
fenced existence : 'There is about such men an air of self-
sufficiency that is vaguely irritating.' Though Priestley takes up
Spedding's 'court jester' idea – Peacock is 'the comedian of the
life of ideas' – he dilutes it with benevolence, and calls attention
to the idyllic settings in the books, where he detects (remembering, no doubt, the garden at Halliford) the fragile outlines of a
'Peacock world'.

Jean-Jacques Mayoux's exhaustive study of *Un Epicurien
Anglais* of 1932 (as yet untranslated save for the extract given
herein) belongs also to this category of appraisal, in a sense,
since it reads Peacock from the end, and seeks to demonstrate the
coherence of his development and the rationality of his route to
the garden in Halliford. However, other aspects of this French
study are new, and indicate a significant shift in critical assumptions. Mayoux examines Peacock's part in intellectual politics
with a new thoroughness (perhaps because of the connection
with French rationalism), and, for almost the first time in a hun-

dred years, makes the clash of ideas sound like something that might be *participated in*. This is to evade 'the Peacockians'; it is also, and more importantly, to evade the vague mental habit of whiggism which afflicted literary history, suggesting that those ideas and values that were at all important must have formed part of the Victorian synthesis, and therefore must somehow form part of our heritage – so that we do not need to study them. This increasingly could be seen not to be the case.

Aldous Huxley also helps to make the controversial Peacock more visible. The dialogue from *Point Counter Point* (which takes place at an awful party) uses Peacock's formula for tying up progress and regress in a nice knot: Webley, the coming man, is positively feudal, while Lord Edward has enlightened conservationist ideas. Setting Phosphorus against Moral Rearmament, too, is reminiscent of Peacock's malicious cocktails. Huxley played his own Shelley, however, and it is seldom that he manages, or tries, to leave his characters alone. Virginia Woolf, though obviously also thinking of Peacock as a writers' writer, is interested in very different aspects of him. She is closer to the text and peers at it with myopic concentration, seeking in the studied surface of the prose a release from the pressures of psychological realism. Peacock's suggestive brevity is an alternative to the earnest exactitudes that have come to be expected of the novel. What both Huxley and Woolf reveal, in fact, is that Peacock's kind of fiction is *not* easily assimilated into tradition, but stands out, and aside: something to be recalled and made use of for special purposes, when realism seems too blunt and ponderous an instrument.

The next phase in criticism bears this out, both positively and negatively. With the 'impartial mocker' discarded, the task of criticism becomes one of finding a new way of placing Peacock in relation to his age (and to ourselves). Olwen W. Campbell argues that his women, especially, show him to have been eccentrically and courageously progressive – out of touch with his age in the best sense. On the opposite side of the question, however, are two major books that set out to chart large regions in the history of literary culture: Mario Praz's *The Hero in Eclipse in Victorian Fiction* (1956) and A. E. Dyson's *The*

*Crazy Fabric* (1965). Both find Peacock's independence and individualism subtly fake, so that for them his standing aside represents a failure of nerve.

Mario Praz sees Peacock as a kind of composite: an 'eighteenth-century spirit', satirical and destructive, and a facile, sentimental optimist, appealing to 'Biedermeier' taste. Each of these he calls 'bourgeois' – rather confusingly, since according to his argument the first is 'positive' and the second is *blamably* bourgeois in the sense of having withdrawn from history and become a mere observer of its processes, a creator of domestic idylls. The terms of the discussion seem to have derived from marxist habits of mind, and the key to Praz's hostile view lies in his observation that, for all Peacock's satiric demolition of 'everything that appears to be superstructure', he still 'fails to find the ultimate truth which alone could justify such devastation'.

A. E. Dyson displays an even livelier antipathy to Peacock's scepticism, which he sees as a plausible cover for what is, in the end, simply a reactionary stance on progress and democracy. Dyson's view, interestingly, seems to rediscover and combine the early responses of the *Westminster* and *Edinburgh* reviewers in deploring Peacock's attacks on those values that tend towards consensus – though, unlike them, he does not believe that Peacock knew what he was doing. What Dyson looks for, and cannot find, in the novels is 'a distillation of human experience'. The point at issue between him and Peacock, in other words, is his assumption that 'synthesis' is the means by which progress occurs in a culture; and that therefore the task of criticism is to build traditions. One problem, however, about this 'whig' approach (see the comments on Mayoux above) is its implication that successful ideas deserve their success. Was Peacock really attacking the *growth-point* of his age in satirising Brougham's policies, and competitive examinations, for example?

More recent criticism has taken a closer view of Peacock in the climate of debate of his age (the *early* nineteenth century), recognising, for example, his intimate relations with radical and Utilitarian thinking – and, at the same time, a longer view of him in terms of the much more abstract 'tradition' of his genre.

This approach (which stems from Northrop Frye's *Anatomy of Criticism* of 1957) suggests a view of the uses of literature more akin to Peacock's own: a view in which abstract roles (like that of the sceptical comedian) subsist through history, to become relevant when certain kinds of cultural crisis occur. How far Peacock was justified in feeling that his age deserved an injection of doubt only a study of the quality of its intellectual life will tell us. And we need, ourselves, to draw on our own experience of the nature of debate. There are signs that what Jean-Jacques Mayoux wrote in 1932 is becoming increasingly true of ourselves: it takes a sceptical age to give sceptical fantasists like Peacock their due.

# PART ONE

# Peacock and Shelley

# 1. PEACOCK ON LITERARY ART

A poet in our times is a semi-barbarian in a civilized community. He lives in the days that are past. His ideas, thoughts, feelings, associations, are all with barbarous manners, obsolete customs, and exploded superstitions. The march of his intellect is like that of a crab, backward. The brighter the light diffused around him by the progress of reason, the thicker is the darkness of anti-quated barbarism, in which he buries himself like a mole, to throw up the barren hillocks of his Cimmerian labours. The philosophic mental tranquillity which looks round with an equal eye on all external things, collects a store of ideas, discriminates their relative value, assigns to all their proper place, and from the materials of useful knowledge thus collected, appreciated, and arranged, forms new combinations that impress the stamp of their power and utility on the real business of life, is dia-metrically the reverse of that frame of mind which poetry inspires, or from which poetry can emanate. The highest inspira-tions of poetry are resolvable into three ingredients : the rant of unregulated passion, the whining of exaggerated feeling, and the cant of factitious sentiment : and can therefore serve only to ripen a splendid lunatic like Alexander, a puling driveller like Werter, or a morbid dreamer like Wordsworth. It can never make a philosopher, nor a statesman, nor in any class of life an useful or rational man. It cannot claim the slightest share in any one of the comforts and utilities of life of which we have wit-nessed so many and so rapid advances. But though not useful, it may be said it is highly ornamental, and deserves to be culti-vated for the pleasure it yields. Even if this be granted, it does not follow that a writer of poetry in the present state of society is not a waster of his own time, and a robber of that of others. Poetry is not one of those arts which, like painting, require repetition and multiplication, in order to be diffused among society. There are more good poems already existing than are sufficient to employ that portion of life which any mere reader and recipient of poetical impressions should devote to them, and these having been produced in poetical times, are far superior in all the characteristics of poetry to the artificial reconstructions of a few morbid ascetics in unpoetical times. To read the promiscuous rubbish of the present time to the exclusion of the select treasures of the past, is to substitute the worse for the better variety of the same mode of enjoyment.

But in whatever degree poetry is cultivated, it must necessarily be to the neglect of some branch of useful study: and it is a lamentable spectacle to see minds, capable of better things, running to seed in the specious indolence of these empty aimless mockeries of intellectual exertion. Poetry was the mental rattle that awakened the attention of intellect in the infancy of civil society: but for the maturity of mind to make a serious business of the playthings of its childhood, is as absurd as for a full-grown man to rub his gums with coral, and cry to be charmed to sleep by the jingle of silver bells.

As to that small portion of our contemporary poetry, which is neither descriptive, nor narrative, nor dramatic, and which, for want of a better name, may be called ethical, the most distinguished portion of it, consisting merely of querulous, egotistical rhapsodies, to express the writer's high dissatisfaction with the world and every thing in it, serves only to confirm what has been said of the semi-barbarous character of poets, who from singing dithyrambics and 'Io Triumphe', while society was savage, grow rabid, and out of their element, as it becomes polished and enlightened.

Now when we consider that it is not the thinking and studious, and scientific and philosophical part of the community, not to those whose minds are bent on the pursuit and promotion of permanently useful ends and aims, that poets must address their minstrelsy, but to that much larger portion of the reading public, whose minds are not awakened to the desire of valuable knowledge, and who are indifferent to any thing beyond being charmed, moved, excited, affected, and exalted: charmed by harmony, moved by sentiment, excited by passion, affected by pathos, and exalted by sublimity : harmony, which is language on the rack of Procrustes; sentiment, which is canting egotism in the mask of refined feeling; passion, which is the commotion of a weak and selfish mind; pathos, which is the whining of an unmanly spirit; and sublimity, which is the inflation of an empty head : when we consider that the great and permanent interests of human society become more and more the main spring of intellectual pursuit; that in proportion as they become so, the subordinacy of the ornamental to the useful will be more and more seen and acknowledged; and that therefore the progress of useful art and science, and of moral and political knowledge, will continue more and more to withdraw attention from frivolous and unconducive, to solid and conducive studies : that therefore the poetical audience will not only continually diminish in the proportion of its number to that of the rest of the reading public, but will also sink lower and lower in the comparison of intellectual acquirement : when we consider that the poet must still please his audience, and must therefore continue to sink to their level, while the rest of the community is rising above it : we may easily conceive that the day is not distant, when the degraded state of every species of poetry will be as generally recognized as that of dramatic poetry has long been : and this not from any decrease either of intellectual power, or intellectual acquisition, but because intellectual power and intellectual acquisition have turned themselves into other and better channels, and have abandoned the cultivation and the fate of poetry to the degenerate fry of modern rhymesters, and their olympic judges, the magazine critics, who continue to debate and promulgate oracles about poetry, as if it were still what it was in the Homeric age, the all-in-all of intellectual progression, and as if there no such things in existence as mathematicians, astronomers, chemists, moralists, metaphysicians, historians, politicians, and political economists, who have built into the upper air of intelligence a pyramid, from the summit of which they see the modern Parnassus far beneath them, and, knowing how small a place it occupies in the comprehensiveness of their prospect, smile at the little ambition and the circumscribed perceptions with which the drivellers and mounte-banks upon it are contending for the poetical palm and the critical chair.

SOURCE: extract from 'The Four Ages of Poetry', *Ollier's Literary Miscellany* (1820); reprinted in *The Four Ages of Poetry*, ed. H. F. B. Brett-Smith (1923).

## ON THE POWER OF RIDICULE (1836)

In respect of presenting or embodying opinion, there are two very distinct classes of comic fictions: one in which the characters are abstractions or embodied classifications, and the implied or embodied opinions the main matter of the work; another, in which the characters are individuals, and the events and the action those of actual life – the opinions, however prominent they may be made, being merely incidental. To the first of these classes belong the fictions of Aristophanes, Petronius Arbiter, Rabelais, Swift, and Voltaire; to the latter, those of Henry Fielding, his Jonathan Wild perhaps excepted, which is a felicitous compound of both classes; for Jonathan and his gang are at once abstractions and individuals. Jonathan is at once king of the thieves and the type of an arch whig.

To the latter class belong the writings of Pigault le Brun. His heroes and heroines are all genuine flesh and blood, and invest themselves with the opinions of the time as ordinary mortals do, carrying on the while the realities of every-day life. There is often extravagance both in the characters and the actions, but it is the mere exuberance of fancy, and not like the hyperboles of Rabelais, subservient to a purpose. Rabelais, one of the wisest and most learned, as well as wittiest of men, put on the robe of the all-licensed fool, that he might, like the court-jester, convey bitter truths under the semblance of simple buffoonery.

Such was also, in a great measure, the purpose of his contemporary Bertrand de Verville, who, although he introduces *Frostibus, Lieutenant-Général de tous les diables*, apostrophizing Luther, in an exceedingly whimsical oration, as *Monsieur de l'autre monde*, was not one of the least strenuous, or least successful, supporters of the cause of the Reformation.

It would be, we think, an interesting and amusing inquiry to trace the progress of French comic fiction, in its bearing on opinion, from the twelfth century to the Revolution; and to show how much this unpretending branch of literature has, by its universal diffusion through so many ages in France, contributed to directing the stream of opinion against the mass of delusions and abuses which it was the object of those who were honest in the cause of the Reformation, and in the causes of the several changes which have succeeded it to the present time, to dissipate and destroy. If, as has frequently happened, the selfishness and dishonesty of many of the instruments has converted the triumph of a good cause into a source of greater iniquities than the triumph overthrew; if use and abuse have been sometimes swept away together, and the evils of abuse have returned, while the benefits of use have been irretrievably lost; if the overthrow of religious tyranny has been made the pretext for public robbery; if the downfall of one species of state-delusion has been made the stepping-stone to the rise of a new variety of political quackery; if the quieting of civil discord has been made the basis of military despotism;[1] if what has been even ultimately gained in the direct object proposed, has been counterbalanced by losses in collateral matters, not sufficiently attended to in the heat of the main pursuit – (a debtor and creditor account well worthy the making out, if the requisite quantity of leisure, knowledge, and honesty could be brought to bear upon it); if the principles which were honestly pursued have been stigmatized as the necessary causes of effects which did not belong to them, and which were never contemplated by those by whom those principles were embraced; and if those who were honest in the cause have been amongst the first victims of their own triumph, perverted from its legitimate results; – we shall find, nevertheless, in the first place, that every successive triumph, however perverted in its immediate consequences, has been a step permanently gained in advance of the objects of the first authors of the Reformation – freedom of conscience and freedom of inquiry; and we shall find, in the second place, not only that comic fiction has contributed largely to this result, but that among the most illustrious authors of comic fiction are some of the most illustrious specimens of political honesty and heroic self-devotion. We are here speaking, however, solely of the authors of the highest order of comic fiction – that which limits itself, in the exposure of abuses, to turning up into full daylight their intrinsic absurdities – not that which makes ridiculous things not really so, by throwing over them a fool's coat which does not belong to them, or setting upon them, as honest Bottom has it, an ass's head of its own.

Ridicule, in the first case, the honest development of the ridiculous *ab intra*, is very justly denominated the test of truth : but ridicule, in the second case, the dishonest superinduction of the ridiculous *ab extra*, is the test of nothing but the knavery of the inventor. In the first case, the ridicule is never sought; it always appears, as in the comic tales of Voltaire, to force itself up obviously and spontaneously : in the second case, the most prominent feature of the exhibition is the predetermination to be caustic and comical. To writers of the latter class most truly applies the axiom – *homines derisores civitatem perdunt*. But an intense love of truth, and a clear apprehension of truth, are both essential to comic writing of the first class. An intense love of truth may exist without the faculty of detecting it; and a clear apprehension of truth may co-exist with a determination to pervert it. The union of both is rare; and still more rare is the combination of both with that peculiar 'composite of natural capacity and superinduced habit', which constitutes what is usually denominated comic genius.

Source: extract from 'French Comic Romances', *The London Review*, ii (October 1836).

NOTE

1. 'Lepidi atque Antonii arma in Augustum cessere : qui *cuncta, discordiis civilibus fessa,* nomine principis, sub *imperio* accepit.' Tacitus, *Ann.*, 1. *Weariness of civil discord* founded the despotisms of Augustus, Cromwell, and Napoleon.

PREFACE TO THE NOVELS (1837)

All these little publications appeared originally without prefaces. I left them to speak for themselves; and I thought I might very fitly preserve my own impersonality, having never intruded on the personality of others, nor taken any liberties but with public conduct and public opinions. But an old friend assures me, that to publish a book without a preface is like entering a drawing-room without making a bow. In deference to this opinion, though I am not quite clear of its soundness, I make my prefatory bow at this eleventh hour.

*Headlong Hall* was written in 1815; *Nightmare Abbey* in 1817; *Maid Marian*, with the exception of the last three chapters, in 1818; *Crotchet Castle* in 1830. I am desirous to note the intervals, because, at each of those periods, things were true, in great matters and in small, which are true no longer. *Headlong Hall* begins with the Holyhead Mail, and *Crotchet Castle* ends with a rotten borough. The Holyhead mail no longer keeps the same hours, nor stops at the Capel Cerig Inn, which the progress of improvement has thrown out of the road; and the rotten boroughs of 1830 have ceased to exist, though there are some very pretty pocket properties, which are their worthy successors. But the classes of tastes, feelings, and opinions, which were successively brought into play in these little tales, remain substantially the same. Perfectibilians, deteriorationists, statu-quo-ites, phrenologists, transcendentalists, political econo-mists, theorists in all sciences, projectors in all arts, morbid visionaries, romantic enthusiasts, lovers of music, lovers of the picturesque, and lovers of good dinners, march, and will march for ever, *pari passu* with the march of mechanics, which some facetiously call the march of intellect. The fastidious in old wine are a race that does not decay. Literary violators of the confi-dences of private life still gain a disreputable livelihood and an unenviable notoriety. Match-makers from interest, and the dis-appointed in love and in friendship, are varieties of which specimens are extant. The great principle of the Right of Might is as flourishing now as in the days of Maid Marian : the array of false pretensions, moral, political, and literary, is as imposing as ever: the rulers of the world still feel things in their effects, and never foresee them in their causes; and political mounte-banks continue, and will continue, to puff nostrums and practise legerdemain under the eyes of the multitude; following, like the 'learned friend' of Crotchet Castle, a course as tortuous as that of a river, but in a reverse process; beginning by being dark and deep, and ending by being transparent.

SOURCE: edition of Peacock's novels in Bentley's 'Standard Novels', vol. LVII (1837).

# 2. SHELLEY ON PEACOCK

ON *Nightmare Abbey* (1819)

Enough of melancholy. *Nightmare Abbey* though no cure is a palliative. I have just received the parcel which contains it, and at the same time the 'Examiners' by the way of [?Malta]. I am delighted with *Nightmare Abbey*. I think Scythrop a character admirably conceived and executed, and I know not how to praise sufficiently the lightness, chastity and strength of the language of the whole. It perhaps exceeds all your works in this. The catastrophe is excellent, – I suppose the moral is contained in what Falstaff says '*For God's sake talk like a man of this world*' and yet looking deeper into it, is not the misdirected enthusiasm of Scythrop what J C calls the salt of the earth? My friends the Gisbornes here admire and delight in it exceedingly. I think I told you that they (especially the lady) are people of high cultivation; she is a woman of profound accomplishments and a most refined taste. Cobbett still more and more delights me, with all my horror of the sanguinary commonplaces of his creed. His design to overthrow bank notes by forgery is very comic.

SOURCE: part of letter from Shelley to Peacock from Italy, June 1819.

'A STRAIN TOO LEARNED FOR A SHALLOW AGE' (1820)

> – his fine wit
> Makes such a wound, the knife is lost in it;
> A strain too learned for a shallow age,
> Too wise for selfish bigots; let his page,

Which charms the chosen spirits of the time,
Fold itself up for the serener clime
Of years to come, and find its recompense
In that just expectation.

SOURCE: extract from Shelley's 'Letter to Maria Gisborne',
written 1820, published in *Posthumous Poems* (1824).

IN DEFENCE OF POETRY (1821)

But poets have been challenged to resign the civic crown to
reasoners and mechanists on another plea. It is admitted that the
exercise of the imagination is most delightful, but it is alleged,
that that of reason is more useful. Let us examine as the grounds
of this distinction, what is here meant by utility. Pleasure or good,
in a general sense, is that which the consciousness of a sensitive
and intelligent being seeks, and in which, when found, it
acquiesces. There are two modes or degrees of pleasure, one
durable, universal and permanent; the other transitory and particular. Utility may either express the means of producing the
former or the latter. In the former sense, whatever strengthens
and purifies the affections, enlarges the imagination, and adds
spirit to sense, is useful. But the meaning in which the Author
of the 'Four Ages of Poetry'[1] seems to have employed the word
utility is the narrower one of banishing the importunity of the
wants of our animal nature, the surrounding men with security
of life, the dispersing the grosser delusions of superstition, and the
conciliating such a degree of mutual forbearance among men as
may consist with the motives of personal advantage.

Undoubtedly the promoters of utility, in this limited sense,
have their appointed office in society. They follow the footsteps
of poets, and copy the sketches of their creations into the book of
common life. They make space, and give time. Their exertions
are of the highest value, so long as they confine their administra-
tion of the concerns of the inferior powers of our nature within

the limits due to the superior ones. But whilst the sceptic destroys gross superstitions, let him spare to deface, as some of the French writers have defaced, the eternal truths charactered upon the imaginations of men. Whilst the mechanist abridges, and the political economist combines, labour, let them beware that their speculations, for want of correspondence with those first principles which belong to the imagination, do not tend, as they have in modern England, to exasperate at once the extremes of luxury and want. They have exemplified the saying, 'To him that hath, more shall be given; and from him that hath not, the little that he hath shall be taken away.' The rich have become richer, and the poor have become poorer; and the vessel of the state is driven between the Scylla and Charybdis of anarchy and despotism. Such are the effects which must ever flow from an unmitigated exercise of the calculating faculty.

It is difficult to define pleasure in its highest sense; the definition involving a number of apparent paradoxes. For, from an inexplicable defect of harmony in the constitution of human nature, the pain of the inferior is frequently connected with the pleasures of the superior portions of our being. Sorrow, terror, anguish, despair itself, are often the chosen expressions of an approximation to the highest good. Our sympathy in tragic fiction depends on this principle; tragedy delights by affording a shadow of the pleasure which exists in pain. This is the source also of the melancholy which is inseparable from the sweetest melody. The pleasure that is in sorrow is sweeter than the pleasure of pleasure itself. And hence the saying, 'It is better to go to the house of mourning, than to the house of mirth.' Not that this highest species of pleasure is necessarily linked with pain. The delight of love and friendship, the ecstasy of the admiration of nature, the joy of the perception and still more of the creation of poetry is often wholly unalloyed.

The production and assurance of pleasure in this highest sense is true utility. Those who produce and preserve this pleasure are Poets or poetical philosophers.

The exertions of Locke, Hume, Gibbon, Voltaire, Rousseau,[2] and their disciples, in favour of oppressed and deluded humanity, are entitled to the gratitude of mankind. Yet it is easy to calculate the degree of moral and intellectual improvement which the world would have exhibited, had they never lived. A little more nonsense would have been talked for a century or two; and perhaps a few more men, women, and children, burnt as heretics. We might not at this moment have been congratulating each other on the abolition of the Inquisition in Spain. But it exceeds all imagination to conceive what would have been the moral condition of the world if neither Dante, Petrarch, Boccaccio, Chaucer, Shakspeare, Calderon, Lord Bacon, nor Milton, had ever existed; if Raphael and Michael Angelo had never been born; if the Hebrew poetry had never been translated; if a revival of the study of Greek literature had never taken place; if no monuments of antient sculpture had been handed down to us; and if the poetry of the religion of the antient world had been extinguished together with its belief. The human mind could never, except by the intervention of these excitements, have been awakened to the invention of the grosser sciences, and that application of analytical reasoning to the aberrations of society, which it is now attempted to exalt over the direct expression of the inventive and creative faculty itself.

We have more moral, political and historical wisdom, than we know how to reduce into practice; we have more scientific and economical knowledge than can be accommodated to the just distribution of the produce which it multiplies. The poetry in these systems of thought, is concealed by the accumulation of facts and calculating processes. There is no want of knowledge respecting what is wisest and best in morals, government, and political economy, or at least, what is wiser and better than what men now practise and endure. But we let '*I dare not* wait upon *I would*, like the poor cat i' the adage'. We want the creative faculty to imagine that which we know; we want the generous impulse to act that which we imagine; we want the poetry of life : our calculations have outrun conception; we have eaten more than we can digest. The cultivation of those sciences which have enlarged the limits of the empire of man over the external world, has, for want of the poetical faculty, proportionally circumscribed those of the internal world; and man, having enslaved the elements, remains himself a slave. To what but a cultivation of the mechanical arts in a degree disproportioned to the presence of the creative faculty, which is the basis of all knowledge, is to be attributed the abuse of all invention for abridging and combining labour, to the exasperation of the inequality of mankind? From what other cause has it arisen that these inventions which should have lightened, have added a weight to the curse imposed on Adam? Thus Poetry, and the principle of Self, of which Money is the visible incarnation, are the God and Mammon of the world.

SOURCE : extract from *In Defence of Poetry*, written 1821, published 1840. (The 1840 version excised all references to Peacock as 'the author of the "Four Ages of Poetry" '.)

NOTES

1. [i.e. Peacock – Ed.]
2. I follow the classification adopted by the Author of the 'Four Ages of Poetry'; but he was essentially a Poet. The others, even Voltaire, were mere reasoners. [Shelley's note.]

# 3. PEACOCK ON SHELLEY

## I. A Society of Cranks

At Bracknell, Shelley was surrounded by a numerous society, all in a great measure of his own opinions in relation to religion and politics, and the larger portion of them in relation to vegetable diet. But they wore their rue with a difference. Every one of them adopting some of the articles of the faith of their general church, had each nevertheless some predominant crotchet of his or her own, which left a number of open questions for earnest and not always temperate discussion. I was sometimes irreverent enough to laugh at the fervour with which opinions utterly unconducive to any practical result were battled for as matters of the highest importance to the well-being of mankind; Harriet Shelley was always ready to laugh with me, and we thereby both lost caste with some of the more hot-headed of the party. Mr. Hogg was not there during my visit, but he knew the whole of the persons there assembled, and has given some account of them under their initials, which for all public purposes are as well as their names.

The person among them best worth remembering was the gentleman whom Mr Hogg calls J. F. N., of whom he relates some anecdotes.

I will add one or two from my own experience. He was an estimable man and an agreeable companion, and he was not the less amusing that he was the absolute impersonation of a single theory, or rather of two single theories rolled into one. He held that all diseases and all aberrations, moral and physical, had their origin in the use of animal food and of fermented and spirituous liquors; that the universal adoption of a diet of roots, fruits, and distilled[1] water, would restore the golden age of uni-

versal health, purity, and peace; that this most ancient and sublime morality was mystically inculcated in the most ancient
Zodiac, which was that of Dendera; that this Zodiac was divided
into two hemispheres, the upper hemisphere being the realm of
Oromazes or the principle of good, the lower that of Ahrimanes
or the principle of evil; that each of these hemispheres was again
divided into two compartments, and that the four lines of divi-
sion radiating from the centre were the prototype of the Christian
cross. The two compartments of Oromazes were those of Uranus
or Brahma the Creator, and of Saturn or Veishnu the Preserver.
The two compartments of Ahrimanes were those of Jupiter or
Seva the Destroyer, and of Apollo or Krishna the Restorer. The
great moral doctrine was thus symbolized in the Zodiacal signs :—
In the first compartment, Taurus the Bull, having in the ancient
Zodiac a torch in his mouth, was the type of eternal light.
Cancer the Crab was the type of celestial matter, sleeping under
the all-covering water, on which Brahma floated in a lotus-flower
for millions of ages. From the union, typified by Gemini, of light
and celestial matter, issued in the second compartment Leo,
Primogenial Love, mounted on the back of a Lion, who produced the pure and perfect nature of things in Virgo, and Libra
the Balance denoted the coincidence of the ecliptic with the
equator, and the equality of man's happy existence. In the third
compartment, the first entrance of evil into the system was
typified by the change of celestial into terrestrial matter – Cancer
into Scorpio. Under this evil influence man became a hunter,
Sagittarius the Archer, and pursued the wild animals, typified
by Capricorn. Then, with animal food and cookery, came death
into the world, and all our woe. But in the fourth compartment,
Dhanwantari or Æsculapius, Aquarius the Waterman, arose from
the sea, typified by Pisces the Fish, with a jug of pure water and
a bunch of fruit, and brought back the period of universal happiness under Aries the Ram, whose benignant ascendancy was
the golden fleece of the Argonauts, and the true talisman of
Oromazes.

He saw the Zodiac in everything. I was walking with him one
day on a common near Bracknell, when we came on a public-
house which had the sign of the Horse-shoes. They were four

on the sign, and he immediately determined that this number
had been handed down from remote antiquity as representative
of the compartments of the Zodiac. He stepped into the public-
house, and said to the landlord, 'Your sign is the Horse-shoes?'
– 'Yes, sir.' 'This sign has always four Horse-shoes?' – 'Why
mostly, sir.' 'Not always?' – 'I think I have seen three.' 'I cannot
divide the Zodiac into three. But it is mostly four. Do you know
why it is mostly four?' – 'Why, sir, I suppose because a horse has
four legs.' He bounced out in great indignation, and as soon as
I joined him, he said to me, 'Did you ever see such a fool?'


## II.  Marital Miseries

The separation did not take place by mutual consent. I cannot
think that Shelley ever so represented it. He never did so to me :
and the account which Harriet herself gave me of the entire
proceeding was decidedly contradictory of any such supposition.

He might well have said, after first seeing Mary Wollstonecraft Godwin, *'Ut vidi! ut perii!'* Nothing that I ever read in
tale or history could present a more striking image of a sudden,
violent, irresistible, uncontrollable passion, than that under
which I found him labouring when, at his request, I went up
from the country to call on him in London. Between his old feelings towards Harriet, *from whom he was not then separated*,
and his new passion for Mary, he showed in his looks, in his
gestures, in his speech, the state of a mind 'suffering, like a little
kingdom, the nature of an insurrection'. His eyes were blood-
shot, his hair and dress disordered. He caught up a bottle of
laudanum, and said : 'I never part from this.'[2] He added : 'I am
always repeating to myself your lines from Sophocles :

> Man's happiest lot is not to be :
>     And when we tread life's thorny steep,
> Most blest are they, who earliest free
>     Descend to death's eternal sleep.'

Again, he said more calmly : 'Every one who knows me must
know that the partner of my life should be one who can feel
poetry and understand philosophy. Harriet is a noble animal,

but she can do neither.' I said, 'It always appeared to me that you were very fond of Harriet.' Without affirming or denying this, he answered: 'But you did not know how I hated her sister.'

The term 'noble animal' he applied to his wife, in conversation with another friend now living, intimating that the nobleness which he thus ascribed to her would induce her to acquiesce in the inevitable transfer of his affections to their new shrine. She did not so acquiesce, and he cut the Gordian knot of the difficulty by leaving England with Miss Godwin on the 28th of July, 1814.

Shortly after this I received a letter from Harriet, wishing to see me. I called on her at her father's house in Chapel-street, Grosvenor-square. She then gave me her own account of the transaction, which, as I have said, decidedly contradicted the supposition of anything like separation by mutual consent.

She at the same time gave me a description, by no means flattering, of Shelley's new love, whom I had not then seen. I said, 'If you have described her correctly, what could he see in her?' 'Nothing,' she said, 'but that her name was Mary, and not only Mary, but Mary Wollstonecraft.'

The lady had nevertheless great personal and intellectual attractions, though it is not to be wondered at that Harriet could not see them.

### III. *Semi-delusions*

In the early summer of 1816, the spirit of restlessness again came over him, and resulted in a second visit to the Continent. The change of scene was preceded, as more than once before, by a mysterious communication from a person seen only by himself, warning him of immediate personal perils to be incurred by him if he did not instantly depart.

I was alone at Bishopgate, with him and Mrs Shelley, when the visitation alluded to occurred. About the middle of the day, intending to take a walk, I went into the hall for my hat. His was there, and mine was not. I could not imagine what had become of it; but as I could not walk without it, I returned to the

library. After some time had elapsed, Mrs Shelley came in, and
gave me an account which she had just received from himself, of
the visitor and his communication. I expressed some scepticism
on the subject, on which she left me, and Shelley came in, with
my hat in his hand. He said, 'Mary tells me, you do not believe
that I have had a visit from Williams.' I said, 'I told her there
were some improbabilities in the narration.' He said, 'You know
Williams of Tremadoc?' I said, 'I do.' He said, 'It was he who
was here to-day. He came to tell me of a plot laid by my father
and uncle, to entrap me and lock me up. He was in great haste,
and could not stop a minute, and I walked with him to Egham.'
I said, 'What hat did you wear?' He said, 'This, to be sure.' I
said, 'I wish you would put it on.' He put it on, and it went over
his face. I said, 'You could not have walked to Egham in that
hat.' He said, 'I snatched it up hastily, and perhaps I kept it in
my hand. I certainly walked with Williams to Egham, and he
told me what I have said. You are very sceptical.' I said, 'If you
are certain of what you say, my scepticism cannot affect your
certainty.' He said, 'It is very hard on a man who has devoted his
life to the pursuit of truth, who has made great sacrifices and
incurred great sufferings for it, to be treated as a visionary. If
I do not know that I saw Williams, how do I know that I see
you?' I said, 'An idea may have the force of a sensation; but the
oftener a sensation is repeated, the greater is the probability of
its origin in reality. You saw me yesterday, and will see me to-
morrow.' He said, 'I can see Williams to-morrow if I please. He
told me he was stopping at the Turk's Head Coffee-house, in the
Strand, and should be there two days. I want to convince you
that I am not under a delusion. Will you walk with me to
London to-morrow, to see him?' I said, 'I would most willingly
do so.' The next morning after an early breakfast we set off on
our walk to London. We had got halfway down Egham-hill,
when he suddenly turned round, and said to me, 'I do not think
we shall find Williams at the Turk's Head.' I said, 'Neither do
I.' He said, 'You say that, because you do not think he has been
there; but he mentioned a contingency under which he might
leave town yesterday, and he has probably done so.' I said, 'At any
rate, we should know that he has been there.' He said, 'I will take

other means of convincing you. I will write to him. Suppose we take a walk through the forest.' We turned about on our new direction, and were out all day. Some days passed, and I heard no more of the matter. One morning he said to me, 'I have some news of Williams; a letter and an enclosure.' I said, 'I shall be glad to see the letter.' He said, 'I cannot show you the letter; I will show you the enclosure. It is a diamond necklace. I think you know me well enough to be sure I would not throw away my own money on such a thing, and that if I have it, it must have been sent me by somebody else. It has been sent me by Williams.' 'For what purpose?' I asked. He said, 'To prove his identity and his sincerity.' 'Surely,' I said, 'your showing me a diamond necklace will prove nothing but that you have one to show.' 'Then,' he said, 'I will not show it you. If you will not believe me, I must submit to your incredulity.' There the matter ended. I never heard another word of Williams, nor of any other mysterious visitor. I had on one or two previous occasions argued with him against similar semi-delusions, and I believe if they had always been received with similar scepticism, they would not have been often repeated; but they were encouraged by the ready credulity with which they were received by many, who ought to have known better. I call them semi-delusions, because, for the most part, they had their basis in his firm belief that his father and uncle had designs on his liberty. On this basis, his imagination built a fabric of romance, and when he presented it as substantive fact, and it was found to contain more or less of inconsistency, he felt his self-esteem interested in maintaining it by accumulated circumstances, which severally vanished under the touch of investigation, like Williams's location at the Turk's Head Coffee-house.

## IV. *Want of reality*

What was, in my opinion, deficient in his poetry was, as I have already said, the want of reality in the characters with which he peopled his splendid scenes, and to which he addressed or imparted the utterance of his impassioned feelings. He was advancing, I think, to the attainment of this reality. It would have given to his poetry the only element of truth which it wanted; though at the same time, the more clear development of what men were would have lowered his estimate of what they might be, and dimmed his enthusiastic prospect of the future destiny of the world. I can conceive him, if he had lived to the present time, passing his days like Volney, looking on the world from his windows without taking part in its turmoils; and perhaps like the same, or some other great apostle of liberty (for I cannot at this moment verify the quotation), desiring that nothing should be inscribed on his tomb, but his name, the dates of his birth and death, and the single word,

'DÉSILLUSIONNÉ'.

SOURCE: extracts from 'Memoirs of Shelley', *Fraser's Magazine*, LVII and LXI (June 1858 and January 1860).

### NOTES

1. He held that water in its natural state was full of noxious impurities, which were only to be got rid of by distillation.

2. In a letter to Mr Trelawny, dated 18 June 1822, Shelley says: 'You of course enter into society at Leghorn. Should you meet with any scientific person capable of preparing the *Prussic Acid, or Essential Oil of Bitter Almonds*, I should regard it as a great kindness if you could procure me a small quantity. It requires the greatest caution in preparation, and ought to be highly concentrated. I would give any price for this medicine. You remember we talked of it the other night, and we both expressed a wish to possess it. My wish was serious, and sprung from the desire of avoiding needless suffering. I need not tell you I have no intention of suicide at present; but I confess it would be a comfort to me to hold in my possession that golden key to the chamber of perpetual rest. The *Prussic Acid* is used in medicine in infinitely minute doses; but that preparation is weak, and has not the concentration necessary to medicine all ills infallibly. A single drop, even less, is a dose, and it acts by paralysis.'

I believe that up to this time he had never travelled without pistols for defence, nor without laudanum as a refuge from intolerable pain. His physical suffering was often very severe; and this last letter must have been written under the anticipation that it might become incurable, and unendurable to a degree from which he wished to be permanently provided with the means of escape. [Peacock is referring to E. J. Trelawny, *Recollections of the Last Days of Shelley and Byron* (London, 1858) pp. 100, 101. That book, along with Charles S. Middleton, *Shelley and his writings* (London, 1858) and Thomas Jefferson Hogg, *The Life of Percy Bysshe Shelley,* 2 vols (London, 1858), provided the occasion for this review article, in which Peacock gave his own, corrective account for the first time. – Ed.]

PART TWO

# Nineteenth-century Appraisals

## '...Very Dull'

Dec. 31st [1818] . . . I read, beginning of the week, *Headlong Hall* – satirical dialogues – an account of a visit to a Welsh squire's seat. The interlocutors represent certain literary parties in the country. There is one who is an optimist, another a deteriorist, who obtrude their speculations on every occasion; there are reviewers, a picturesque gardener, etc.; but the commonplaces of the literators of the day are not preserved from being tiresome by original humour or wit, so that the book is very dull.

> SOURCE: *Henry Crabb Robinson on Books and their Writers*, ed. E. J. Morley (London, 1938) p. 226.

## WILLIAM HAZLITT (1826)

## *Art versus Utility*

SENTIMENTALIST: . . . I have sometimes thought that the great professors of the modern philosophy were hardly sincere in the contempt they express for poetry, painting, music, and the Fine Arts in general – that they were private *amateurs* and prodigious proficients *under the rose*, and, like other lovers, hid their passion as a weakness – that Mr. M——[1] turned a barrel-organ – that Mr. P——[2] warbled delightfully – that Mr. Pl——[3] had a manuscript tragedy by him, called 'The Last Man', which he withheld from the public, not to compromise the dignity of philosophy by affording any one the smallest actual satisfaction during the term of his natural life.
RATIONALIST: Oh, no! You are quite mistaken in this supposition, if you are at all serious in it. So far from being proficients, or having wasted their time in these trifling pursuits, I

believe not one of the persons you have named has the least taste or capacity for them, or any idea corresponding to them, except Mr Bentham, who is fond of music, and says, with his usual *bonhomie* (which seems to increase with his age) that he does not see why others should not find an agreeable recreation in poetry and painting.

[At this point Hazlitt adds a footnote:] One of them has printed a poem entitled 'Rhodope';[4] which, however, does not show the least taste or capacity for poetry, or any idea corresponding to it. *Bad poetry* serves to prove the existence of *good*. If all poetry were like 'Rhodope', the philosophic author might fulminate his anathemas against it (floods of ghastly, livid ire) as long as he pleased; but if this were poetry, there would be no occasion for so much anger: no one would read it or think any thing of it!

SOURCE : extract from 'The New School of Reform', *The Plain Speaker* (1826).

NOTES

1. [James Mill or J. R. McCulloch (cf. MacQuedy in *Crotchet Castle*) – Ed.]
2. [Peacock – Ed.]
3. [Francis Place – Ed.]
4. [Whether by accident or design, Hazlitt gets the title of Peacock's poem *Rhododaphne* (1818) wrong; his judgement that Peacock was not a poet, however, is closer to the truth. – Ed.]

ANONYMOUS (1831)

*The Questionable Liberal*

The author of *Headlong Hall* is a bitter persecutor of the singularities and excrescences of science. He is a prose Peter Pindar, writing however with a vast deal of knowledge on the topics about which he is occupied, but with the keenest eye upon the absurdities of all who come under his cognizance. Dr. Walcot represented sir Joseph Banks as boiling fleas, in order to ascertain whether they turned red like lobsters; and the traveller Bruce as cutting his beefsteaks from a living animal, and then sending the bullocks to graze. Who now doubts at this time of day that sir Joseph Banks and Bruce were benefactors of society; there will be as little hesitation on the question, whether the phrenologists, the conchologists, and the political economists, with numerous other tribes of scientific devotees, who are described by the Greek termination ιοτης, of the present day, are to be considered as the patrons of human happiness, and the benefactors of their race by our successors in the next age, and in coming centuries. We do not mean, that all who boast the name of science will be so considered; for, as soon as any science or branch of knowledge has made a certain progress, it necessarily follows, that it will be professed by numerous pretenders, who will probably greatly magnify its importance, and at any rate possibly make an outcry, of which the real originators are heartily ashamed. We believe, sincerely, that it is not the warriors, but the followers of the camp, against which Mr. Peacock levels his shafts; he would probably be himself the first to regret his prowess if he thought he had put the whole army to the rout, and we are quite certain that he would much grieve, did he know, that by his very able sharpshooting upon the stragglers he was mistaken for the advance corps of the enemies of all improvement, whether in science or politics.

It is a pity, that men are most inclined to satirise that of which they know the most. Juvenal, hot from the stews, Petronius Arbiter, fresh from the garden of Epicurus, in the first moments of re-action employed their genius upon the exposure of their partners in vice: it is thus with Mr. Peacock, he does not satirize the boroughmongers, for he is not of their click; he does not attack the money-brokers, for he is not a regarder of pelf; were he of the Stock Exchange he would rail against waddlers and men of straw; were he of the Universities, a fellow of some musty college, he would run down the malappropriation of testamentary funds, and the misdirection of the courses of instruction; the idleness which passes under the name of learned ease, the ignorance which is called erudition. Had he been a lawyer or a police magistrate, the chicaneries of the law, or the absurdities of society would have been his food. We should, perhaps, have laughed as much, but not so wisely. Mr. Peacock happens to be well acquainted with those studies on which men at the present day chiefly pride themselves, he consequently detects more acutely than others the hollowness and emptiness of the pretensions of the trainbearers of these particular sciences. Being himself a master of the art, he can instantly discover the clumsy efforts of a sciolist – having a great susceptibility of the ridiculous, he is forced upon comparisons of the most laughable description. In order to be understood, however, he aims at the most distinguished representatives of the science, where others would have satirized the pretenders.

The most conspicuous personage of Crotchet Castle is Mr. MacQuedy, the economist; he is represented in colours not to be mistaken; and it is very possible that they who are incapable of understanding the writings of the author satirized are quite equal to the comprehension of the satire. Political Economy has enemies enough in the ranks of those who are ignorant of it; weapons are now supplied from its own arsenal. Under the name of Mr. Skionar, the professor of the transcendental school of poetry is ridiculed, and we have no objection. We can also forgive the vagaries of the antiquary, Mr. Chainmail, who lives in the twelfth and thirteenth century. Dr. Folliott is the representative of Common Sense, according to the author's idea of it. Common Sense, then, is a divinity doctor, of a great wine capacity, a parson of uncommon pugilistic force, as clever at knocking down an antagonist with a classical quotation, as with his cudgel. . . .

[Mr. Peacock] is learned and he plays with his erudition, he is well acquainted with modern discoveries and he laughs at them, he is liberal in all his political opinions, and he attacks liberals only. The hero of the church and the ring, Dr. Folliott is precisely the jovial and narrow-minded athletic grammarian, whom *Blackwood's Magazine* would deify as the model of men, a pattern for all Christendom in religion, politics, and morals, a gormandizer of sensual things, a wielder of the fist, a knockerdown of arguments. It is true that he is the antipodes of cant, which implies professions of disinterestedness : the model of men despises all generosity, and does not pretend to a virtue which no hypocrisy could procure him credit for. It does not become us to assume the direction of the efforts of a man of Mr. Peacock's genius, more particularly after suffering ourselves to be so greatly entertained by the perusal of one of his works, nevertheless we cannot help beseeching him to apply his most tranchant qualities to the extirpation of the greater nuisances which prey upon the well being of society, and impede the future improvement of mankind.

> S o u r c e : extracts from anonymous review of *Crotchet Castle*, *Westminster Review*, xv (July 1831).

LEIGH HUNT (1832)

*On Poetical Utilitarians*

And last, not least, the Utilitarians themselves are poetical ! . . . If you want a proper Bacchanalian uproar in a song, you must go to the author of *Headlong Hall*, who will not admire utility itself unless it be jovial.

> S o u r c e : extract from Preface to *Poetical Works* (1832). The Preface is reprinted in the O.U.P. edition of *The Poetical Works of Leigh Hunt*, ed. Sir H. S. Milford (1923).

JAMES SPEDDING (1839)

## The Court Jester

There was an officer attached to one of the ancient regal estab-
lishments whose business was to appear before the king every
morning, and gravely remind him that he was mortal. How long
this office was endured, and what was the fate of the person who
first held it, we are not informed. It probably soon sunk into a
sinecure, its active duties being discharged in deputy by a death's
head, till the times of change came when, among other bulwarks
of that constitution, it was swept away altogether. But though
names change and salaries cease, wants remain. Courts still stood
in need of some such monitor; and in the person of the king's
jester the old office was revived in an improved form, and with
additional duties. The jester was licensed to utter other and
newer truths than that one, so long as he did not seem to be
uttering them in earnest; and the king could listen patiently to
speeches by which his own follies were anatomized, so long as it
was understood that the speaker, not himself, was the fool. The
profession of the jester was simply to make sport for the great;
but his real use was to tell unwelcome truths; his privilege to tell
them without offence; and his great art and faculty (supposing
him duly qualified for his office) was one in which no lover of
truth should omit to exercise himself, – that of detecting secret
resemblances between things most distant, and, in common estimation, most unlike; and of searching the substance of popular
judgments, by turning the seamy side outward. It was a sad day
for kings when that divine right passed from them of hearing
reason only from the lips of fools. It came, however, in its appointed time. Truths of the most uncourtly kind found their way
to court unbidden and undisguised; and the jester's office became obsolete. But though in courts it is now perhaps but little
needed, there are many places in which it might, we think, be
revived with great advantage. The immunity which passed from
the Crown was divided among the public. Every man's house
became his castle. Every man's peculiar set, creed, system, or

party became a kind of court, in which he might live surrounded
by the echoes of his own thoughts, and flattered by a convincing
uniformity of sentiment, as secure as kings were once from the
intrusion of unwelcome censures. But this is a security which a
man who duly distrusts his own skill or courage in self-dissection
can hardly wish to enjoy; though if he distrusts likewise his
resolution to court annoyances because they are wholesome,
which he might exclude because they are disagreeable, he will
wish it broken as inoffensively as possible; and with as few of
those shocks and mortifications from which correction, in whatever form it comes, can never be wholly free. It is for this purpose
that, if it were possible to restore dead fashions to life, we would
revive the office of jester. It is by the squandering glances of the
fool that the wise man's folly is anatomized with least discomfort.
From the professed fool he may receive the reproof without feeling the humiliation of it; and the medicine will not work the
worse, but the better, for being administered under the disguise
of indulgence or recreation. It would be well, indeed, if every
man could keep a licensed jester, who, whether in thought or
action, has too much his own way. All coteries, literary, political,
or fashionable, which enjoy the dangerous privilege of leading
the tastes and opinions of the little circle which is their world,
ought certainly to keep one as part of their establishment. The
House of Commons, being at once the most powerful body on
the earth, and the most intolerant of criticism, stands especially
in need of an officer who may speak out at random without fear
of Newgate. Every philosopher who has a system, every theologian
who heads a sect, every projector who gathers a company, every
interest that can command a party, would do wisely to retain a
privileged jester. The difficulty is to find a becoming disguise
under which the exercise of such a privilege would be pleasant
or even endurable. The motley and the coxcomb are obsolete.
They belonged to the 'free and holiday-rejoicing' youth of
England, and have no mirth in them for us. To the nineteenth
century, in which every hour must have its end to attain, and its
account to render, and every soul must be restlessly bent on providing wares for the market, or seeking a market for its wares
(which is what we now mean by 'doing well'), the foolishness

of fools is only folly. A modern Jacques, desirous of a fool's license to speak his mind, and of procuring from the infected world a patient reception of his cleansing medicines, must find some other passport into its self-included and self-applauding circles, – some other stalking-horse than professional foolery under which to shoot his wit. But in one form or other the heart of man will have its holiday; and whichever of the pursuits of the day has in it most of relaxation and amusement and least of conscious object, whichever is most popular yet least prized – the favourite that has no friend – will supply a suitable mask under which freedom of speech may still be carried on. This, in our day, is unquestionably the novel. It is over novels in three volumes that the mind of this generation relaxes itself from its severer pursuits, into that state of dreamy inadvertency which is the best condition for the alterative treatment which we recommend. It is a maxim that 'the mind is brought to any thing better, and with more sweetness and happiness, if that whereunto you pretend be not first in the intention, but *tanquam aliud agendo*,' – and certainly the mind of a modern novel reader, forgetting its graver purposes in a pleasurable anxiety for the marriage of the hero and heroine, – purified by terror and pity, – perpetual pity for their crosses, and occasional terror for their fate, – may be brought by the way to imbibe many strange and salutary lessons, which, if formally addressed to it, would have been rejected at once as tedious, mischievous, or unprofitable. The truth of this has in practice been largely recognised. Politics, religion, criticism, metaphysics, have all used this introduction to the heart of the public; and the disguise is at least equally well fitted for the purposes of that philosophy, the function of which is to detect the sore places in favourite creeds, doctrines, or fashions, by the test of half-earnest ridicule; to insinuate the vanity of popular judgments which are too popular to be openly assailed with success; to steal on men's minds some suspicion of the frauds, and corruptions, and inanities, and absurdities, which pass current in the world under the protection of names too sacred to be called in question without impiety.

The author of the works which we are about to review is in many respects eminently qualified for this office; in which he has for some years been labouring with great skill and assiduity. His influence, indeed, does not seem as yet to have been considerable. The popularity of his works has been just sufficient to make them scarce; which implies that they are highly esteemed, but by a limited circle of readers. In fact, an early popularity was not to be expected for them; and it may be doubted whether they will ever attain a place in our circulating literature. Their rare excellence in some qualities carries them too high above the taste of ordinary readers; while their serious deficiency in some others will prevent them from obtaining a permanent value in the estimation of a better class. The refined beauty of the composition, pure as daylight from the flaring colours by which vulgar tastes are attracted, 'as wholesome as sweet, and by very much more handsome than fine', is of itself sufficient to keep them on the upper shelves of circulating libraries; while certain shallows and questionable regions in the author's philosophy will make them uninteresting to many deeper judges.

For our own parts, however, we are not so easily deterred. Good books are not so plentiful that we can afford to throw them away because they are not better; and though fully prepared to be just judges in public, we must take the liberty to be familiar in private, and keep a copy of these questionable volumes within reach of our easier chair. In truth we much doubt the wisdom of living only in the company of such as are perfect. It is to go out of the world before our time; to deal with the children of the world as if they were no wiser in their generation than ourselves. Doubtless, mental and moral obliquities are to be censured wherever we meet them, and if possible amended. Yet it cannot be denied that they help to perform much necessary service, which could not be done so well without them. The economy of the world requires characters and talents adapted to various offices, low as well as high; and it is vain to deny that the lower offices will be most readily undertaken and most efficiently discharged by minds which are defective in some of the higher attributes. There is work to be done in the state which a man may be too good to qualify himself for without in some degree contracting the circle of his goodness; and there is work to be done in the province of knowledge and literature to which the deepest and largest and best balanced intellects cannot address themselves with eager interest or undivided attention. We must have spies as well as soldiers, hangmen and informers as well as magistrates and lawgivers, advocates as well as judges, antiquaries as well as historians, critics as well as poets, pullers down as well as builders up, scoffers to scourge falsehood as well as philosophers to worship truth. There is a place as well as a time for all things, and a hand for every work that is done under the sun.

Whether, indeed, these works are so necessary as to justify us in *educating* workmen to excel in them, we are happily not concerned to enquire. There is no danger of a scarcity. When we have done all we can to extend education and raise the tone of public feeling, and train all men to the noblest functions of which they are capable, there will still be more than enough of coarse grain and tortuous growth, whose abilities will be well enough adapted to the narrower spheres, whose aspirations will not rise higher, and who will really, in performing these necessary works, be cultivating their talents to the best advantage. Being there, the only question is how they shall be dealt with; whether they shall be acknowledged, as good after their kind, or cast out as unworthy of our better company; praised for being faithful over a few things, or condemned because so few have been entrusted to them. For ourselves we have no hesitation in preferring the humaner alternative. It is our favourite belief that there is in every man and in every thing a germ of good, which, if judiciously educed and fostered, may be made gradually to prevail over the surrounding bad, and convert it more and more into its own likeness. But this must be one by favour and encouragement. It is not by whipping the faults, but by expressing a just sympathy with the virtues that the final predominance of the better nature is to be brought about. And if it is for their interest that this treatment should be adopted, it will be our own fault if we do not turn it to advantage for ourselves. The labours of men who are pursuing any thing with an earnest desire to find it, can never be positively worthless. They are sure to make out something which is worth knowing; the possession of which can only be injurious when improperly applied, or valued at more than its real worth; the pursuit of which can only become mischievous or unprofitable when it involves the sacrifice, or interferes with the attainment, of something better. Wealth, distinction, power, though not worth living for, are well worth having while we live. A fragment of truth is a good thing, so far as it goes. Wit does not lose its value as wit, when it mistakes itself for wisdom. The things themselves are of sterling worth; they lose the value which they have only by arrogating a value which they have not; and it is our own fault if we cannot restore them to their proper place, and make that good for us by regarding it in its true character, which is bad where we find it only because it affects a higher.

It is not to be denied that this faculty is called into unusual activity by the works before us. The reader must bring with him his own philosophy, moral, religious, and political. The feast is ample and various, but every man must help and digest for himself. Indeed the very aim and idea of them requires that it should be so. That the author should come before us, not as a teacher, but as a questioner of what others teach, is of the essence of his privilege. For this purpose something of waywardness and levity; – some apparent looseness, inconsistency, or absurd liberty; some daring claim to allowance and indulgence too extravagant to be meant or taken in earnest, – is as necessary to him as motley to the jester, or bluntness and oddity of manners to the humorist. It is the pretext and excuse for his raillery; the illusion (more or less discerned, but willingly submitted to) which disarms resentment, and makes censure and earnest opposition seem ridiculous and out of place; which enables us, in the words of Jacques, –

> To weed our better judgments
> Of all opinion that grows rank in them.
> That he is wise.

He must not mean all he says, or he could not say all he means. It is for us to find out for ourselves how much is to be taken in earnest. He appears not as a judge, but as an advocate; licensed to espouse either side, and to defend it by bad evidence as well as good; by sophistry where sound arguments are not forthcoming; and by improvements on the truth where the simple truth will not serve his turn. It is for his opponent to argue the question

on the opposite side; and for us the judges to bear a wary eye
and catch the truth which is struck forth from the collision of the
two. The motto which he has prefixed to his earliest work gives
us the key to all —

> All philosophers who find
> Some favourite system to their mind;
> In every point to make it fit,
> Will force all nature to submit.

He is the disturber-general of favourite systems, the self-retained
advocate of nature against all philosophers who affect to discern
her secrets.

Among the various offices, high and low, by which the purposes of society are served, and for which a supply of fit candi-
dates is never wanting, we shall not be suspected, after what we
have said, of placing this too high in point of dignity, whatever
we may think of its usefulness. But that which justifies a man
in following any vocation, is not its dignity, but it adaptation to
his own nature; and it would be hard to find another for which
our author is so well fitted by natural constitution and capacity
as for this. A wandering and contemplative turn of mind; a
patient conviction of the vanity of all human conclusions; an
impatient sense of the absurdity of all human pretensions, quick-
ened by a habitual suspicion of their insincerity; an eye and a
heart open enough to impressions and opinions of all kinds, so
that vanity be the end of all; a perception of the strangeness and
mystery which involves our life, — keen enough to enliven the
curiosity, but not to disturb or depress the spirit; with faith in
some possible but unattainable solution just sufficient to make
him watch with interest the abortive endeavours of more sanguine
men, but not to engage him in the pursuit himself; a questioning,
not a denying spirit, — but questioning without waiting for an
answer; an understanding very quick and bright, — not narrow
in its range, though wanting in the depth which only deeper
purposes can impart; a fancy of singular play and delicacy; a
light sympathy with the common hopes and fears, joys and
sorrows of mankind, which gives him an interest in their occupa-
tions just enough for the purposes of observation and intelligent

amusement; a poetical faculty, not of a very high order, but quite capable of harmonizing the scattered notes of fancy and observation, and reproducing them in a graceful whole; – such, if we have read him rightly, are the dispositions and faculties with which he has been turned forth into this bustling world of speculation, enterprise, imposture, and credulity, with its multiplying spawn of cant, quackery, and pretension; – such the original constitution which seems to point out as his natural and genial vocation the hue and cry after folly in its grave disguises; the philosophy of irreverence and incredulity; the light and bloodless warfare, between jest and earnest, against all new doctrines, accepted or proclaimed for acceptance, – clamorously hailed by the many, or maintained in defiant complacency by the self-constituted 'fit and few'.

The impartiality with which he quits himself in this warfare is marvellous, and scarcely explicable unless on the supposition that he has within a deeper and more substantial faith to repose on than any which he allows to appear. Naked scepticism, – blank privation of faith and hope, – can never be really impartial; it is an uncertain succession of fleeting partialities; vain, querulous discontented, full of quarrel and unquietness, full of spite and favouritism, full, above all, of itself. Not so with our author. He stands, among the disputing opinions of the time, a disengaged and disinterested looker-on; among them, but not of them; showing neither malice nor favour, but a certain sympathy, companionable rather than brotherly, with all; with natural glee cheering on the combatants to their discomfiture, and as each rides his hobby boldly to the destruction prepared for him, regarding them all alike with the same smile of half compassionate amusement. Of all the philosophies which are encouraged to expose themselves in these pages, we have endeavoured in vain to conjecture which enjoys the largest, or which the smallest share of his sympathy. Could we find one constantly associated with more agreeable personal qualities, or with more brilliant conversation, or with sounder argument than any other; – were there any which he seemed to handle with peculiar tenderness, or in the showing up of which he appeared to take peculiar pleasure; we might suspect that we had discovered the secret of his preference or aversion. But no such clue is offered to us. The instances of the kind which we have been able to detect serve only, when rightly understood, to baffle us more completely. It might certainly seem that his respect for the good old times of roast-beef and quarter-staff, and his contempt for the 'march of intellect', have a touch of earnestness in them; – that of all theories of human life, that which maintains the superiority, in all that concerns man's real welfare, of the twelfth century to the nineteenth, has most of his secret sympathy; and, that that which is advocated in broken Scotch by certain imaginary members of our own fraternity, and which may be called the politico-economical theory, is most to his personal distaste; – that of all characters his favourite is the worldly man who boldly proclaims and acquiesces in his infirmity; his aversion, the worldly man whose weakness is disguised by himself under the affectation of something better, or protected from the censure of society by the sanctity of his profession or his order. But, rightly considered, these apparent sympathies and antipathies are not to be taken as an index to his real feelings. It is not their greater or less conformity to his own tastes, but their greater or less acceptance in the world, by which he is repelled or attracted. We see in them only the working of a scepticism truly impartial and insatiable, which, after knocking down all the opinions which are current in the world, proceeds to set up an opinion made up of all that is *not* current in the world, that when that falls too, the desolation may be complete. Hence his tenderness to the twelfth century. The worshippers of the twelfth century are a race extinct. It is a fallen image, to insult which would be to flatter not to oppose the dogmatists of the time. That which has no friends he can treat with tenderness; that which others have thrown aside as false, his vocation requires or his genius moves him to seek some truth in. Our own philosophy, on the contrary, is of a newer fashion. It draws the largest audience; therefore the largest variety of folly, pretension, and credulity, as well as of their opposites. It is the article which best meets the wants of the time, and is therefore most puffed, hawked, and counterfeited. It provides him, we need not care to confess, with a great deal of legitimate work; nor do we desire to exclude him from our precincts. The light shafts which he employs cannot hurt us where we are sound; and where they do touch us, we are not above profiting by the hint. We will not fall into the common error of taking, what we see to be good physic in our neighbour's case, to be poison in our own. His apparent predilections with regard to personal character are to be explained in the same way. Some predilection for something, it was necessary to feel or feign. Otherwise, his fictions would have wanted warmth and a body. They would have wanted that reference to something positive, without which his world of negations could not have been made palpable; that standard of substance, without which the emptiness of the surrounding shadows could not have been explained. Being obliged to represent some character or other as an object of sympathy, he naturally fixes on that with which no one professes to sympathize. Projects for the diffusion of knowledge, the suppression of vice, the advancement of science, the regeneration of philosophy, or the purification of politics, are entertained as amusing vanities; but a genuine devotion to good eating and drinking, neither disguised nor excused, but studiously indulged, and boldly professed, as the natural occupation of a sound mind in a sound body, is a quality on which his eye pauses with an enjoyment almost akin to love. Not that he really esteems it (we know nothing of him, but imagine him a temperate man, with a thorough contempt for made dishes), but because it is his calling and his delight thus audaciously to reverse the opinion of the world; and to make all the idols for the worship of which men quarrel, appear hollow and ridiculous in the presence of that which they agree in despising. On the same principle it may be observed that the desire of Dinner is, in these novels, the one touch of nature that makes the whole world kin; the one thing good for man all the days of this vain life which he spendeth as a shadow, on which all philosophers agree, – the one thing which abides with him of his labour. All conflicting theories shake hands at the sound of the dinner-bell. All controversies, however divergent, where the disputants are growing ever hotter and wider asunder as they proceed, strangely converge and meet in the common centre of the dinner table. . . .

The spirit of frolic exaggeration in which the characters are

conceived, – each a walking epitome of all that is absurd in
himself, – the ludicrous felicity of self-exposure with which they
are made to talk and act, – and the tone of decided though
refined caricature which runs through the whole, unite to set
grave remonstrance fairly at defiance. And while the imagination is thus forced into the current of his humour, the taste is
charmed by a refinement of manners, and by a classical purity
and reserved grace of style, which carries all sense of coarseness
or vulgarity clean away; and the understanding is attracted and
exercised by the sterling quality of the wit, the brilliancy, fulness,
and solidity of the dialogue, the keenness of observation, the
sharpness and intelligence, if not the delicacy or philosophical
depth, of satire; and a certain roguish familiarity with the
deceitfulness of human nature, from which we may derive many
useful hints, to be improved at pleasure. Add to this, that
although he dwells more habitually among doubts and negations
than we believe to be good for any man, he is not without positive impulses, – generous and earnest, so far as they go, – which
impart a uniformly healthy tone to his writings. There are many
things both good and bad which he does not recognise; but the
good which he does recognise is really good; the bad really bad.
Explicit faith of his own he seems to have none; the creeds,
systems, and theories of other men he treats alike as toys to play
with; his humour, though pure, is shallow : his irony covers little
or none of that latent reverence and sympathy, – rarely awakens
within that 'sweet recoil of love and pity', – which gives to irony
its deepest meaning, and makes it in many minds the purest, if
not the only natural language of tender and profound emotion;
his general survey of life has something of coldness and hardness,
so that much good seed falls in vain and withers on the surface.
But his nature bears no weeds, and the natural products of the
soil are healthy and hardy. Inhumanity, oppression, cant, and
false pretensions of all kinds are hated with a just hatred; mirth,
sunshine, and good fellowship are relished with a hearty relish;
simplicity, unassuming goodness, and the pure face of nature
never fail to touch him with natural delight. It is most pleasant
and encouraging to observe these better qualities gradually prevailing and exercising in each successive production a larger in-

fluence. The humour seems to run deeper; the ridicule is informed with a juster appreciation of the meaning of the thing ridiculed; the disputants are more in earnest, and less like scoffers in disguise; there is more of natural warmth and life in the characters; and, altogether, there is a humaner spirit over his later works, and a kindlier sympathy with his subject.

A corresponding improvement may also be observed in the management of his plots – in the skill with which the incidents are interwoven with the conversations, and made to assist in developing the humours of the dialogue. In the two earliest of them, indeed, *Headlong Hall* and *Melincourt*, the whole story might be stripped off, so as to leave a series of separate dialogues scarcely injured by the change. We should miss only, what, indeed, we should be very sorry to miss, the picturesque grouping and lively satirical narrative by which they are accompanied and relieved. In *Nightmare Abbey* this could not be so easily done. Without the successive situations which form the story, the humour of *character* (which is more considerable in this than in the two foregoing tales) could hardly be brought out. Scythrop, the gloomy and mystical regenerator, who builds morbid hopes for the future upon a morbid discontent with the present; – Mr Glowry, the large-landed misanthropist, to whose table all men are welcome, who can find nothing in the world for a reasonable man to enjoy; – and Mr Toobad, the Manichean millennarian, who can see nothing there except the devil himself, having great wrath – could hardly have been displayed in full character without the loves, jealousies, and contradictions which it is the business of the narrative to develope. In *Maid Marian* and *Crotchet Castle*, the interest lies in a kind of running commentary on the action; which would lose its meaning if the scene and story were taken away. In *Crotchet Castle*, the incidents are employed to bring out the humours of individual character, and are so well wrought into the texture of the work, that, slight as they are, they could not be separated from it without material injury. It is not that truth to nature is more strictly preserved in the later than in the earlier tales, for the spirit of exaggeration and caricature is still kept up; but that the caricature is deeper and more pervasive, and better harmonized. In the latter, the characters *live* upon their hobbies; in the former, they only mount them to dispute upon.

But though the management of the plots is in this respect very skilful, the author has wisely abstained (except in one instance, which we shall notice presently) from attempting to give them any independent interest as stories. They are of the simplest construction, and the incidents are taken from everyday life. A hospitable house, a variety of guests, and an occasion which may bring them together on easy terms, are all he wants : no matter whether it may be a Christmas party, a wedding party, a party of speculators in philosophy or in the stocks, or a party of rival suitors to an attractive heiress. The course of true love cannot run too smoothly; virtue cannot triumph with too little help from accident or superhuman effect, – need not indeed triumph at all; the true heir cannot be in too little danger of losing his inheritance; the meeting of the guests cannot be too easily brought about, or the parting cause too few tears. The business of the fiction lies in the dialogues, and would only be injured and embarassed by any independent interest that might be combined with it of an exciting or pathetic nature.

The importance of observing this principle may be best seen in the effect which, in the instance to which we have alluded, is produced by a departure from it. Anthelia Melincourt is an heiress endowed with all virtues of mind and body, – not without an estate of ten thousand a-year to make them manifest to the apprehension, and operative upon the happiness, of mankind. These combined attractions draw together a sufficient variety of suitors, and supply them with a fair opportunity for exhibiting their peculiarities. Aristocracy, landed propriety, established churchmanship, political economy, match-making maternity, barouche-driving baronetcy, and chivalry in modern attire, – all gather round her as principals, or as seconds. They must disperse again as soon as her choice is made. In the mean-time, there is plenty of mutton to eat, of wine to drink, and of subjects to dispute about. Such circumstances would, in the common course of things, breed crosses and misunderstandings quite enough for all the author's purposes, without extorting from nature any unnecessary exertions. But, instead of contenting him-

self with these, he has borrowed on this one occasion the com-
mon-place-book of a melodramatist, and tried the fortitude of
his heroine by a forcible abduction, and the constancy of his hero
(and, indeed, of his reader), by an anxious pursuit. She is
carried off by a noble suitor, and shut up in a solitary castle,
nobody knows where. Her lover sets off on foot to find her; accompanied by a political economist with whom he may hold dialogues by the way. He wanders about for some days, discussing
in a very calm and philosophical spirit a variety of questions suggested by the scenes through which they pass – such as paper-
money, surplus population, epitaphs, apparitions, the probable
stature of the Patagonians, mountains, and the hopes of the
world – but meets with no trace whatever of the heroine; till at
length, by the most forunate accident in the world, he suddenly
stumbles upon her, at that precise moment of time when, if he
had not, – the author must have found some difficulty in going
on. The dialogues and conversations by which the weariness of
this journey is beguiled, are most of them very elegant and
spirited compositions; but they have so little to do with the
heroine or the story, that they might be left out without diminish-
ing the interest of the tale, and published as separate papers
without losing any of their own. And, indeed, every reader who
feels anxious for the fate of Anthelia – which, to confess the truth,
we ourselves do not – had better pass at once from the first
chapter of the third volume to the last; and read the rest at his
leisure, as an independent work of a quite different character.
He cannot have sympathy in him for both at once.

Nor is this the only demand which is made on the reader in
this work for moods of sympathy incompatible with each other.
It presents a worse combination than that of moving accidents
and melodramatic escapes, with miscellaneous dialogue of a
philosophical cast; – a combination, to our taste still more in-
harmonious, of the reality with the masquerade of life; the
comedy, with the farce; of grave questions for the conscience,
with the merest buffooneries of wit; of touching appeals to the
affections, with absurd assaults upon risibility; and no attempt
seems to have been made to reconcile these incompatible moods –
to make them blend with each other by the interfusion of some

sentiment common to both, or relieve each other by the force of just and harmonious contrast.

It was probably from a consciousness of these defects that the author determined to exclude this tale from the collection before us, though it is evident that no small pains have been bestowed on it; and we suspect that at the time of composition it was a favourite. Its purposes appear to be graver, its pretensions loftier than the others; and although, from the defects we have mentioned, it must be pronounced a comparative failure, it contains, if we mistake not, indications of a capacity for a better and a higher strain than he has yet attempted.

To make this appear, it will be necessary to go somewhat into detail, and to hazard another speculation as to the history and development of his mind. The pains will be well repaid, if he should be induced to reconsider the capabilities of the work, and recast it for some future collection in a more perfect form.

Our theory is, that during the composition of *Melincourt* a struggle was going on in his mind between his better and his worse genius, and that the contest was neither decided nor compromised, but drawn, – each party claiming the victory, and setting up a trophy, after the fashion of the Greek armies in Thucydides, on its own side of the field. We have already adverted to his tenderness for the former times, and ascribed it to the natural reaction in a mind like his against the clamorous pretensions of modern refinement. And we have little doubt that it began in this; but had the tale before us been fresher in our memory, we should not perhaps have asserted so roundly that his mind was really as free from bias in this direction as in others. He began in joke, but he seems to have narrowly escaped ending in earnest. He amused his fancy, or gratified his spleen, by setting forth the rival pretensions of the barbarous ages, till he fell in love with the picture he had drawn, – half persuaded himself that civilisation was a downward progress, and had more than half a mind to turn preacher against it in good faith. But here his habitual scepticism, aided probably by his sound sense of the ridiculous, stands in the way. He has not faith enough to turn devotee. He shrinks from the solemnity of the task in which the consistent pursuit of such a purpose must involve him; and, after a brief struggle, during which he wavers indecisively between the graver service of truth, and the more exciting persecution of error, he relapses into the original condition which we have already endeavoured to describe – betakes himself to the work of destruction rather than of edification – to the pulling down of other men's systems instead of building up a better of his own. . . .

Yet though this transient passion – this struggle towards a more earnest life – has yielded to a relapse, its salutary effects have not been wholly obliterated. The hope may have faded, the pursuit may have been abandoned, but the genial glow which it inspired has not departed with it; and its influence may still be traced, mellowing the under thoughts, softening the harsher touches, making the heart and head work more harmoniously together. Even in *Nightmare Abbey*, which was produced in the following year, we seem to perceive traces of this improvement, especially in a point which we have already noticed; – the better development of the humour of *character* as distinguished from the mere battle of opinions. This is a quality which it is of course difficult to exhibit in an extract; but we may refer, as a striking illustration, to the difference between the two representations of transcendentalism in this and the preceding work – between Moly Mystic, whose conversation seems to be mere jargon, quite unworthy of the writer, – exposing nothing except his own inability to see any meaning in what he is laughing at; and Ferdinando Flosky, in whose person he deals many sharp and dexterous strokes, which, though passing wide enough of the individual at whom they appear to have been aimed, do much wholesome execution elsewhere. . . .

Mr Skionar, transcendentalist of *Crotchet Castle*, is yet again an improvement upon Mr Flosky; the rather perhaps because he says very little. What he does say has so much of the sound and movement of the tone of transcendentalism, that it requires some knowledge of the matter to detect the counterfeit. Our limits forbid us to pursue this comparison further. But as many of the characters re-appear in each succeeding Tale under new names, the progress of the author's mind may be easily traced by comparing them with each other. Compare, for instance, Squire

Headlong in the earliest of them, with Mr Hilary in the next;
and again with the Baron in *Maid Marian*; – all belonging to
that class of men who takes life as it comes, and enjoy it, without
caring to understand or to mend it. Observe how crude and
thin a creation is Mr Escot, with his wild man of the woods, and
his skull of Cadwallader, when compared with Mr Chainmail,
and his old baronial hall hung with old armour and banners; –
his boar's head and wassail bowl, his old poetry and old manners
copied from the twelfth century. Or observe the various representatives of the Church established, – the Rev. Dr Gaster, the
more genial Mr Larynx, and the most genial Dr Folliot. It is
easy to see that the difference is not accidental, but springs from
the deeper and kindlier impulses under which the later characters
were moulded. It is like the difference between a Bobadil and a
Falstaff, which might be taken as a measure of the humanity of
the hearts, not less than of the pregnancy of the wits in which
they were conceived. But this progressive triumph of the gentler
nature is nowhere displayed so strikingly as in his heroines. The
mere misses and coquettes who fill that place in his earlier
works (Anthelia Melincourt we have already noticed as an exception, though not a very successful one) seem to have been
created solely for the purpose of making a story to set the dialogues in; yet even there, the secret delight in beauty shows itself
at intervals in shy touches of delicacy and grace. Gradually the
feeling growing stronger and more impatient insists on a fuller
utterance, and is at length permitted to have its way, and to
mould the entire characters of Maid Marian and the heroine of
Crotchet Castle at its own delighted will, for its own pure satisfaction.

> Source: extracts from 'Tales by the Author of *Head-*
> *long Hall*', *Edinburgh Review*, LXVIII (January 1839).

W. M. THACKERAY (1850)

*On Peacock*

. . . Peacock – did you ever read *Headlong Hall* and *Maid Marian*? – a charming lyrical poet and Horatian satirist he was when a writer; now he is a white-headed jolly old worldling, and Secretary [*sic* – Ed.] to the E. India House, full of information about India and everything else in the world.

> SOURCE: extract from *A Collection of Letters of W. M. Thackeray, 1847–1855*, ed. Jane Brookfield (London, 1887); letter of July 1850 to Jane Brookfield.

T. B. MACAULAY (1851)

*Meeting with Peacock*

December 31 [1851] – I met Peacock, a clever fellow, and a good scholar. I am glad to have an opportunity of being better acquainted with him. We had out Aristophanes, Aeschylus, Sophocles, and several other old fellows, and tried each other's quality pretty well. We are both strong enough in these matters for gentlemen.

> SOURCE: extract from G. O. Trevelyan, *The Life and Letters of Lord Macaulay* (1876).

SIR MOUNTSTUART E. GRANT DUFF (1853)

*A New Use for Utilitarians*

*November* 10 [1853]. Mr. Peacock talked to me to-day at much
length about Jeremy Bentham, with whom he had been extremely intimate – dining with him *tête à tête*, once a week for
years together. He mentioned, amongst other things, that when
experiments were being made with Mr. Bentham's body after
his death, Mr. James Mill had one day come into his (Mr.
Peacock's) room at the India House and told him that there had
exuded from Mr. Bentham's head a kind of oil, which was almost
unfreezable, and which he conceived might be used for the oiling
of chronometers which were going into high latitudes. 'The less
you say about that, Mill,' said Peacock, 'the better it will be for
*you*; because if the fact once becomes known, just as we see now
in the newspapers advertisements to the effect that a fine bear is
to be killed for his grease, we shall be having advertisements to
the effect that a fine philosopher is to be killed for his oil.'

SOURCE: extract from *Notes from a Diary, 1851–1871*
(1897) p. 60.

ANONYMOUS (1861)

*'Quaint, hearty, unostentatious Paganism'*

. . . *Gryll Grange* is a very strange book, full of learning, of odd
opinions, of jokes, good and bad; but what binds it together, and
invests it with a peculiar charm, is its quaint, hearty, unostentatious Paganism. Most modern Paganism is offensive. It either
shows itself under the form of a coarse opposition to Christianity,
or under that of a longing for a forbidden license. There is nothing of that sort in *Gryll Grange*. There is no sneering, no coarse-

ness, no sensuality. But the author lives in a world of thought
from which Christian notions are excluded. He has imbibed the
classical spirit so thoroughly that he cares for nothing except
what might commend itself to a virtuous Pagan, and thinks only
as men thought before Christianity awoke them to the consciousness of sin, of suffering, and of immortality. His one view of life
is to drink wine and indulge his genius, to love and to joke before
the end comes when wine and sport will be no more. There never
perhaps were collected together so many mottoes as in this volume
expressive of a desire for classical festivity, for cups, and garlands,
and the pleasures of to-day. The effect produced is totally distinct from that produced by Moore's Anacreontics. The author
is not inviting Christians to a debauch, nor is he glorifying the
classical past at the expense of all that seems most precious in
the modern world. He simply ignores all that does not fit in with
the creed of the writers whom he most admires. It seems out of
place to judge him by our ordinary rules of right and wrong. If
we came across an old lady whose sole pleasure it was, and from
her childhood had been, to draw landscapes in the Chinese style,
we should never think of spoiling her happiness by intruding on
her the criticism suggested by the art of perspective. We should
yield ourselves to the amusement of contemplating the oddity of
her pursuit, and the sunny gaiety which accompanied its exercise. In the same way, *Gryll Grange* is beyond the pale of ordinary
criticism. The author, however excellent a Christian he may be in
practical life, in his literary moments is simply a learned Pagan,
and his book is a very entertaining specimen of the Paganism he
loves.

His learning and his Paganism together have enabled him to
write what learned people at least may read with instruction and
pleasure. He has so thoroughly identified himself with his favourite authors, that he can write about them or refer to them so
easily and naturally as to escape any strong tinge of pedantry
and antiquarian tiresomeness. It ought not, however, to be supposed that it is only with the classical authors that he is familiar.
He knows the standard English and Italian authors thoroughly,
but he looks at them always under the influence of the ideas
which the great writers of Greece and Rome have printed in-

delibly on his mind. Very various subjects have also attracted his attention. He is great on cooking. He is great on the fine arts. When he sets himself seriously to make a remark, it is generally good and true. There are many capital suggestions and dis- quisitions in the volume on the most miscellaneous subjects. He has much to say about the Greek musical scale; he discusses the reasons why the Greek painters attended so little to their back- grounds; he explains difficult passages in Homer, in Petronius Arbiter, in Persius; he gives his reasons for preferring one edition of Boiardo rather than another. There is no point too remote or various for him to take up, settle, and dismiss. The volume reads like a few numbers of *Notes and Queries* jumbled up with a funny love story, and pervaded by a fine Pagan morality. The greatest tribute to its merits than can be paid is to say – what may be said with perfect truth – that all this queer mixture flows easily along, and that we never feel that we have been delivered over to a learned bore.

The author is a man of dislikes as strong as his likes, and the discursive nature of his book enables him to have a fling at almost everything that he hates. Often what he says is shrewd and true, even when exaggerated; and even when he seems to us to go wrong, we enjoy the relish with which this veteran Pagan slashes at all modern innovations that he detests. He has two especial objects of attack. His whole soul revolts against the Social Science Association and Competitive Examination. He is never tired of springing little mines of attack upon the 'Pantopragmatic Society, under the presidency of Lord Facing-both-ways', and he has been at the trouble of writing what he calls an Aristo- phanic comedy, in order to get in a scene that will blast competi- tive examination, if comedy can blast it. It is complicated by a side attack on spirit-rapping, but still enough is directed against examiners to make their hair stand on end. . . .

S o u r c e : extract from anonymous article, *'Gryll Grange'*,
*The Saturday Review* (16 March 1861) 274–5.

ANONYMOUS (1866)

*'A satirist who shot Folly as it flew'*

The name of Peacock as a writer of fiction is too little known by the readers of our generation; but Shelley's executor, the author of *Headlong Hall, Nightmare Abbey, Maid Marian* (with its charming lyrics), *Crotchet Castle, Melincourt*, and, the other day, *Gryll Grange* – the friend and collaborator of Bentham, and Mill, and Grote, must not pass to his rest, at the patriarchal age of eighty, without a tribute to his racy wit, his quaint reading, and his quiet command of our mother-tongue. Rated among novelists, Peacock, in one respect, counts for little. He never tried for plot; he had small descriptive power. Rated as a satirist who shot Folly as it flew, and could exhibit the philosophies and paradoxes of the time with an epigrammatic keenness, and withal a genial recognition of all that is best, highest, and most liberal, he demands no common praise, and will hold no common place whenever the story of ultra-liberal literature comes to be written.

> SOURCE: extract from anonymous notice in *The Athenaeum* (10 February 1866).

GEORGE BARNETT SMITH (1873)

*'Negative Gifts'*

Wit dissects and destroys, but it has no creative force, is almost devoid of enthusiasm, and is no respecter of dignities and persons. There is much truth, however, which can in nowise come within its scope; hence it is a fallacy to call it the test of truth. It is rather the discoverer of error. There is something in the mental constitution of the satirist which prevents him from taking an optimist view of things. He is all the more useful on that account. The negative gifts of the satirist, while not lifting him to an equality with the being who originates, still entitle him to a high place in the world's regard. It should be borne in mind, too, that though it will be generally found he lacks enthusiasm, yet he possesses a sensitiveness as real, while differing in quality, as that of the artist and the poet.

Thomas Love Peacock had every opportunity for becoming the calm, contemplative cynic. His life was long but uneventful. His fourscore years did not embrace ten events to be remembered even in an ordinary life. . . .

It is not a little singular to find one whose tastes were those of the recluse taking up in his writings the burning questions of the day and mingling in the fray of politics. His observation, however, was most extensive; like his learning, it seemed to embrace all matters and topics which came to the surface of public life. In his own political views he must have been ardently progressive – Liberal in the highest sense of the word, and to the backbone. He would be as opposed to a Whig job as to a Conservative monopoly. The deep-rooted conviction he had of the rights of man, the individual, caused him to loathe injustice in whatever quarter it was perceived. It is impossible to read his works and not to admire his denunciations of the base, and his scorn of the petty, sins which are sometimes hugged so closely. He had many pagan qualities, and among them a pagan kind of rectitude.

As to his humour, it is exclusively his own; one never meets with its precise flavour either before or after him. Mingled sometimes with a dash of effrontery, it is very searching, attaining its end by a kind of intellectual travesty. To the quack and the mountebank he is a most dangerous person, wielding a power of castigation that is amazing. To his honour, however, it can be said that throughout his whole works there is no demonstration of personal feeling. Considering his endowment and the great temptation to wield the lash which invariably accompanies it, his self-repression was very great. Principles, not men, were the objects of his satire, and if occasionally individuals recoiled from the smart, it only showed how true had been his perceptions of character. Some humorists gently play with their subjects and tease them as a cat does a mouse; others knock them down with a bludgeon; whilst others again make them despise themselves by inverting their natures, and showing them their vanity, hollowness, and pretence. Peacock adopted the last method with all the human excrescences he dealt with. To rebuke incapacity in attempting to deal with things too high for it, and to tear the glazed mask from the hollow cheek of pretence, were the objects to which he devoted himself. . . .

Other works may have their own special charm, but that which is richest in the exhibition of the most prominent gift of the author is *Headlong Hall*. Before the publication of this work there had been no writer who so boldly flung himself into the arena against contemporary humbugs. It is infinitely refreshing to read his straightforward scathing denunciations as well as his insinuating facetiousness and inuendo. He seems to revel in a tilt against all that the world praises as proper and respectable. An intellectual and material epicureanism pervades his pages, and when the rollicking wit ceases to flow it is only to give time for the passing of the bottle. We not only get 'the feast of reason and flow of soul', but an unswerving devotion to those creature comforts in which the clergy – first in good works – have ever been our leaders. Mr. Headlong, the representative of the ancient Welsh family of the Headlongs, claiming superior anti-quity to Cadwallader, contracts a strange taste in a Welsh squire – the taste for books. He next desires to pass for a philo-sopher and a man of taste, and comes up to Oxford to inquire for other men of taste and philosophers; but 'being assured by a learned professor that there were no such things in the Univer-sity', he proceeds to London, where he makes as extensive ac-quaintance with philosophers and *dilettanti* as his ambition could desire. Several of these he invites to Headlong Hall, and the staple of the volume is composed of their doings and their discussions. The four leading personages who sustain the brunt of the battle are – Mr. Foster, the perfectibilian, who takes the bright view of everything; Mr. Escot, the deteriorationist, who takes the dark view of everything; Mr. Jenkison, the statu-quo-ite, who has arguments to advance on both sides, but is nearly always in favour of allowing things to remain as they are; and the Rev. Dr. Gaster, a worthy divine who can deliver a learned dissertation on the art of stuffing a turkey, and to whom the consumption of a bottle of port is a very slight matter. It is amusing to note how the various classes of thinkers are trotted out one after another on their respective hobbies, and how impartial the author is in dividing his favours amongst them. Nor is it a little singular that all his specimens of the clergy whom Peacock has drawn are of one type; they are all jolly men of the world. About fifty or sixty years ago, the time at which he wrote, the conventional parson was very frequently of this stamp. His life was passed between fox-hunting, card-playing, and drinking. Since then the muscular Christian and other excellent men have arisen. But there have also sprung up with them men almost of a more mischievous type than the old fox-hunter. There are too many pitiful shepherds left who, in quiet, out-of-the-way villages make the life of the poor a burden to them. These continually enlarge on the duty of the labourers to keep their proper stations, and to revere the clergy and the squirearchy – the former of whom are to provide for them their opinions and their spiritual food, the latter their temporal comforts. Many of the later clergy are in the eyes of sensible men little less contemptible than the old; the venue of our contempt has been changed, that is all. But there is the same difficulty existing now that there was in Peacock's time, and indeed has been in all ages, – the difficulty of persuading the clergy to take one step towards reform in any direction, till nearly all other classes have taken ten. Progress, to them, has generally meant the destruction of their cherished rights. . . .

In *Crotchet Castle* the author still writes with the pen of wormwood and ink of gall. The motto sufficiently indicates in the outset what a pungency of wit may be expected – 'Le monde est plein de fous, et qui n'en veut pas voir, doit se tenir tout seul, et casser son mirroir.' The complacency of many people is effectually destroyed by the way the author himself breaks the mirrors in which they have been wont to survey their own perfections. Possibly there may be those who think that in this work he has overstepped the just bounds of ridicule, and endeavoured to bring into contempt persons who are really useful to their generation. This is the conclusion to which a merely surface-reading of his books would lead, and probably many would rise from their perusal with an impression as unjust to the writer as could well be. Because Peacock ruthlessly condemns the pretenders of science, it is not to be supposed, and will not be by the really candid judge, that he has no sympathy with its true and earnest devotees. A Newton would receive his homage equally with an Æschylus or a Homer. He only wishes to prick the windbag; to show upon what a very little a reputation which the world chooses to honour is sometimes built. It is the bubble which he desires to burst – the unsoundness in our social and political economics he endeavours to expose. Probably there was no one who would have felt it more deeply than he, if he had imagined that what he was writing would be turned from its purpose, either wilfully or ignorantly, and the writer made to appear an enemy of truth. It is hard, at times, to get rid of the idea that he is laughing at all the rest of the world, which, in any, is the surest test of folly, for the mighty wisdom of the cachinnatory great one himself is only a river into which the lesser streams of wisdom in others have flowed. There is no human being who can afford to laugh at and despise the whole race, simply because there is no human being who is not indebted to it. But we absolve our author at once from any such charge as this. Having comprehended in some degree the stand-points from which he has shot his arrows, we are bound to confess, not only that his aim is true, but that he has not chosen his subjects thoughtlessly or unjustifiably. Adam Smith lived long before him, and his principles were well established in the public mind, and acknowledged to be in many respects unassailable. It is not to be imagined for a moment that either he or his true followers were satirised in the person of the Scotch political economist who figures in these pages. Yet, strange to say, there have been critics who have credited him with some such aims, and have employed their acumen in discovering how he has transfixed this and that personage who has hitherto been held as an authority in the branch of literature or science to which he has devoted himself. Nothing could be more fallacious. Peacock was a man who was thoroughly abreast with the intellectual progress of his time; he was deeply interested in it, and capable of sympathizing to the full with all those men whose solid attainments and brilliant talents have been of service to humanity.

Source: extracts from 'Thomas Love Peacock', *Fortnightly Review*, xx (August 1873).

ROBERT BUCHANAN (1875)

*The Survivor*

> And did you once see Shelley plain,
> And did he stop and speak to you?...
> How strange it seems, and new![1]

And this old man had spoken with Shelley, not once, but a thousand times; and had known well both Harriet Westbrook and Mary Godwin; and had cracked jokes with Hobhouse, and chaffed Proctor's latinity; and had seen, and actually criticised, Malibran; and had bought 'the vasty version of a new system to perplex the sages',[2] when it first came out, in a bright, new, uncut quarto; and had dined with Jeremy Bentham; and had smiled at Disraeli, when, resplendently attired, he stood chatting in Hookham's with the Countess of Blessington; and had been face to face with that bland Rhadamanthus, Chief Justice Eldon; and was, in short, such a living chronicle of things past and men dead as filled one's soul with delight and ever-varying wonder. 'How strange it seemed, and new!'. . . .

His chief, almost his only, correspondent was Lord Broughton, who had been his friend through life. The two old gentlemen interchanged letters and verses, and capped quotations, and doubtless felt like two antediluvian mammoths left stranded, and yet living after the Deluge – that Deluge being typified to them by the submersion of Whig and Tory in one wild wave of Progress, and the long career of Lord Brougham as a sort of political

Noah. The old landmarks of society were obliterated. Lord Byron was a dim memory, and the stage-coach was a dream. The poetry of Nature had triumphed, and the poetry of Art had died. Germany had a literature, and it was part of polite education to know German. Beards were worn. Rotten boroughs were no more. The *Times*, like a colossal Podsnap, dominated journalism, but the *Daily Telegraph* was stirring the souls of tradesmen to the sublime knowledge of Lemprière's Dictionary and Bohn's *Index of Quotations*. Special correspondents were invented, competitive examination was consecrating mediocrity, and a considerable number of Englishmen drank bad champagne. What was left for an old scholar, but, like the Hudibrastic Mirror of Knighthood,

> To cheer himself with ends of verse,
> And saying of philosophers!

For the rest, the world was in a bad way; best keep apart, and let it wag. Ψῦξόυ τὸυ οἶυου, Δωρι! Quaff a cool cup in the green shade, and drink confusion to Lord Michin Mallecho and the last Reform Bill!

Source: extracts from 'Thomas Love Peacock: A Personal Reminiscence', *New Quarterly Magazine,* IV (April 1875).

NOTES

1. Robert Browning.
2. Byron's description of Wordsworth's 'Excursion'.

EDITH NICOLLS (1875)

*Old Age and Death*

In society, my grandfather was ever a welcome guest, his genial manner, hearty appreciation of wit and humour in others, and the amusing way in which he told stories made him a very delightful acquaintance; he was always so agreeable and so very witty that he was called by his most intimate friends the 'Laughing Philosopher', and it seems to me that the term 'Epicurean Philosopher', which I have often heard applied to him, describes him accurately and briefly. In public business, my grandfather was upright and honourable; but as he advanced in years, his detestation of anything disagreeable made him simply avoid whatever fretted him, laughing off all sorts of ordinary calls upon his leisure time. His love of ease and kindness of heart made it impossible that he could be actively unkind to any one, but he would not be worried, and just got away from anything that annoyed him. He was very fond of his children, and was an indulgent father to them, and he was a kind and affectionate grandfather; he could not bear any one to be unhappy or uncomfortable about him, and this feeling he carried down to the animal creation; his pet cats and dogs were especially cared for by himself, the birds in the garden were carefully watched over and fed, and no gun was ever allowed to be fired about the place. After he retired from the India House he seldom left Halliford; his life was spent among his books, and in the garden, in which he took great pleasure, and on the river. May-day he always kept in true old English fashion; all the children of the village came round with their garlands of flowers, and each child was presented with a new penny, or silver threepenny or fourpenny piece, according to the beauty of their garlands; the money was given by the Queen of the May, always one of his grand-daughters, who sat beside him, dressed in white and crowned with flowers, and holding a sceptre of flowers in her hand. He loved to keep up these old English customs. It was the habit of my grandfather's life to rise every morning at 5 a.m., and read till 8 a.m. In the winter he

used to light his own fire, and always from the top. All day we
saw but little of him unless we sought him in the library. When
he joined us at seven o'clock dinner (which, by-the-by, he always
ordered himself) his genial manner, sparkling wit, and very
amusing stories were welcomed by us all – his hearty laugh was
most infectious. About a year before his death, he took to reading
the works of Charles Dickens afresh; he found them a rest from
more serious study, which fatigued him latterly a good deal; he
was continually in fits of laughter over *Pickwick*, with which he
was greatly delighted; but *Our Mutual Friend* was, perhaps, his
favourite. He declared that 'Lizzie Hexam' was the perfection of
womanhood, and he was often heard to say, he would give anything if some artist could paint his ideal of her. He talked of her
often with great pleasure, saying that he had quite 'fallen in love
with Lizzie'. His grandchildren loved him – 'Grandpapa was
such a good playfellow.' He entered with great amusement into
any of our games in the garden; in the house we were apt to
grow too noisy, and he hated noise. Towards the close of his life
he grew much depressed in spirits; the loss of his two daughters
was a terrible grief to him, and a very short time before his death
he was greatly shaken by a fire breaking out in the roof of his
bedroom. He was taken to his library, which, being at the other
end of the house, was away from the danger and the water. At
one time it was feared the fire was gaining ground, and that it
would be needful to move him into some one of the houses in
the neighbourhood, but he refused to move. The curate who
came kindly to beg my grandfather to take shelter in his house,
received rather a rough and startling reception, for in answer to
the invitation, my grandfather exclaimed with great warmth and
energy, 'By the immortal gods, I will not move!'

He would not leave his books; and fortunately the danger
passed. He never recovered that fire; he had been weak and ailing
all the winter, and he took to his bedroom almost entirely after
that; he died in a few weeks, in his eighty-first year.

Source: extract from 'A Biographical Notice of
Thomas Love Peacock', in Peacock's *Works*, ed. H. Cole
(1875) vol. I.

E. W. GOSSE (1875)

## The 'Last Man'

A commonplace of conversation, which is only too sadly true, is for ever reminding us that the activity and energy of this age, with its quenchless thirst for physical and mental movement, has swept off the face of the earth a certain very interesting type of the human individual. All English generations before our own have had time to produce a race of men who, without much creative power, have possessed a passion for learning, a craving for reflective intellectual exercise, a faculty for the successful cultivation of *belles-lettres*, which, indeed, have added little to the stores of our literature except some verses, some scholia, or some reflections, but which have done inestimable service in making broad and solid the culture of the educated minority. A quiet practical life, without strain and without the possibility of poverty, has enabled them to cultivate what was called a hundred years ago 'an elegant retirement'. Now the fever of business and the widening of all intellectual interests, the fight for life and the claims of society, conspire to reduce to a minimum the numbers of those who are able and willing to devote themselves to the study of letters for its own sake. The 'people of quality' who did so much in a quiet way for poetry, classical learning, archæology, and music in the eighteenth century are either tempted into the wasting circle of the politics of the hour, or if they give themselves to intellectual exercise at all, it is rather in the channel of experimental science. The gentlemen who met seventy years ago to quote Pindar over their wine, or to discuss Lord Byron's poems over a cup of green tea with my lady, now flock, with geological specimens in their pockets, to the meetings of the British Association, or argue about the acoustic transparency of the atmosphere with scientific ladies from Girton. It would be idle to discuss the advantage or disadvantage of the new state of things. The times change, and we change with them. No doubt the port-wine was heady, the classic quotations monotonous, the criticism dreary and stupid, in the old-world days of elegant retirement. Possibly the present fashion for the anatomy of phenomena may one day seem to have been a scraping among dry bones. The fact is indisputable that the race of gentlemen who combined ease and the *belles-lettres* with an affectionate study of the classics has completely passed away. And Thomas Love Peacock was the last and by no means the least worthy of them.

Many of the characteristics of a 'last man' clung about Mr Peacock. He was suspicious, resentful and dolorous in his aspect towards the world in general, hopeless for the future, regretful of the past, using satire as punishment, not as correction, and saved only by his affectionate and generous inner nature from the moroseness of disappointment and despair.

SOURCE: extract from 'Thomas Love Peacock', *London Society*, XXVII (June 1875).

GEORGE MEREDITH (1879)

*Dr Middleton/Peacock*

The leisurely promenade up and down the lawn with ladies and deferential gentlemen in anticipation of the dinner-bell was Dr. Middleton's evening pleasure. He walked as one who had formerly danced (in Apollo's time and the young god Cupid's), elastic on the muscles of the calf and foot, bearing his broad iron-grey head in grand elevation. The hard labour of the day approved the cooling exercise and the crowning refreshments of French cookery and wines of known vintages. He was happy at that hour in dispensing wisdom or nugae to his hearers, like the western sun, whose habit it is when he is fairly treated to break out in quiet splendours, which by no means exhaust his treasury. Blest indeed above his fellows, by the height of the bow-winged bird in a fair weather sunset sky above the pecking sparrow, is he that ever in the recurrent evening of his day sees the best of it ahead and soon to come. He has the rich reward of a youth and manhood of virtuous living. Dr. Middleton misdoubted the future as well as the past of the man who did not, in becoming gravity, exult to dine. That man he deemed unfit for this world and the next.

An example of the good fruit of temperance, he had a comfortable pride in his digestion, and his political sentiments were attuned by his veneration of the powers rewarding virtue. We must have a stable world where this is to be done.

The Reverend Doctor was a fine old picture, a specimen of art peculiarly English, combining in himself piety and Epicurism, learning and gentlemanliness, with good room for each and a seat at one another's table. . . .

SOURCE: extract from *The Egoist* (1879) ch. 20, 'An Aged and a Great Wine'.

# PART THREE

# Twentieth-century Interpretations

*Carl Van Doren*

# PEACOCK'S REPUTATION (1911)

. . . the novels probably suffer from being placed in a class of
writings to which they belong only by a vague extended resemblance. The novel-reader finds in them little which conforms to
his notion of what a novel should be like : little plot, little attempt
at characterisation, little 'human interest', no passion. He probably feels that the persons of the story indulge in protracted
gossip of which he is not invited to partake any more than he is
asked to share in their frequent banquets. Even if he be interested
in the opinions which form the staple of these arguments, he finds
it confusing to perceive that Peacock, although himself concerned with opinions to the exclusion of almost everything else,
does not seem to care for any one in particular, but plays them
against each other, weighing out alternative victories with easy
impartiality, and finally dismissing them all with a song or a
glass of wine. There is always the difficulty of fitting preconceived
modes of thought to the eccentric angles of Peacock's little world.
Everywhere there is tipsy-turvy : laughter extinguishes reverence,
words play tricks with logic, wine leaves sobriety lurching, up
go the heels of dignity, and folly splits its sides at the jest, wit is
as unpartisan as it is unerring, irony shows its head where it is
least expected, humour bestows its caresses where it will. A
woman may be an angel – an intellectual angel in a pelisse and a
poke-bonnet – or she may be an abstraction to be treated with
the mockery generally meant for men. A man may be a man, a
lay figure, or an ape; presumably he is a fool. It takes good self-
possession not to feel that the reader is being treated with some
of the contempt from which wit can scarcely be disassociated in
the minds of most people. And Peacock's public is treated with
contempt in the sense that he pays only the slightest attention to
its tastes or desires. He wrote his books for his own pleasure, to

a degree unusual even in wilful England. Thus he was bent on
pleasing an audience of the smallest proportions. 'He was
utterly unlike any one I have ever met before or since,' said one
of his friends. Wilfulness, a strong bent towards singularity, was
one of his most prominent intellectual qualities. To it was due
his choice of the novel as the form which gave him the greatest
latitude of expression. It showed him a hospitality which he
could not easily have found elsewhere. Neither the drama, the
lyric, the long poem, nor the essay would have afforded him
such facilities. In the novel he could indulge himself in the dialogue which would have been his chief staple as a writer of
comedy; he could add lyrics at his will; and though he took no
opportunity to include long poems, yet he could make his personages deliver as many oral essays as he pleased. The novel gave
him leisure, without the attention to plot which a comedy would
have demanded, to record his observations of human character
in the terms of the caricaturist. Peacock's eye for 'humours', as
the seventeenth century called them, never slept. His judgment
had in it a peculiar turn which seems almost obliquity of vision.
He saw the world by twists and angles. As in scholarship he
delighted in fantastic learning, so in his novels he neglected
normal human beings to sport with eccentricity.

This does not mean that Peacock's comprehension, his sober
judgment both of men and books, could not often be just, but
so far as his own literary work went, he limited himself to a
narrow field out of which he did not try to stray. He deliberately
avoided discussion of the larger problems which confront serious
thinkers. Lofty speculations, all that concern the origin and
destiny of mankind, he turned away from. The world is in the
hands, it was his habit to say, of Necessity, before whom Jupiter
and his successors are alike helpless. What have men to do with
gods or the business of gods? They sit in 'tranquil abodes which
neither winds do shake nor clouds drench with rains nor snow
congealed by sharp frost harms with hoary fall', and have as little
care for the men beneath their feet as men have power to draw
them down to earth. It is better for men to think only of the
time that passes too rapidly, and best if they regard its flight
with eyes undimmed by gazing into mysteries. The poetry of

faith, intense devotion to ideals too high ever to be realised, magnificent sacrifices where there is no hope, these Peacock comprehended only from a distance, and left to other hands. And even in the world to which he confined himself he did not pretend to be a guide. His apparent denial of moral responsibility repels many who might otherwise, forgiving an occasional obviousness in his satire or lack of point in his ironic criticism, still find his books delightful. It seems almost as if to him the Me of existence were the power to ridicule, and the Not-Me the state of being ridiculous. A speech of Friar Tuck may serve as a text for Peacock's sermon to his readers.

None shall laugh in my company, though it be at my expense, but I will have my share of the merriment. The world is a stage, and life is a farce, and he that laughs most has most profit of the performance. The worst thing is good enough to be laughed at, though it be good for nothing else; and the best thing, though it be good for something else, is good for nothing better.[1]

A man who holds such doctrine has made out of laughter an inaccessible seat from which he will despise the world and be as lonely on his merry throne as the desolate sublime, if there is bitterness mixed with his mirth. In Peacock, however, there is little bitterness. His pessimism was the theme of his daily talk, but it was a half-humorous pessimism, laughing at a hundred things which bitterness would have made him hate. If he despised his generation, it was due chiefly to the consciousness of his intellectual superiority to the huzzas of the rabble. 'I am more afraid of deference to popular clamour than I am of anything under heaven,' he said before one of the parliamentary committees.[2] From the first Peacock felt out of touch with the world he lived in. The fact has given him a reputation for Toryism which cannot be properly said to have characterised his intellect. That he was constitutionally a lover of the past, there is no denying; but to think that his intelligence was submerged by devotion to antiquity, is an error. Nearly the only friends he had were liberal thinkers. His seal bore the line from Horace, 'Nec tardum opperior nec præcedentibus insto' (I neither follow in the rear, nor pursue those who run before me). He considered that his

intellectual position, as a sensible man, was indicated by the
motto. When, in *Crotchet Castle* and *Gryll Grange*, the present
seems to suffer rough handling, it is done less to prove its inferiority to the past than to prove the superiority to either of a
common-sense world of simplicity and peace, which, of course,
never existed, but which Peacock created from the fragments
of the ancient world. It was its offences against peace which
made him scorn the doctrine of progress. That the world needed
to be made better, he had no doubt; it was difficult for him to
see in the midst of the reforming spirit which surrounded his
later life, that anything was being done by the very generation
which actually achieved so much. To fall into paradox, if he had
not been so detached from his contemporaries, he would have
been more so; that is to say, but for his intellectual liberalism,
he would have been temperamentally driven to an affection for
prerevolutionary days which might have spoiled utterly the independence which generally marks his ironic criticism.

If one judges Peacock by the highest qualities of literature,
loftiness to inspire, wisdom to instruct, nobility to incite, or
beauty to enchant, one will simply depreciate him, as by such
standards one must, for failure to achieve excellence in directions
to which he never turned his attention. He fully accepted his
limitations, at any rate after he had reached maturity, and confined his efforts resolutely to the field in which he was proficient.
Subtracting from his praise still further, and without argument,
the power to amuse as Scott or Cervantes amuses, there still
remains excellence, a little narrow, somewhat unvaried, but still
excellence that amounts to supremacy in a type which requires
no mean ability. Satire of a restricted kind, bristling with
eccentricities of opinion and originality of expression which repel
the normal intelligence; without didactic intention to a degree
which estranges sober thinkers; with a sharpness of wit and a
nicety of learning lost upon casual readers – such satire must look
to an audience composed of individuals who unite to liberality
of opinion, quickness of perception, and extent of learning, either
a temper as full of crotchets as Peacock's, from the testimony of
his novels, seems to have been, or else a capacity for sheer enjoyment in the exercise of wit, who or what may be its objects, as

great as Peacock, by the testimony of his life, actually had. Peacockians are wont to plume themselves upon a taste denied to the vulgar as if it conferred upon them some peculiar credit. The credit, as a matter of fact, may belong quite as much to a congenital singularity of perception as to an intelligence sophisticated enough to find in caprice and whim a pleasant diversion after long pedestrian inquiry for firm grounds of opinion. . . .

It is to his adroitness in maintaining a point of view, and to his care as an artist, rather than to his mental or moral power, that Peacock owes his place in English literature. In that literature, and his face will reach few who do not read it with native eyes, he seems to belong to a class which he exhausts, standing alone in laughter as Landor stands in wrath. Inferior to Lamb in personal charm and humour, far to the rear, when it comes to scope, of Fielding, Thackeray, Meredith, Mark Twain, he can by no means be ranked with the ephemerides. Among the wits in whom the first half of the century abounded he enjoys the pre-eminence of having given his work a classical finish that bodes well for the permanence, if not for the extent, of his fame.

Few books in the English language are as compact of sense and learning as the little edition of 1837 which contains *Headlong Hall, Nightmare Abbey, Maid Marian* and *Crotchet Castle.* That year saw the completion of a work which begins a new chapter in mirth, but *The Pickwick Papers* obscured no minor humorist who seems more likely to endure side by side with the great Dickens than Peacock. The slightness of his output, which has enabled a twentieth-century printer to include all the novels in a single small volume, serves only to rank him with the fastidious of the literary tribe who forestall the winnowing action of time voluntarily. One who desires to assign Peacock a rank among his contemporaries will probably put him with Hood, when Hood was not merely journalistic, and with Praed. To go to periods with which Peacock has more in common, he is like Gay and Prior, or Congreve and Sheridan. But these unsatisfactory attempts at classifying prove nothing beyond the often-repeated contention that Peacock is unique. He derives little from any predecessor and bequeaths little to any follower. Except indirectly through Shelley, he exerted small influence upon thought and letters. At the same time, he belonged to a liberal movement in English thinking which has changed the face of belief, and he was perhaps the keenest critic the English romantic movement had to endure.

Witty men are likely to be suspected of some coldness of heart. Peacock, indeed, had a large share of the sardonic in his make-up, and he was almost devoid of mental and spiritual humility. But he did not lack either tenderness or earnestness. He loved truth, he hated injustice; he was upright in business, charitable to the unfortunate, affectionate towards his family and friends. The tenderness which occasionally finds exquisite reflection in his lyrics arose from a sensitiveness of spirit which appears but indirectly in his books. That romantic melancholy, bordering upon sentimentalism, which he had manifested in his youth, had been an outward sign of the shocks which he felt at contact with reality. To them he attempted to give voice in his early poems, but his pride asserted itself, and, retreating from the dangerous grounds of sentiment, he took up a position from which he could defend himself against all attacks with the unconquerable weapons of laughter. His old sensitiveness persisted. It lent his work an occasional touch of pathos and frequent passages of delicate beauty. His pride persisted, and it imposed upon him cautious restraint, ironic aloofness, satiric scorn. Almost all the apparent contradictions in his character can be understood if they are looked upon as the results of an endless opposition within him of sensitiveness and pride. The use which he made of laughter secured him immunity from many a disturbing incident which could not overcome his mirth, and it gave him fame. But because he laughed without responsibility he belongs less with the writers of power than with those of whom laughter has exacted a great, as of all laughter exacts a certain, penalty.

SOURCE: extracts from *The Life of Thomas Love Peacock* (London, 1911; repr. New York: Russell and Russell, 1966) pp. 271–7, 279–81.

1. *Works,* II 83.

2. *Report from the Select Committee on Steam Communication with India* (1837) p. 56.

# A. Martin Freeman

# 'A TRUE RELIC OF SHELLEY'S CIRCLE' (1911)

. . . *Gryll Grange* was probably written during the eighteen months between the publication of the first and second parts of the *Memoir of Shelley*; it was in any case completed during the years when Peacock's mind was habitually dwelling upon the time, more then four decades before, when he and Shelley had been intimate friends. In the interval Peacock had acquired a lifetime of experience, in surroundings utterly unlike those in which the friends had lived, or those they had imagined or desired. Spiritually he had conquered in the ordeal. Recognition and success had mellowed and not spoiled him. As a natural concomitant, he had remained unchanged in other less funda-mental but more daily noticeable characteristics; incorruptibility in his case implied and included a lack of adaptability. He had thus lived on, a true relic of Shelley's circle at Bracknell and Marlow, into another age. . . .

Shelley's devotion to types of ideal beauty, his tendency to live in the immaterial rather than the material world, and to confuse the two, and the disillusionment that Peacock thought would have been his lot if he had lived on, are explicitly set forth in the *Memoir*. They are all expressed with equal distinctness in *Gryll Grange*, and may be most shortly illustrated in three scraps of dialogue, in whose sentiments there is a strange intermixture of the Shelley of 1817, and the hypothetical Shelley of forty years later, while his interlocutor is Peacock at the time of writing. Here for the last time we shall take the liberty of re-translating the names of Peacock's characters into those of their originals:

PEACOCK: At present your faith is simply poetical. But take care, my young friend, that you do not finish by becoming the dupe of your own mystification.

SHELLEY : I have no fear of that. I think I can clearly distinguish devotion to ideal beauty from superstitious belief. I feel the necessity of some such devotion to fill up the void which the world as it is leaves in my mind. . . . And the saint whom I have chosen presents to my mind the most perfect ideality of physical, moral, and intellectual beauty.

PEACOCK : I cannot object to your taste. But I do hope you will not be led into investing the ideality with too much of the semblances of reality. I should be sorry to find you far gone in hagiolatry. I hope you will acquiesce in Martin, keeping equally clear of Peter and Jack.

SHELLEY : Nothing will more effectually induce me so to acquiesce than your company. (Ch. 9.)

PEACOCK : You are determined to connect the immaterial with the material world, as far as you can.

SHELLEY : I like the immaterial world. I like to live among thoughts and images of the past and the possible, and even of the impossible, now and then.

PEACOCK : Certainly there is much in the material world to displease sensitive and imaginative minds; but I do not know anyone who had less cause to complain of it than you have. . . .

SHELLEY : It is not my own world that I complain of. It is the world on which I look 'from the loopholes of retreat'. . . . I look with feelings of intense pain on the mass of poverty and crime; of unhealthy, unavailing, and unremunerative toil, blighting childhood in its blossom, and womanhood in its prime; of 'all the oppressions that are done under the sun'.

PEACOCK : I feel with you on all these points; but there is much good in the world; more good than evil, I have always maintained. (Ch. 11.)

PEACOCK : You look as little like a disappointed man as any I have seen. . . .

SHELLEY : We are all born to disappointment. It is as well to be prospective. Our happiness is not in what is, but in what is to be. We may be disappointed in our everyday realities, and if not, we may make an ideality of the unattainable, and quarrel with Nature for not giving us what she has not to give. It is unreasonable to be so disappointed, but it is disappointment not the less. . . .

PEACOCK : I am afraid I am too matter-of-fact to sympathise very clearly with this form of ætheticism : but here is a charming bit of forest scenery! Look at that old oak with the deer under it.... (Ch. 4.)

The most obvious passage to be pointed out in the above extracts as a repetition from the *Memoir* is that containing the image of Falconer looking upon the world 'from the loopholes of retreat'; but is there not also observable more than one touch of Scythrop and Mr. Hilary?

There is one more fact which cannot be overlooked, indicating how the recollection of the old days at Bracknell and Marlow was drawn upon for the composition of this book. The paragraph in Chapter 12 containing the account of the forest dell, to which Mr. Falconer walks when trying to rid himself of the obsession of Morgana's image, is merely an expansion of the two sentences in *The Last Day of Windsor Forest*, describing the Bourne, a spot which Peacock tells us he had not seen since he was in the habit of visiting it with Shelley. With the memory of this friend he ends up his life as a novelist, as he had begun it with his company. This reincarnation seems a remarkable proof both of the mighty influence exercised by Shelley upon Peacock, and of the intimate nature of his writings. The more we knew of his life, the better would be our understanding of his novels. The impression given by *Gryll Grange* is, that it is a very strong case in point; in reading it, the conviction grows that it could only have been fully commented by those who knew Peacock at Halliford, during the years intervening between his retirement and his death, early in 1866.

Thus many of the regular elements of the Peacockian novel are present, though in a less obvious form, in this work of his old age. Compared with the rest it is more subdued and reflective, and even more personal and idiosyncratic. Already in *Crotchet Castle* it is noticeable that Peacock is introducing more of himself and less of other people than in his earlier books. In this epilogue to all his works – in poetry, fiction, criticism – the tendency to write about himself is seen to have grown strong enough to become the leading element of the book. This is accompanied, perhaps necessarily, by a remarkable artistic carelessness and by a supreme neglect of his public. He is now writing purely and simply to please himself, and he has grown garrulous.

Peacock is so personally popular with his readers that we are willing to forgive him many things. We suffer him, with but a faint protest, to tell us under cover of fiction, that he once knew a man who tried hard to cut the figure 9 on the ice, and could only succeed by fitting it in between two 8s; to recapitulate the stages whereby he satisfied himself that the hair of the Vestals was allowed to grow again, once their heads had been shaved; to repeat long passages of Bojardo, and translate them; to express a puerile contempt for geological discoveries. But to say truth, the licence of this book is not compensated by the violent, witty exaggerations of the first novels. *Gryll Grange* is far from his masterpiece, and it would be interesting to know if any one, unacquainted with his other works, had read it and remained much impressed. The sympathetic handling of its characters is undoubtedly an attraction; but the story is preposterous and long drawn out. We can feel no anxiety for the fate of Harry and Dorothy, of Algernon and Morgana, of Lord Curryfin and Miss Niphet. The interest is inevitably centred in the author. We must be content to listen to him while he talks to us of his tastes and habits, chats to us about things which have been occupying his attention, tells us anecdotes.

He is a genial and kindly old man, but easily upset by anything that worries him. He seldom dines out nowadays, except with one friend of his own age, at whose table he is sure his palate will not be annoyed and his taste for quiet conviviality and good conversation will be indulged. Dinners at strange houses are such a risk. On one of the last occasions when he ventured upon one, he was served with the tail of a mullet, followed by the drumstick of a fowl. And then the after-dinner bore is so intolerable. He was present not so very long ago when a long-winded individual held forth to the uttermost limit of patience on 'what's wrong with India', passing from city to city and from province to province in a merciless harangue, until he was forced to pause for breath. The man seated next took the opportunity to start another topic; but the social tyrant touched his arm and said: 'Excuse me; now I come to Madras.' Of course, on an occasion like that, the only thing to do is to take one's departure, and leave those who like it to listen to it. Reading is safer and

more satisfying, especially Greek. There is enough Greek literature extant to provide interest for even a long lifetime, particularly if you go into side issues, the less known tracts of mythology
and archæology. How much there is that we still do not know
about the Attic theatre! Their resonant vases must have had a
wonderful effect; but the principle seems to be lost now, perhaps
irrecoverably. What a pity that we cannot find out more about
their music! The Greeks were people of such exquisite sensibility, and their poetry and sculpture reached such a pitch of
perfection, that it is impossible to believe their music was as bare
and monotonous as the experts would make out. Their melodies
at least must have been beautiful. Yes, most beautiful things, most
wise pronouncements, were made more than two thousand years
ago. But the classical languages as used after the break-up of
antiquity are not entirely to be despised. The latinity of many
hymns and sequences is tolerable, and their sentiments very
acceptable as an offset to the spirit of our machine-made civilisation. Almost all old things are good. Old fashioned dances are
charming to watch; the card games that were popular long ago
form an interesting study, and they are so much more sociable
than the modern play. Quadrille, for instance, is a *game*, and
not like whist, a mere excuse for dogmatism and bad temper.
Then the thoughts of age will be dwelling a good deal on the past :

> I played with you 'mid cowslips blowing,
> When I was six and you were four; ...

Time has softened and sweetened most memories; that can best
be enjoyed in retirement, and are rudely disturbed by reports of
current affairs. What a detestable thing a newspaper is! It contains little that is pleasant or profitable to know, and is chiefly
made up of the accounts of crimes and disasters, the speeches of
insincere politicians, scandals ventilated in the law courts, meetings of ridiculous societies, fraudulent business concerns, and
lying advertisements of useless or harmful medicines. To read
the papers is to become misanthropic, whereas life among
friends, and in one's own garden and library, conduces to
geniality and cheerfulness. . . .

SOURCE: extracts from *Thomas Love Peacock: A
Critical Study* (1911) pp. 330–1, 335–42.

*L. Conrad Hartley*

# A LINK WITH THE VICTORIANS
## (1915)

Gentleman, scholar, and keen observer of men and things, he is a vital link between the early Victorians and ourselves for he lived so late as to come into the times we knew when young, and we ought to find a peculiar interest in his thoughts. From an epicurean pinnacle on wisdom's height he watched the conflict of those who descended into the arena to fight for renown. His mind was no mean temple. It was unprofaned, for instinct, reason, and training, alike forbade him to traffic with what was vulgar. The dirt of the eighteenth century, in literary things, was never noticed by him. His judicial temper, keen analytical power, his sense of humour, and his bantering satire were ever directed against those things that were unreasonable or unseasonable. The impulse behind literature varies, and in the satirist may come from a sense of injustice or the rioting of a disordered liver, but, Peacock was ever genial, and his light satire was natural to him. It has been said that Peacock's peculiar satire was due to the fact that he was never recognised as a poet. With such a pronouncement I cannot agree. The romantic vein in his nature, and the Bacchic humour, rollicking and fun-provoking, along with his more or less assumed inquisitorial attitude towards everything, and his love for the quiet of intellectual exercise, are quite enough to account for all that he wrote after his early years, and also for the particular channels where he studied in the classics. The poetic instinct was in Peacock, but he could never be a great poet, because of his limitations. He had never been into the deeps of life, nor had he suffered in stress of soul. He was never swept off his feet by any grand idea. He was humorous in the extreme, but he was not witty. The true wit is allied to poetry, for wit is fearless, jumps into the abyss of things, and returns with the torch of truth. Heine was witty, Peacock humorous : both were satirical. Then clever, discerning and epigrammatic as he was, he was not so human, so searching, nor so wistful as Meredith. There, again, Peacock was lacking, for he had not experienced. That cool judicial mentality was as an impassable barrier. The form of his satire makes it very difficult for the reader to discover his real thoughts, though he says so much on every conceivable subject. He is entirely wanting in the formative and creative, but the speculative and contentious loom large, in certain fields of thought, and are fit vehicles for his satire. Of original ideas he is virtually barren. A controlling wisdom directs his shafts and they are never directed against the holier things of life. His shield is his love for sheer fun and mischief. In the old and strict sense of the word he was an epicurean; not a mere pleasure-seeker, but a pain-avoider. He will so indulge himself as to obtain the highest good compatible with a keen use and enjoyment of the good things of life. Philosophically making himself comfortable, intending to be happy, come what may, he reduces his muse to a level where she will be a jolly companion, and indulges his genius to the full. A motto from *Gryll Grange*, translated by Peacock from Persius, expresses his attitude :

> Indulge thy genius, while the hour's thine own :
> Even while we speak, some part of it has flown.
> Snatch the swift-passing good : 'twill end ere long
> In dust and shadow, and an old wife's song.

It is well that some of our fellow-travellers through life should journey laughingly, and give cheer to their more sober-minded brethren. I see nothing unnatural in Peacock. Though he laughed well and often, he laughed wisely. He seems to me to have gained as much pleasure from his writing as he has given to his readers, and they are not many, for to most people Peacock is *caviare.* But I can see his leonine head thrown back in hearty laughter after his well-directed shaft of satire has found the centre of the target. Why ought not the healthy artist to take delight in his pictures?

He had no love for metaphysics or theology, and the cold anatomical reasonings of philosophers were as little welcomed. His sense of humour kept him within prescribed limits. I grant that there is an indefiniteness of aim in some of his 'novels', but they are worthy of study to-day; for the follies of men change not. His writings are sprinkled with classical references, and one may overlook his conscious pride in his ability to bring before us so many choice analogies and well translated passages. To shew that human nature does not change he quotes from Horace or Euripides. If he would point out the tendencies and humours of life, he prefers the classical to the modern illustration; and, whether commonplace, or odd, he prefers the old to the new. Here is an illustration taken from *Gryll Grange* :

Rev. Dr. Opimian [speaking of Miss Niphet] : She is silent and retiring, but obliging in the extreme; always ready to take part in anything that is going forward. She never needs, for example, being twice asked to sing. She is free from the vice, which Horace ascribes to all singers, of not complying when asked, and never leaving off when they have once begun.

Quaint and out of the way classical allusions are a feature in his work. His knowledge of Greek and Latin impels him to coin words, and the reader is not infrequently forced to consult his Latin Dictionary or his Lexicon. I think some of his words were coined in order to satirize the use of the dead languages in the making of new words for scientific treatises and metaphysical works. On one occasion he was good enough to translate a word; philotheoparopteism, – this means the 'roasting by a slow fire for the love of God.' The word is found in *Maid Marian*, and refers to a good, old English custom.

He led a kind of Dr. Jekyll-and-Mr. Hyde life. Look at his business life ! There, a man with grave responsibilities, on personal terms with many statesmen, and a power in the good conduct of the affairs of the great East India Company. Look at his intellectual life ! Not a word about London in his books : the place might never have existed. One wonders what form his letters took, and whether his humour and satire found their way into the lines on the blue foolscap that passed through his hands. If so, that would have been excellent commentary upon himself and his correspondents.

It is said that he was particularly exact, neat, and methodical in his work. No doubt that judicial mentality of his conduced to his success at his work, just as readily as it commanded the form of his 'novels'. The keen commercial man must be able to stand as easily in his correspondents' shoes as in his own, and must be able to answer questions before they are put to him. As a controversialist, Peacock would have few equals; he was a mental Colossus, with one foot on the *pro*, the other on the *con*. Those knowing him in the city held him in high esteem, for he was so genial. He was 'our Peacock', he was 'everybody's Peacock'; so it has been said. Apart from his writings, he was valued highly as a man and a comrade. Possibly he was misunderstood by some of his intimates, especially in later years, for the shield of self may have brought some to regard him as a misanthrope. As time went on, he was the more inclined to withdraw behind that impenetrable shield, and as we know that the man of independent spirit is always open to attack, Peacock may have suffered under misjudgment. He avoided ordinary society, not because he disliked his fellows, but because intellectual exercise was essential to his happiness and was as the very air that he breathed. So he withdrew from petty cares into the atmosphere that he best loved, that of his books; for such was his need. In summer he spent most of his time in the open air, for he loved the Thames valley; in winter he was usually in his study. He had friends, true friends, but as the years passed over his snow-white head, he never replaced those who had gone into the eternal silence.

In spite of this withdrawal into his library, where he buried himself in his books, he could not escape from his times. He may have pretended to ignore his times, and may have deceived some of his fellows, but his works shew that his correspondence with his times was intimate, real, and large. The greater a man is, the more firmly does he stand in his times: the power to rise above them, to oversee them, is only given because his feet are in them, for you cannot jump into the air without first using the earth.

As frost is to rock, so is satire to hardened custom, or privilege, or folly, because each has a disintegrating effect, and exposes faults. Peacock has no scheme of regeneration save his own object lesson that he laughingly puts before us. I find him stimulating, and am convinced of his faith in human nature and of his integrity of purpose. Ever behind his satire, flashed that will-o-the-wisp of a gentle and very playful humour. Having played his part, he quitted life's stage with a gentle adieu. He had poured scorn upon vain things, but he had never soured himself or others, and the year of his death found him the same good-humoured and intellectual aristocrat that he had ever been.

SOURCE: extract from 'Thomas Love Peacock', *Manchester Quarterly*, xxxiv (1915).

*John W. Draper (1918)*

# THE SOCIAL SATIRES

All but the last of the satiric novels of Thomas Love Peacock are compassed within the sixteen years from 1815 to 1831, a time when – although Europe was outwardly given over to reaction – the social ideas, rationalistic and sentimental, of the French Revolution were still smoldering issues, and when most serious writers felt, at least distantly, the tidal waves of the great cataclysm. Born in 1785, twelve years after Coleridge and seven before Shelley, and living on until 1866, Peacock stands between the older generation of Coleridge, Wordsworth and Southey, and the younger generation of Shelley and Keats. During the French Revolution, he was, like his friend Shelley, too young to understand and sympathize with the revulsion against radicalism during the Terror and Napoleon's conquest of Switzerland. This might lead one to suppose Peacock, like Shelley, a radical; but he seems scarcely more in accord with the 'isms' of the day than with the Tory conservatives. Somewhat older than his friend, and of more incisive, analytic temper, he saw many flaws in the doctrines which Shelley and his fellow-radicals championed. Thus is Thomas Love Peacock at once arch-critic of things-as-they-are, and arch-critic of reforms-as-they-are-proposed. This was, perhaps, the thought of Richard Garnett when, in the *Encycl. Brit.*, he wrote of Peacock's 'skeptical liberalism', a liberalism skeptical even of itself.

This was sometime a paradox, but criticism gives it proof. Indeed, a brief summary of opinions shows strange contrasts. Saintsbury, in his introduction to *Maid Marian*, finds in Peacock 'evidence of that latent conservatism' which turns one into a 'stout reactionary'. Ingpen, in his edition of Shelley's letters (p. 37), notes: 'What views, political and social, Peacock possessed were the very reverse of Shelley's [which were radical].'

And Gummere, in *Democracy and Poetry* (p. 12), speaks of 'a whole literary life devoted to reactionary prose and verse'. Some criticisms, in direct contradiction, term him a radical; among them Van Doren's biography, which speaks of 'a reputation for Toryism which cannot be properly said to have characterized his intellect' (p. 275). Freeman, moreover, refers to his contributions to the *Westminster* as 'distinctly radical,' and characterizes Peacock himself as 'notoriously an exposer of abuses and implicitly a reformer' (p. 283). Some writers, however, take neither stand definitely. Hartley thinks that 'Peacock has no scheme of regeneration save his own object lesson that he laughingly puts before us' (p. 283–4) [pages 108–9 above]. And Paul asserts: 'Peacock held at the same time, and in reference to the same subject-matter, opinions which the utmost ingenuity cannot reconcile' (p. 654). Thus, satirist of liberal and conservative alike, he has been put now in one camp, now in the other, now adjudged a freebooter.

Peacock could scarcely have chosen a vehicle more exasperating to the expositor of his theories. He invents a puppet to typify each current social theory, packs them all into the geographical confines of one house-party, and lets them talk 'about it and about'; but, unfortunately, the whole discussion merely comes out at the same door 'wherein it went', having progressed nowhere in particular. Often the reader is puzzled to know where – if anywhere – Peacock's preferences lie; for he often sets the puppets dallying, and then stands aside to watch for broken heads, with the genially malicious unconcern of the innocent bystander. At times, by comments in his own person, he makes known his point of view; at times, an unwonted partiality for one character betrays a preference; but, even so, one commonly finishes a volume with the wish that Peacock would, like Bernard Shaw, prefix a preface to make certain just what he wants the whole thing to mean. With some pains, however, a fairly accurate interpretation can be attained. In the present study, I propose to discuss his general attitude toward current practices in education, marriage, religion and government. . . .

Peacock believed that neither sex was being properly educated. In almost every novel, he rails at the great universities where

England's youth had for centuries imbibed its Latin, Greek, and
mathematics. In *Nightmare Abbey* (p. 140), he says of Scythrop
that college cured him 'of the love of reading in all its shapes'.[1]
And in *Crotchet Castle* (p. 228), when the house-party makes a
pilgrimage in a body to Oxford, Peacock tells us : 'The Rev. Dr.
Folliott laid a wager with Mr. Crotchet that in all their perlustra-
tions, they would not find a single man reading, and won it.' The
professors, according to Peacock, are quite as bad as the students;
for, when Squire Headlong went to Oxford to look for 'men of
taste and philosophers', he was 'assured by a learned professor
that there were no such things in the University' (p. 6). If one
remembers that Peacock had learned his own Greek – which he
always wrote in an unorthodox fashion without accents – sans aid
or comfort of any university education; and, when one adds to
this consequent feeling of independence, the satirist's natural
sympathy for the collegiate martyrdom of his friend Shelley, one
can, I think, understand the subconscious motives behind his
censure of university education.

In the case of woman, however, he finds the situation even
worse. In *Melincourt*, he describes Sir Henry as 'one of those who
maintained the heretical notion that women are, or at least may
be, rational beings; though, from the great pains usually taken
in what is called education to make them otherwise, there are
unfortunately few examples to warrant the truth of the theory'
(p. 9). In *Nightmare Abbey*, Scythrop, a humorous caricature
of Shelley, declares : 'The fault is in their [women's] artificial
education, which studiously models them into mere musical dolls
to be set out for sale in the great toy-shop of society' (p. 131).
In a later novel, Peacock describes his heroine as having received
'an expensive and complicated education, complete in all the
elements of superficial display' (p. 148). In *Maid Marian*, moreover, he ridicules even the household virtues, preferring above
them learning and determination. One of the characters ventures
to query : ' "Has she not . . . learning and valor?" "Learning!"
exclaimed the little friar, "what has a woman to do with learning?
And valor ! who ever heard a woman commended for valor?
Meekness . . . and obedience to her husband, and faith in her
confessor, and domesticity, or, as learned doctors call it, the

faculty of stay-at-homeitiveness, and embroidery, and music, and pickling, and preserving, and the whole complex and multiplex detail of the noble science of dinner . . . these are the female virtues" ' (p. 10). Mary Wollstonecraft, who married the philosopher Godwin, had earlier raised the question of woman's education in her *Vindication of the Rights of Women* (1792). She saw the inconsistency in Rousseau's *Emile*, that gave Sophie a mere Oriental, sex-education, with submission to father and husband as its final goal, whereas it endowed Emile with individualized selfhood. She demanded equal education for women, and declared them endowed with minds capable of a rational training. Peacock unquestionably knew of her work; for not only was it widely read, but also his friend Shelley, son-in-law to the authoress, was interested in the problems it raised.

Holding so pessimistic a view of the education of both men and women, Peacock could scarcely hope much for their union in marriage. The very attitude of his characters toward it is unhealthy. Two, at least, of his heroes, like so many young radicals of the day, victims of the *Weltschmerz*, are nympholepts: 'Scythrop's romantic dreams', says Peacock, 'had indeed given him many *pure anticipated cognitions* of combinations of beauty and intelligence' (p. 148); and Forester also is searching for a soulmate through the purlieus of this degenerate but perfectable universe – a somewhat hazy and impractical concept of marriage! The women, on the other hand, are nothing if not practical; and fare even worse in the satirist's esteem. 'Musical dolls to be set out for sale in the great toy-shop of society', most of them can only degrade the married state, and are fit to raise their children to no higher ethical ideal than money for its own sake and for the things that money can buy. In *Melincourt*, Miss Pinmoney – with her own foreknowledge and consent – is being disposed of by her mother 'according to the universal practice of this liberal and enlightened generation, in the most commercial of all bargains, marriage' (p. 14). Older generation and younger are alike debased. Peacock agrees with Mary Wollstonecraft in condemning the practical workings of marriage as an institution, but with this difference: in *Mary* and *The Wrongs of Woman*, she looks upon woman as downtrodden by a false, double standard of sex-

morality super-imposed upon her from without. To Mary Wollstonecraft, the fault was in the marriage-laws of England; to
Peacock, in the basic nature of woman herself. Godwin also
attacks the institution of marriage, and indeed suggests its abolition. Peacock sees men and woman mis-educated and mis-allied,
sees marriage cankered by false ideals and greed of money, made
a thing of mockery, and to that mockery, adds his own Juvena-
lian laughter.

But even though the marriage-tie be corrupt, optimism has still
a chance : society has still the Church and the State, two great
potentialities of good. The Church, however, shares in his re-
proach. He pictures the clergy as given over to good living, brain-
less gluttons in the earlier novels, in the latter novels refined but
quite unspiritual hedonists. In *Headlong Hall* (pp. 9 ff.), the
Rev. Dr. Gaster, whose name Peacock derives from the Greek
γαστήρ, *i.e.*, 'paunch', is discovered anxiously awaiting breakfast; he manages to secure the best place at the inn; when his
somewhat hearty refreshment arrives, he wishes to have the time
for partaking extended (p. 20); he does his intellectual browsing
in the *Almanach des Gourmands* (p. 26) – but no more! The
worthy Doctor is but the first in a gallery of Peacockian clerics.
Through the bibulous symposia of *Melincourt*, the Reverend Mr.
Portpipe swims into the reader's ken; *Maid Marian* boasts not
only a sort of Friar Tuck, but also the whole vinous fraternity
of Rubygill; *Crotchet Castle* limns 'The Reverend Dr. Folliott,
a gentleman endowed with a tolerable stock of learning, an interminable swallow, and an indefatigable pair of lungs' (p. 148).
And the very first line of *Gryll Grange* introduces the inimitable
Dr. Opimian genially discoursing upon the virtues of Palestine
soup.

But what happens when these gentlemen of the cloth engage in
their strictly clerical duties? *Maid Marian* contains several unequivocal suggestions : The Reverend Lord Abbot, upon receiving
a thump on the head, indulges in the 'pious and consolatory
reflection on the goodness of Providence in having blessed him
with such a thickness of skull, to which he was now indebted for
his temporal preservation, as he had before been for spiritual
promotion' (p. 63). Thus 'spiritual promotion' is due to 'thick-

ness of skull.' Furthermore, Peacock explains of the noble heroine's confessor: 'he never ventured to find her in the wrong, much less to enjoin anything in the shape of penance, as was the occasional practice of holy confessors with or without cause, for the sake of pious discipline, and what in those days was called social order, namely, the preservation of the privileges of the few who happened to have any, at the expense of the swinish multitude who happened to have none' (p. 68). If, then, the clergy work merely for a selfish class-benefit, what do this 'swinish multitude' think of it? After a satirical description of the oppressions of Longchamp, Bishop of Ely, Peacock adds: 'The ignorant impatience of the swinish multitude with these fruits of good living, brought forth by one of the meek who had inherited the earth, displayed itself in a general ferment' (p. 72). His iteration of 'swinish multitude' – a phrase borrowed from one of Burke's reactionary tirades – is final proof that he intended contemporary satire. The author of *Maid Marian* looks upon the clergy of his day as corrupt worldlings, sunk in luxury, blind mouths, that neither can nor will perform any ecclesiastical function other than the safeguarding of their own petty interests.

Does no purity reside even in the State? Peacock's answer is a derisive negative. It was the fashion for young intellectual bloods of the day to fulminate against the tyranny of kings and the license of their courts; but George IV had been giving England an especially apt occasion; and Peacock was not slow in borrowing revolutionary thunder of his friend Shelley. *Maid Marian* is full of implied criticisms both of the theory of divine right and of the actual practices of the government; for those were the days before the passage of the Reform Bill, and the country was undergoing a period of domestic upheaval: ' "Robin Hood",' says Friar Tuck, ' "is king of the forest both by dignity of birth and by virtue of his standing army: to say nothing of the free choice of his people, which he has indeed, but I pass it by as an illegitimate basis of power. He holds his dominion over the forest, and its horned multitude of citizen-deer, and its swinish multitude or peasantry of wild boars, by right of conquest and force of arms. He levies contributions among them by free consent of his archers, their virtual representatives" ' (p. 82). So much for the very un-

divine George IV and his rotten-borough Parliament which ruled
England by 'virtual representation'. In foreign affairs, Peacock
is equally caustic against the Holy Alliance which had lately
dominated Europe, and satirizes it bitterly in *Maid Marian*
(p. 71); and, indeed, the criticism is largely justified. Not only
royal policies at home and abroad, but also the immediate court,
especially the royal bard, probably Southey, who was laureate at
the time, receive castigation in almost every satire : *The Misfortunes of Elphin* speaks of the prince's 'bard of all work, who
was always willing to go to any court with any character or none'
(p. 130).

But not only is royalty decayed, but the great aristocracy of
England, the great land-owners, are incompetent and vicious.
This class is pictured as being recruited from the successful
merchants and bankers who have made fortunes chiefly through
the fraudulent manipulation of paper currency. They then
spread their wings, and acquire nobility and a coat of arms 'after
proper ceremony (payment being the principal)' (*Crotchet
Castle*, p. 144). They carry the petty tyranny of the counting-
house into their estates as far as their tastes permit by 'game-
bagging, poacher-shooting, trespasser-pounding, footpath-stop-
ping, common-enclosing, rack-renting, and all the other pursuits
and pastimes which make a country gentleman an ornament to
the world, and a blessing to the poor' (p. 145).

In *The Misfortunes of Elphin* (p. 47), he refers to the squires
as 'our agrestic kakistocracy'. Further quotation seems needless :
the country gentlemen, like the clergy, are shown sunk in their
own selfish motives, a source only of weakness and discord. Yet
by the wretched electoral system, they controlled even the House
of Commons; and, in fact, in *Melincourt*, a squire actually
returns to Parliament from his borough an Angola monkey.

Society, then, is filled with corruption : family, church, and
state. None of the parts function properly; for the individuals
composing each class are sunk in selfishness. Such a society is disintegrating into anarchy; and, indeed, the problems caused by
the rise of industrialism, were at the time, racking England's
vitals. The restoration of economic equilibrium in Europe after
Napoleon's fall, aggravated the difficulty; and, in 1819, Parlia-

ment found it necessary to pass six acts against industrial and agrarian rioting. This movement for reform later became known as Chartism, and, in spite of the Reform Bill of 1832, lasted down into the fifties. Peacock saw the struggle seething within; and, to him, the great English institutions seemed to have become a mockery: he might have written a philosophy of clothes, had his temperament been such; instead, he has left us a series of argumentative house-parties for which he is not without honor. But Peacock's is not an indictment of society merely, but of humanity, not merely of this or that class, but of the individuals that make up every class: for him, human-nature is gone wrong.

S O U R C E : extract from 'The Social Satires of Thomas Love Peacock', *Modern Language Notes*, XXIII (December 1918) 456–63.

NOTE

1. Page references in this extract are to *The Novels of Thomas Love Peacock*, ed. George Saintsbury (New York and London, 1895–7).

# J. B. Priestley

## THE MAN AND HIS WORK (1927)

### I. Peacock's character

. . . There never was a man, it would appear, with less desire
for novelty of any kind than Peacock. Very early in life he seems
to have made up his mind that certain things would give him
all the pleasure he wanted, and ever afterwards we find him
serenely enjoying those things. This is well illustrated by his taste
in books. He was, as we have seen, a hard reader for two-thirds
of a century, and was familiar with five literatures, Greek, Latin,
English, French and Italian. In his old age he added a sixth,
Spanish. In addition, he had made some study of Welsh. With
German he would have nothing to do, probably because he
heartily disliked the German philosophy and ultra-romantic
poetry, drama and fiction, that were so fashionable in his youth.
There is here sufficient breadth of scholarship, but his own
personal tastes were comparatively narrow. He soon discovered
what he wanted and thereafter was not inclined to make experiments. His favourites he read over and over again. These were
Homer, Sophocles, Aristophanes and Nonnus, whose *Dionysiaca*
he called 'the finest poem in the world after the *Iliad*', but was
not unaware of the fact that most of his hearers had never set
eyes on it; Virgil, Horace, Cicero, Petronius and Tacitus, who
undoubtedly had an influence upon his own style; Pulci, Ariosto,
Bojardo, among the Italians, and Rabelais and Voltaire among
the French. His English favourites were probably Shakespeare,
Chaucer and the author of Hudibras, but perhaps it is hardly
fair to single out these or any other three writers because his
taste in English literature was fairly catholic, more so than one
would at first imagine. It is easy to understand his pleasure in
the Restoration dramatists and the Augustan wits, but his
judgment of contemporary literature is rather surprising. Thus,

in spite of his persistent mockery, he had a genuine appreciation of Wordsworth and Coleridge as poets. He saw the weakness of Byron and Byronism, but he admired Byron's best work and could be enthusiastic over *Don Juan*. He has been accused of being indifferent to Shelley's genius, but a glance at the *Memoirs*, in which the nature of that genius is admirably described, will show that there is no truth in the charge. Indeed, when we consider the difference in temperament and point of view, we must admit that his appreciation of all these poets, who were contemporaries, to be liked or disliked at will, and not great figures in some past golden age, proves that at times his purely literary judgment was so good that it frequently got the better of him, for undoubtedly he would have found it more convenient to have disliked all contemporary Romantics. This he contrived to do with Keats and Tennyson, whom he dismissed with pedantic quibbles. On the other hand, if he sometimes mistook a swan for a goose, he never fell into the opposing error of mistaking geese for swans : the Campbells and Tom Moores and Barry Cornwalls never received any of Peacock's suffrages.

It is, however, his attitude towards the great writers of the past that reveals the man. That list of favourite authors already quoted is significant. A list of those authors, of equal stature, who were not to his taste, would be equally significant, and such a list would probably include such massive figures as Euripides, Lucretius, Dante, Milton. As Buchanan remarked : 'His sympathies, indeed, were less with the grand, the terrible, and the sublimely pathetic, than with the brilliant, the exquisite, and the delicately artistic'. The adjectives are none too well chosen, but we shall not quarrel with the judgment. Peacock's tastes were obviously those of a humanist. Mysticism he disliked, and even an intense moral earnestness left him uncomfortable. He was not one of those persons who feel that they are spirits exiled here for a season. He did not see this world as a place cloudy with doom or this life as a brief and bitter trial. He turns aside even from the satirists if their voices are too harsh and their laughter too embittered, and we do not find Juvenal and Swift among his chosen companions. He looks in literature for laughter and sunlight and ease, gracious forms and pleasant green places, roaring

farce or light keen mockery, human relations that are droll
or affectionate, touched with tenderness but undisturbed by
deep passion, all going their way beneath the fair sky of good
sense.

Peacock has been unfortunate in appearing before the reading
public so frequently as a figure in the various biographies of his
friend Shelley. There, as he coolly strolls through one perfervid
chapter after another, he is apt to seem a very cold and supercilious person. Many Shelley enthusiasts, who, unlike their idol,
have not been able to escape from *Nightmare Abbey* and to
laugh at the antics there, have made no secret of their dislike
for the creator of Scythrop. Other people, more detached, have
yet been influenced in their attitude towards Peacock, as a man
if not as a writer, by vague memories of a detached shrugging
figure in the brief shining chronicle of Shelley's life. Even so fine
a critic as Richard Garnett, for example, who clearly rejoices
in the task of praising the writer, immediately cools when he turns
to the man. It is difficult to avoid the suspicion that the critic is
involuntarily seeing Peacock against the background of Shelley's
life. Peacock did not love humanity and die young. Peacock
laughed at humanity, made himself snug, and could still be discovered sipping his port and Madeira when he was eighty. This
contrast, making itself felt somewhere at the back of the mind,
has been too compelling for many critics. But there are other
reasons, too, why Peacock as a man should irritate, if not actually
repel, so many critics and students of literature. To begin with,
there was in him not a little of the amateur, not the eager
appealing amateur but the disdainful aristocratic amateur of
letters, who writes for his own pleasure and shows no particular
anxiety to be commended for what he has done. There is about
such men an air of self-sufficiency that is vaguely irritating. And
Peacock was peculiarly self-sufficient both as a writer and a man.
If he had misfortunes, he kept them to himself; he made no
demand whatever upon public sympathy; he appeared to be for
ever cool and comfortable. His poetry seemed the occasional indulgence of a scholar and gentleman; his fiction, for the most
part published anonymously, was not unlike a domestic joke;
and his official life, in which he was apparently very efficient,

very successful, was almost entirely hidden from the public view. Such independence is not altogether to our taste. Not only are we robbed of any opportunity for indulging in posthumous pity, one of the pleasantest and cheapest of emotions, but we are not even favoured with the usual demand for our suffrages. Thus, retiring somewhat baffled, we cannot help feeling that the man was too successful, too comfortable; hence the cool references to him, the talk of 'self-indulgence', as if all critics and readers were fasting friars.

At this point it would be well to glance at some facts of his life and some of his more obvious characteristics. He was fond of ease and comfort and good living, and as he grew older 'his detestation of anything disagreeable made him simply avoid whatever fretted him, laughing off all sorts of ordinary calls upon his leisure time'. This type of elderly man, touched with a genial selfishness, is not unfamiliar. But Peacock was obviously free from the grosser forms of selfishness, and such egoism as his was frank and open, humorously paraded, and not, as egoism so often is, subtly disguised, hidden away, to gnaw at the roots of his character. We know that in his public business he was upright and honourable. His more serious convictions were honestly arrived at, tenaciously held, and courageously expressed. He was Shelley's friend during the time when it was not very convenient nor even safe to act in that capacity. It is true that he was under obligations to Shelley, but so were a great many other people who all contrived to be missing when the poet most needed sympathy and help. Years later, as we have seen, Peacock sturdily defended Harriet's memory and drew down upon himself the wrath of those who were busy fighting Shelley's battles for him at a remove of forty years. And whatever views, progressive or reactionary, Peacock put forward, they were never the easy fashionable ones. Shelley admired him in his youth, and Meredith admired him in his old age. Men like Thackeray and Macaulay enjoyed his company and would have been glad to have had more of it. There is no evidence that he ever lost a friend, a significant fact; and if he would seem to have had few friends it is merely because he never asked for more. There is a familiar type of public man who has such an intense love of humanity in general that he has no

affection left for human beings in particular, and frequently con-
trives to wreck the happiness of all the people near him, his
charity beginning anywhere but at home. Peacock belongs to the
opposing type. He makes no pretence of loving everybody, but
he did really care for the human beings nearest to him, who may
have had to submit to a few whims and little pieces of self-
indulgence, but whose lives were never ruined by any egoistical
pranks of his. He was a good son, a good husband, and a good
father, not simply coldly dutiful, but tender and affectionate.
He appears to the mind's eye probably as he would have wished
to appear, as a figure of easy prosperity, a laughing philosopher
against a background of gardens and libraries and tables shining
with old silver and decanters. But in his private life he was sorely
tried by fortune: his favourite child died when she was three;
his wife became an invalid; his eldest daughter was quickly
widowed and then made her tragic marriage with Meredith; his
son was unstable and a constant source of anxiety; his youngest
daughter lost her two children and died herself not long afterwards; few men have known more misfortunes in their domestic
life. The man who wrote *Gryll Grange*, around which some of
these tragic events are grouped, must have had a brave heart or
a very unfeeling one, and we have ample testimony that Peacock
was anything but insensitive.

We have called him self-sufficient, and undoubtedly it was his
desire, within the limits of an affectionate nature, to be self-
sufficient. Unlike a familiar type of author, who is very vain but
not at all proud, ready to do almost anything for a little applause,
Peacock was very proud but not at all vain. His lack of vanity
explains the curious anonymity of his life and works. Few writers
have shown themselves less eager for praise or even common
recognition. But if this is explained by his lack of vanity, it is also
explained by his pride, which made him stand apart and not
compete, and turned his authorship into a gentlemanly whim.
Once he had passed his early youth, when fortune gave him
several hard buffets (the greatest of them the tragic conclusion
of his first love affair, which left a deep impression), Peacock
wished to be always a little detached from life, to be always master
of circumstance. In addition, as we have seen, he reacted almost

violently from the ultra-romantic tendencies that he observed in Shelley and his set and in so much of the literature of the period, in which characters drifted helplessly on the tide of passion and changing mood. The fact that he had for a time played this character himself, and not with any conspicuous literary success, only hastened this reaction. Nevertheless, as one or two astute critics have noticed, he always remained a Romantic at heart. People who see him as nothing but the spokesman of common sense have mistaken their man, just as those who regard him mainly as a political satirist (on their own side of the question) have mistaken their man. In this they have been helped by Peacock himself. He chose for his seal the Horatian line : *Nec tardum opperior nec præcedentibus insto*. This is how he liked to see himself, as a cool, moderate man, occupying a sensible middle position. But in his heart of hearts, he knew he was nothing of the kind and may often be found, in the curious fashion of his type, laughing at himself. His very courtship and marriage were as whimsical as anything in his novels, and there is hardly anybody in *Crotchet Castle* more crotchety than its author. As for his politics and political satire, they will be discussed later; it is only necessary here to point out that they are so odd that he can be claimed by all political parties with some show of reason and by none with complete justice. All these simple explanations of his character are superficial, and the slightest critical examination of his work will demonstrate how inadequate they are fully to account for it. It asks us to look for a more complicated character with a tangle of motives. Like every humorist who is something more than a mere joker, Peacock was really a secret and baffled idealist. He laughed at the world because it was incongruous and droll, and he saw it was incongruous and droll because he had compared it with another and better world, hidden away in his dream. His extraordinary passion for Greek is in part explained by the fact that it enabled him to escape into what seemed to him an ideal world.

There is nothing of the true realistic temper in his works. Even their astonishing conviviality is an idealisation. Even their love passages, which do not play an important part but would be more important to himself and his contemporary readers than

they are to us, who find them stilted and perfunctory, bear witness to the idealist in him. His novels laugh at most things, but
they do not laugh at love, and he did not fill them with happy
young lovers to please the novel-reading public, for which he
cared not a rap, but to please himself. Indeed, his satire is never
directed against what we might call private life. This was clearly
seen by Raleigh, who has left us a tiny chapter on Peacock in a
posthumously published volume of notes. This chapter exagger-
ates one side of Peacock's character, but Raleigh's opening
remarks are extraordinarily penetrating :

There is nothing misanthropical about Peacock. He admires, and
loves. All that is simple and matter of affection, and private, is dear
to him. He laughs at idealists, and makers of systems. Yet – here is
the strange thing – he is not common sense against the idea. He has,
deep down in him, a great love for ideas. How easy to make fun
of Rousseau, Mme. de Genlis, Thomas Day – all that world of
theory which belongs to the French Revolution! Peacock does make
fun of it, but he has been touched by it.

The rest of the passage should be read, though Raleigh goes
wrong in places, chiefly because he argues too much from
*Melincourt*, which in some respects, as we have already seen, is
not typical of its author. But Raleigh touches Peacock's secret
when he indicates briefly (the above are notes that were verbally
expanded in lectures) Peacock's attitude towards ideas. If Peacock had cared nothing for ideas, had been the servant of down-
right common sense that some of his critics imagine him to have
been, he would never have taken the trouble to explore ideas so
thoroughly, would never have studied the hundred and one
authors he quotes in his footnotes and parodies in his text. The
truth is that he was at once attracted and repelled by those large
simple philosophic theories and systems that were the mental
diet of Godwin and his circle or the Bracknell set. The crank
or crotcheteer is his prey not because he himself is far removed
from one but because he himself only just stops short of being
one. Indeed, he has his own crotchets. His mind, like Shelley's,
lived in the kingdom of philosophic theories and systems and
ideals, and if Shelley was its bard, Peacock was its Court Jester.

It is this position, as the comedian of the life of ideas, that makes Peacock a unique figure in English Literature.

We shall see later, when we come to examine his fiction, what use he made of this position. We have first to discover – and the inquiry is pertinent to any discussion of his character – how he came to hold such a position. Perhaps the best line of approach will be a comparison and contrast with his friend, Shelley. We think of them representing two different halves of humanity. There never was, at first sight, such a piquant association. But when we begin to consider their personalities and their relation more closely, we discover that they are not so sharply opposed as we first imagined. We remember that Peacock could be influenced by Shelley, that Shelley could admire Peacock. And probably there was a time, during the first year or so of their friendship, when the likeness between them would be far more apparent than the difference. They shared a passion for certain pursuits; they were both in rebellion against conventional thought and belief; they were both romantic and idealistic. We can imagine them for a time keeping step together. But very soon their ways diverge, until at last they have almost lost sight of one another. In this matter of idealism, it might be said that Shelley was bold and Peacock was shy. Shelley had intensity, could easily kindle his imagination into a blaze, and had the faculty of believing what he wanted to believe and seeing what he wanted to see. Peacock, cooler, with an exquisite sense of proportion (which is of course precisely what is lacking in all cranks and crotcheteers) that forced the ludicrous upon his attention, was inevitably compelled to be more detached. He could not possibly hurl his whole mind in one direction as Shelley could. His sense of humour was for ever warning his pride that he was about to make a fool of himself. He could not accept the world and he could not begin to mend it; he could not help being drawn to the idealists and makers of systems and he could not help discovering how inadequate they were; he could not fall out of love with ideas and yet he could not marry them; thus he was left, a Mahomet's coffin, in mid-air. So situated, a man must either laugh or be laughed at, so Peacock laughed. By his laughter he doubly revenged himself on a world that he could not accept and reformers he could not join: he mocked the complacency of a world that imagined itself to be in no need of reformation, and equally mocked the complacency of those who thought they were capable of reforming it. His singular position left his energetic and powerful mind without proportionate objects on which to fasten, and inevitably it sought relief, outside scholarship, in wit and intellectual mischief, soaring into sheer high spirits. He became the playboy of the intellectual world.

Both he and Shelley wished to escape from the present, but when they did escape they turned different ways. Shelley jumped forward into the future. Peacock returned to the past, but not to the real past, but to some golden age of classic myth and poetry. He knew himself that it was not the real past; but this little dream world, filled with unenclosed forests and quiet gardens, pure air, food and liquor, a fit habitation for poets and philosophers and fair women, concretely represented the good life, whatever Peacock could solidly accept, and thus served as a basis for sardonic comparison with the present world. And his Epicureanism is not unconnected with this pretended belief in a past that never existed. It must not be taken too seriously for it is largely an attitude, part mischievous, part defensive. Feeling compelled, at times, to make some affirmative gesture, Peacock played the pagan. But when a blow really fell, he dropped the part and retired until the wound healed and he was ready to laugh again. We know how, when his favourite child died so suddenly, he said to his friend Strachey: 'There are times when the world cannot be made fun of.' A tragedy is being played simultaneously with the comedy of this life. There is something in Peacock's remark that suggests that he liked to pretend to himself that the tragedy, with which he did not know how to cope, was not really there, until there came a time when it forced itself upon him and he could pretend no longer. The Friar's famous speech, in *Maid Marian*, beginning: 'The world is a stage, and life is a farce, and he that laughs most has most profit of the performance', does not apply to a world that contains the deaths of little children. Peacock's philosophy was an excellent one for fine afternoons in the garden and untroubled evenings in the library, enabling him to endure the occasional trials of a corked wine and a mislaid folio; but it would be as useful to a man really grappling with this life as a toy whip would be to a lion-tamer. All this would be very damaging if Peacock made any pretence of being a serious interpreter of life, but he made no such pretence and only begged leave to make fun of the world. He kept his troubles to himself, but liberally shared his pleasures. His laughter is not harsh, misanthropical, a revenge for joys left untasted. His humour is like a ripe old sherry, dry yet genial, with sunshine in the heart of it.

## II.   The Novels of Talk

. . . All his characters that are of any importance exist in order to talk. Once Peacock has brought them into his country house and set the wine in front of them, he retires as a narrator, merely letting us know who is speaking by putting a name above the speech, like a dramatist. The moments when the talk is in full flood are the real crises of these novels, the action of which exists either to bring about these moments or as a droll or sardonic commentary upon them. When we think about these novels we do not remember what was done but what was said, and on reading them again we are generally surprised to find that they offer us even some semblance of a plot. In the earlier novels, particularly *Headlong Hall*, not only is Peacock at no pains to conciliate the ordinary novel-reading public but in places he is deliberately flying in its face. This is his intellectual mischievousness. He will laugh at novels while apparently writing one. Thus, he begins *Headlong Hall* by indicating four travellers in the Holyhead mail coach. They begin to talk about the weather, and 'the ice being thus broken, the colloquy rambled to other topics, in the course of which it appeared, to the surprise of every one, that all four, though perfect strangers to each other, were actually bound to the same point, namely Headlong Hall. . . .' All these four gentlemen are provided with names whose convenient etymology is explained by the ingenious author in footnotes. The story might be said to have a conventional plot, for it has an ardent young man in love with a beautiful girl, whose father he saves from drowning, and the father, in the best tradition, refuses his consent and brings forward a richer suitor, and is not won over until the very end of the story. On this data the story is the conventional romance of the time. But when most of the events connected with this plot, such as the rescue of the father, are described very briefly and drolly; when all the personages concerned always dismiss their own affairs to talk about things in general; when the father is a Mr. Cranium, the phrenologist, and is won over by being presented with the skull of Cadwallader; when the reader is coolly informed that the rejected suitor, on being condoled with by the father, 'begged him not to distress himself on the subject, observing, that the monotonous system of female education brought every individual of the sex to so remarkable an approximation of similarity, that no wise man would suffer himself to be annoyed by a loss so easily repaired'; it becomes obvious that whatever the author is doing, he is certainly not plotting in the conventional manner. After being tricked in this fashion, the ordinary novel-reader retires in disgust from the study of Peacock, not being like Mr. Panscope above, who would not suffer himself to be annoyed by a loss so easily repaired. And if anything is needed to confirm that reader's suspicion that the author is laughing at him, it is probably supplied by the end of the story, when characters are paired off at an astonishing rate. 'Here', says the Squire to Mr. Escot, 'are three couple of us going to throw off together, with the Reverend Doctor Gaster for whipper-in : now, I think you cannot do better than make the fourth with Miss Cephalis.' This is indeed Headlong Hall.

This deliberate flouting of the conventionalities of fiction is never entirely absent from any of Peacock's novels, but there is less and less of it as we move forward. Indeed, before he has done, he commits himself to a little half-serious plotting. The affairs of Captain Fitzchrome and Lady Clarinda, of Mr. Chainmail and Miss Susannah Touchandgo, in *Crotchet Castle*, of Mr. Falconer and Miss Gryll, of Lord Curryfin and Miss Niphet, in *Gryll Grange*, are all handled with a certain serious- ness, romantic zest, in spite of their droll setting. Peacock, who, as we have already seen, always remained something of a roman- tic at heart, really enjoyed these passages of young and triumphant love, enjoyed them, we suspect, more than he would have cared to admit. In the earlier *Nightmare Abbey* there is none of this half-serious romantic interest, but in its place there is almost sufficient action, revolving about Scythrop's simultaneous love affairs, but augmented by a certain amount of comic by-play, to make the novel entertaining to readers who may not appreciate to the full its capital talk. In *Melincourt*, however, Peacock undoubtedly presented the ordinary novel-reader with a choke-pear. Yet it is well to remember that Mr. Forester and his Anthelia, that excessively solemn, long-winded and priggish pair of lovers, who seem to us to put such obstacles in the way of any reader, can be matched in a good deal of the conventional fiction of the time. Most of the action of the novel, however, has for its protagonist the civilised orang-outang, known as Sir Oran Haut-ton, a character not to be matched in the fiction of any time. Sir Oran does exactly what the hero of conventional romance always does : he is always on hand to rescue the heroine from mountain torrents and kidnappers; and he may be said to be the first of our strong silent heroes. This is one of Peacock's most impudent strokes. For the rest, the most spirited chapters in *Melincourt* are those that describe the election, a piece of glorious Aristophanic burlesque that is worlds away from either the romance or realism of ordinary fiction.

Let us admit, then, that the personages in these novels do little but talk and that most of them – the Milestones and Sir Simon Steeltraps and Henbanes and Feathernests – are not creatures of this world but simply so many personified ideas or interests. Does this mean that *Headlong Hall* and the rest cannot really be considered novels at all? Are they best approached as so many comic dialogues? So some critics would seem to think, and one of them has described the Peacock novel as 'a Platonic dialogue as Aristophanes might have caricatured it'. This is an excellent description so long as we are allowed to assume that Aristophanes (who was certainly Peacock's greatest master) would have turned his dialogue into what we now call fiction. Otherwise it is misleading. Peacock's critics have been so anxious to point out that he did not write conventional fiction that they have frequently driven him away from the novel altogether. This, however, is a mistake because Peacock is, in his own queer way, a novelist, and his five tales of talk are just as far removed from philosophical dialogues and the like as they are from ordinary realistic fiction. They occupy a position – perhaps a unique position – between the two. It is one of the secrets of their appeal, this curious intermediate character of theirs, which makes them less concrete and documented than novels proper and yet far less abstract than such things as dialogues and allegories. Indeed, they are far less abstract, are nearer the earth, than a great many of the old artificial comedies. If these novels of his do not give us fully human records, neither do they transport us entirely to some abstract region of ideas. Their action passes in a world, even though it is a world at some remove from the one we know. It is easily recognised and quite unlike any other, so that we can say there is a Peacock world just as we say there is a Dickens world. Peacock, so unlike the great original novelists in almost every particular, at least resembles them in this, that he has created a world of his own. And whatever difference there may be between *Headlong Hall* and *Gryll Grange*, *Melincourt* and *Crotchet Castle*, one and all take us to the same Peacock world.

It is of course a world of talk and talkers. Its personages are almost completely themselves when they are happily seated behind the decanters, each hammering away at his own theory. But there are also some women, fair and pleasant-spoken, and some romantic young lovers. Moreover, this world is provided with the scenery of romance. Consider this passage in the best of these novels, *Crotchet Castle* :

One day Mr. Chainmail traced upwards the course of a mountain-stream, to a spot where a small waterfall threw itself over a slab of perpendicular rock, which seemed to bar his farther progress. On a nearer view, he discovered a flight of steps, roughly hewn in the rock, on one side of the fall. Ascending these steps, he entered a narrow winding pass. between high and naked rocks, that afforded only space for a rough footpath carved on one side, at some height above the torrent.

The pass opened on a lake, from which the stream issued, and which lay like a dark mirror, set in a gigantic frame of mountain precipices. Fragments of rock lay scattered on the edge of the lake, some half-buried in the water : Mr. Chainmail scrambled some way over these fragments, till the base of a rock, sinking abruptly in the water, effectually barred his progress. He sat down on a large smooth stone; the faint murmur of the stream he had quitted, the occasional flapping of the wings of a heron, and at long intervals the solitary springing of a trout, were the only sounds that came to his ear. The sun shone brightly half-way down the opposite rocks, presenting, on their irregular faces, strong masses of light and shade. Suddenly he heard the dash of a paddle, and, turning his eyes, saw a solitary and beautiful girl gliding over the lake in a coracle. . . .

There is a passage that any romance might wear as a jewel. Nor would it be difficult to find companion passages, in which remote and beautiful places are described in a style that is vivid in spite of its obvious restraint. Even the comic debaters and crotcheteers are always provided with a charming or wild and picturesque background, far removed from bustle and noise and dirt. Thus the opening paragraph of *Crotchet Castle* takes us to an Arcadian countryside :

In one of these beautiful valleys, through which the Thames (not yet polluted by the tide, the scouring of cities, or even the minor defilement of the sandy streams of Surrey) rolls a clear flood through flowery meadows; under the shade of old beech woods, and the smooth mossy greensward of the chalk hills (which pour into it their tributary rivulets, as pure and pellucid as the fountain of Bandusium, or the wells of Scamander, by which the wives and daughters of the Trojans washed their splendid garments in the days of peace, before the coming of the Greeks); in one of those beautiful valleys, on a bold round-surfaced lawn, spotted with juniper, that opened itself in the bosom of an old wood, which rose with a steep, but not precipitous ascent, from the river to the summit of the hill, stood the castellated villa of a retired citizen.

And Headlong Hall is in the romantic Vale of Llanberis; Anthelia Melincourt has an old castle 'in one of the wildest valleys in Westmoreland', where daily she sees 'the misty mountain-top, the ash-fringed precipice, the gleaming cataract, the deep and shadowy glen, and the fantastic magnificence of the mountain clouds'; Nightmare Abbey very naturally has a more dismal setting, being situated somewhere between the sea and the Fens in Lincolnshire, but is equally picturesque and remote; and Gryll Grange, 'on the borders of the New Forest, in the midst of a park which was a little forest in itself, reaching nearly to the sea, and well-stocked with deer', is clearly only a stone's-throw from Arden itself. This world of Peacock's, then, though it would seem a world of intellectual comedy, is filled with Arcadian countrysides and wildly romantic solitudes. The droll debates and the bumpers of Madeira are set against a background of quiet rivers and green shades, of the gleaming cataract and the deep and shadowy glen. It is the poet, the romantic, the idealist, in Peacock who has touched in this background purely for his own good pleasure.

If satire pure and simple – political, literary, social satire – were his object, then it is curious that he should have given us these idyllic or romantic settings instead of taking us to London, that he should have assembled all his characters in these remote places instead of displaying them in their native haunt, the Town. It is true that his house-party method, bringing all his people under one roof and leaving them to entertain one another, gives him a certain advantage, but this is far outweighed by the advantage offered by the London scene, which obviously is far richer in possibilities for the satirist. But being something more than satirist, being also a poet and humorist, Peacock preferred to set his scene against these backgrounds because, we repeat, their creation gave him pleasure. His imagination took refuge in these idyllic or romantic settings, which represent one side of his mind just as the intellectual farce that is played there represents another. The poet in him, who once wrote *The Philosophy of Melancholy* and *Rhododaphne*, now found satisfaction in idealising the scenes of the novels, and this he could do quite safely, without any fear of being laughed at, because he was already protected by the mockery in their action and characterisation. If the foreground in his fiction is mostly filled in with a caricature of what actually goes on in the world, its background gives us a sketch of what ought to go on in the world, of the author's ideal realm. There is something very piquant in the contrast, and piquancy, so welcome to sophisticated minds, has long been noted as one of Peacock's characteristics. If its presence has been noted, however, it has not been explained, simply because no explanation is possible so long as the satirist in him is allowed to hide completely the poet in him, so long as he is seen as a writer of comic dialogues only and not as a novelist, creating a world of his own in which his imagination can happily play. It is a very queer world, but it suited Peacock, whose novels were primarily a recreation, and, in spite of its obvious limitations, it is capable of providing rest and refreshment for any reader who brings to it a sense of humour. . . .

SOURCE: extracts from *Thomas Love Peacock* (London, 1927) pp. 98–110, 133–41.

*Aldous Huxley*

# A PEACOCKIAN CONFRONTATION IN *POINT COUNTER POINT* (1928)

. . . Everard Webley had got Lord Edward into a corner and was trying to persuade him to support the British Freemen.

'But I'm not interested in politics,' the Old Man huskily protested. 'I'm not interested in politics. . . .' Obstinately, mulishly, he repeated the phrase, whatever Webley might say.

Webley was eloquent. Men of good will, men with a stake in the country ought to combine to resist the forces of destruction. It was not only property that was menaced, not only the material interests of a class; it was the English tradition, it was personal initiative, it was intelligence, it was all natural distinction of any kind. The Freemen were banded to resist the dictatorship of the stupid; they were armed to protect individuality from the mass man, the mob; they were fighting for the recognition of natural superiority in every sphere. The enemies were many and busy.

But forewarned was forearmed; when you saw the bandits approaching, you formed up in battle order and drew your swords. (Webley had a weakness for swords; he wore one when the Freemen paraded, his speeches were full of them, his house bristled with panoplies.) Organization, discipline, force were necessary. The battle could no longer be fought constitutionally. Parliamentary methods were quite adequate when the two parties agreed about fundamentals and disagreed only about trifling details. But where fundamental principles were at stake, you couldn't allow politics to go on being treated as a Parliamentary game. You had to resort to direct action or the threat of it.

'I was five years in Parliament,' said Webley. 'Long enough to convince myself that there's nothing to be done in these days by Parliamentarism. You might as well try to talk a fire out. England can only be saved by direct action. When it's saved we can begin to think about Parliament again. (Something very unlike the present ridiculous collection of mob-elected rich men it'll have to be.) Meanwhile, there's nothing for it but to prepare for fighting. And preparing for fighting, we may conquer peacefully. It's the only hope. Believe me, Lord Edward, it's the only hope.'

Harassed, like a bear in a pit set upon by dogs, Lord Edward turned uneasily this way and that, pivoting his bent body from the loins. 'But I'm not interested in pol . . .' He was too agitated to be able to finish the word.

'But even if you're not interested in politics,' Webley persuasively continued, 'you must be interested in your fortune, your position, the future of your family. Remember, all those things will go down in the general destruction.'

'Yes, but . . . No. . . .' Lord Edward was growing desperate. 'I . . . I'm not interested in money.'

Once, years before, the head of the firm of solicitors to whom he left the entire management of his affairs, had called, in spite of Lord Edward's express injunction that he was never to be troubled with matters of business, to consult his client about a matter of investments. There were some eighty thousand pounds to be disposed of. Lord Edward was dragged from the fundamental equations of the statics of living systems. When he learned the frivolous cause of the interruption, the ordinarily mild Old Man became unrecognizably angry. Mr. Figgis, whose voice was loud and whose manner confident, had been used, in previous interviews, to having things all his own way. Lord Edward's fury astonished and appalled him. It was as though, in his rage, the Old Man had suddenly thrown back atavistically to the feudal past, had remembered that he was a Tantamount, talking to a hired servant. He had given orders; they had been disobeyed and his privacy unjustifiably disturbed. It was insufferable. If this sort of thing should ever happen again, he would transfer his affairs to another solicitor. And with that he wished Mr. Figgis a very good afternoon.

'I'm not interested in money,' he now repeated.

Illidge, who had approached and was hovering in the neighbourhood, waiting for an opportunity to address the Old Man, overheard the remark and exploded with inward laughter. 'These rich!' he thought. 'These bloody rich!' They were all the same.

'But if not for your own sake,' Webley insisted, attacking from another quarter, 'for the sake of civilization, of progress.'

Lord Edward started at the word. It touched a trigger, it released a flood of energy. 'Progress!' he echoed, and the tone of misery and embarrassment was exchanged for one of confidence. 'Progress! You politicians are always talking about it. As though it were going to last. Indefinitely. More motors, more babies, more food, more advertising, more money, more everything, for ever. You ought to take a few lessons in my subject. Physical biology. Progress, indeed! What do you propose to do about phosphorus, for example?' His question was a personal accusation.

'But all this is entirely beside the point,' said Webley impatiently.

'On the contrary,' retorted Lord Edward, 'it's the only point.' His voice had become loud and severe. He spoke with a much more than ordinary degree of coherence. Phosphorus had made a new man of him; he felt very strongly about phosphorus and, feeling strongly, he was strong. The worried bear had become the worrier. 'With your intensive agriculture,' he went on, 'you're simply draining the soil of phosphorus. More than half of one per cent. a year. Going clean out of circulation. And then the way you throw away hundreds of thousands of tons of phosphorus pentoxide in your sewage! Pouring it into the sea. And you call that progress. Your modern sewage systems!' His tone was witheringly scornful. 'You ought to be putting it back where it came from. On the land.' Lord Edward shook an admonitory finger and frowned. 'On the land, I tell you.'

'But all this has nothing to do with me,' protested Webley.

'Then it ought to,' Lord Edward answered sternly. 'That's the trouble with you politicians. You don't even think of the important things. Talking about progess and votes and Bolshevism and every year allowing a million tons of phosphorus pentoxide to run away into the sea. It's idiotic, it's criminal, it's . . . it's fiddling while Rome is burning.' He saw Webley opening his mouth to speak and made haste to anticipate what he imagined was going to be his objection. 'No doubt,' he said, 'you think you can make good the loss with phosphate rocks. But what'll you do when the deposits are exhausted?' He poked Everard in the shirt front. 'What then? Only two hundred years and they'll be finished. You think we're being progressive because we're living on our capital. Phosphates, coal, petroleum, nitre – squander them all. That's your policy. And meanwhile you go round trying to make our flesh creep with talk about revolutions.'

'But damn it all,' said Webley, half angry, half amused, 'your phosphorus can wait. This other danger's imminent. Do you *want* a political and social revolution?'

'Will it reduce the population and check production?' asked Lord Edward.

'Of course.'

'Then certainly I want a revolution.' The Old Man thought in terms of geology and was not afraid of logical conclusions. . . .

SOURCE: extract from *Point Counter Point* (London, 1928) ch. 5, pp. 76–80.

*Virginia Woolf*

# PEACOCK'S STYLE (1929)

. . . When we open *Crotchet Castle* and read that first very long sentence which begins, 'In one of those beautiful valleys, through which the Thames (not yet polluted by the tide, the scouring of cities or even the minor defilement of the sandy streams of Surrey)', it would be difficult to describe the relief it gives us, except metaphorically. First there is the shape which recalls something visually delightful, like a flowing wave or the lash of a whip vigorously flung; then as phrase joins phrase and one parenthesis after another pours in its tributary, we have a sense of the whole swimming stream gliding beneath old walls with the shadows of ancient buildings and the glow of green lawns reflected in it. And what is even more delightful after the immensities and obscurities in which we have been living, we are in a world so manageable in scale that we can take its measure, tease it and ridicule it. It is like stepping out into the garden on a perfect September morning when every shadow is sharp and every colour bright after a night of storm and thunder. Nature has submitted to the direction of man. Man himself is dominated by his intelligence. Instead of being many-sided, complicated, elusive, people possess one idiosyncrasy apiece, which crystallizes them into sharp separate characters, colliding briskly when they meet. They seem ridiculously and grotesquely simplified out of all knowledge. Dr. Folliott, Mr. Firedamp, Mr. Skionar, Mr. Chainmail, and the rest seem after the tremendous thickness and bulk of the Guermantes and the Stavrogins nothing but agreeable caricatures which a clever old scholar has cut out of a sheet of black paper with a pair of scissors. But on looking closer we find that though it would be absurd to credit Peacock with any desire or perhaps capacity to explore the depths of the soul, his reticence is not empty but suggestive. The character of

Dr. Folliott is drawn in three strokes of the pen. What lies between is left out. But each stroke indicates the mass behind it, so that the reader can make it out for himself; while it has, because of this apparent simplicity, all the sharpness of a caricature. The world so happily constituted that there is always trout for breakfast, wine in the cellar, and some amusing contretemps, such as the cook setting herself alight and being put out by the footman, to make us laugh – a world where there is nothing more pressing to do than to 'glide over the face of the waters, discussing everything and settling nothing', is not the world of pure fantasy; it is close enough to be a parody of our world and to make our own follies and the solemnities of our institutions look a little silly.

The satirist does not, like the psychologist, labour under the oppression of omniscience. He has leisure to play with his mind freely, ironically. His sympathies are not deeply engaged. His sense of humour is not submerged.

But the prime distinction lies in the changed attitude towards reality. In the psychologists the huge burden of facts is based upon a firm foundation of dinner, luncheon, bed and breakfast. It is with surprise, yet with relief and a start of pleasure, that we accept Peacock's version of the world, which ignores so much, simplifies so much, gives the old globe a spin and shows another face of it on the other side. It is unnecessary to be quite so painstaking, it seems. And, after all, is not this quite as real, as true as the other? And perhaps all this pother about 'reality' is overdone. The great gain is perhaps that our relation with things is more distant. We reap the benefit of a more poetic point of view. A line like the charming 'At Godstow, they gathered hazel on the grave of Rosamond' could be written only by a writer who was at a certain distance from his people, so that there need be no explanations. For certainly with Trollope's people explanations would have been necessary; we should have wanted to know what they had been doing, gathering hazel, and where they had gone for dinner afterwards and how the carriage had met them. 'They', however, being Chainmail, Skionar, and the rest, are at liberty to gather hazel on the grave of Rosamond if they like; as they are free to sing a song if it so pleases them or to debate the march of mind.

The romantic took the same liberty but for another purpose. In the satirist we get not a sense of wildness and the soul's adventures, but that the mind is free and therefore sees through and dispenses with much that is taken seriously by writers of another calibre.

There are, of course, limitations, reminders, even in the midst of our pleasure, of boundaries that we must not pass. We cannot imagine in the first place that the writer of such exquisite sentences can cover many reams of paper; they cost too much to make. Then again a writer who gives us so keen a sense of his own personality by the shape of his phrase is limited. We are always being brought into touch, not with Peacock himself, as with Trollope himself (for there is no giving away of his own secrets; he does not conjure up the very shape of himself and the sound of his laughter as Trollope does), but all the time our thought is taking the colour of his thought, we are insensibly thinking in his measure. If we write, we try to write in his manner, and this brings us into far greater intimacy with him than with writers like Trollope again or Scott, who wrap their thought up quite adequately in a duffle gray blanket which wears well and suits everything. This may in the end, of course, lead to some restriction. Style may carry with it, especially in prose, so much personality that it keeps us within the range of that personality. Peacock pervades his book.

SOURCE: extract from 'Phases of Fiction', *The Bookman*, LXIX (1929); reprinted in *Granite and Rainbow* (London, 1958) pp. 131–3.

*Jean-Jacques Mayoux*

# RADICAL AND EPICUREAN (1932)

## I. The Turncoat Poets: The Tories and their Journals

*Headlong Hall* and *Melincourt* – in this respect resembling *Sir
Proteus* – are in part a denunciation and a satire of the political,
social and religious system of the day, from the pen of a radical
and Voltairean reformer. The end of the Napoleonic Wars,
albeit victorious for England, found the country in a very poor
way. The wretched condition of the working class grew worse
after the end of the wars and up to about 1821. Their plight
stirred many hearts and minds. A previous generation of reformers had turned in on itself with the French Revolution's be-
trayal of the first high ideals. And a new generation arose in the
midst of oppressive measures at a time when the unity of the
nation in the face of external threat had worn thin and ceased
to be a vital force. The workers, forbidden by legislation to combine in any way to fix the terms and conditions of labour, tended
to avenge their misery in riots, sabotage and machine-breaking
rather than to seek remedies. One of the most notable of the new
reformers, William Cobbett – formerly an upholder of order but
now a turncoat of a very unusual sort – strove to give them a
wider view and to persuade them by firm and simple arguments
that their troubles arose mainly from bad and hostile legislation,
and that they should devote all their efforts to achieving parliamentary reform, from which better laws would emerge.

If government *for* the people was far from being a strong
feature of England at this time, government *by* the people was
even more remote. The principle of representation was present,
it is true, but in an eccentric and oligarchical form; and corruption figured prominently at all levels within the system. Corruption scandalised the reformers and sharpened their bitter feelings.
This bitterness appeared particularly strongly in their attitude to

their elders. Godwin, for example, had got stuck in a kind of crankiness of mind; and his reputation had sunk, along with his ideas, into such obscurity that Shelley, writing to him early in 1812, artlessly said he thought he had died. Mistaken as he was about Godwin, he knew only too well that very much still alive was aging Southey, author of the insurrectionary poem *Wat Tyler*:

> Why are not all these empty ranks abolished,
> King, slave and lord ennobled into man?
> Are we not equal all?

The younger generation recalled what their elders had once been. The recollection of an earlier radical fervour was a source of embarrassment and irritation for the older men and of bitter disillusion for the young. Shelley, who could not prevent his eyes from seeing and his ears from hearing, concluded: 'I am not sure that Southey is *quite* uninfluenced by venality. He is disinterested so far as respects his family, but I question if he is so as far as respects the world. His writings solely support a numerous family. . . .'[1] Southey, Coleridge and Wordsworth were still alive; but quite dead now was the project, dreamed of in their days of democratic enthusiasm, of setting up a pantisocratic community in America on the banks of the Susquehanna. They had become loyal subjects, upholders of order. By an unfortunate conjunction, Southey (Poet Laureate), Wordsworth (Distributor of Stamps in Westmorland) and Coleridge (ministerial journalist) all depended on the established order for much of their livelihood. In their former camp there was but one opinion: they had betrayed a sacred mission, prostituted their talents. Apostles once, they were now apostates and, in the vocabulary of politics, 'bought men'.

The new democrats had suffered more than a loss of personnel: the whole political atmosphere was changed, and among those who were not too exalted in spirit (as Shelley was) to perceive it, mistrust and cynicism tended to replace hope and faith. Listen to Hazlitt:

The tone of politics and of public opinion has undergone a considerable and curious change, even in the few short years I can remember. In my time . . . the love of liberty (at least by all those whom I came near) was regarded as the dictate of common sense and common honesty. . . . The dawn of a new era was at hand. Might was no longer to lord it over right, opinion to march hand in hand with falsehood. The heart swelled at the mention of a public as of a private wrong – the brain teemed with projects for the benefit of mankind. . . . Mr Burke had in vain sung his *requiem* over the 'age of chivalry' : Mr Pitt mouthed out his speeches on the existence of social order to no purpose : Mr Malthus had not cut up Liberty by the roots by passing 'the grinding law of necessity' over it, and entailing vice and misery on all future generations as their happiest lot : Mr Ricardo had not pared down the schemes of visionary projectors and idle talkers into the form of Rent : Mr Southey had not surmounted his cap of Liberty with the laurel wreath; nor had Mr Wordsworth proclaimed Carnage as 'God's Daughter'; nor Mr Coleridge, to patch up a rotten cause, written the *Friend*.[2]

We need to be aware of this atmosphere if we are to have a proper appreciation of the degree of faith and scepticism, of idealism and materialism, of conviction and irony in Peacock's writings. The tendency is always to contrast him with Shelley; but if we see his position as an amalgam of reaction, of Cobbettism and of the utilitarianism that had rendered obsolete the dreamy fancies he clung to as a young poet, we shall come to realise what a remarkable thing the Peacockian compromise is : one which does not preoccupy itself with demolishing systems that are already crumbling, but rather pictures them as personalised expressions of belief and attitude, and accommodates itself as best it can to the human interests of the new vision.

In *Sir Proteus* we see his animosities violently revealed. It is unfortunate for a poet who changed his opinions in so flagrant a manner that Southey should have dedicated one of his poems to the god Proteus. The opportunity was too good to be missed, and Peacock was swift to devour the easy prey. Hence the first face of Proteus :

> He first appeared a folio thick,
> A glossary so stout
> Of modern language politic
> Where conscience was left out.[3]

A footnote of Peacock's explains 'language politic' thus: 'This language was not much known to our ancestors; but it is now pretty well understood by the majority of the H—— of C——, by the daily, weekly, monthly, and quarterly venders of panegyric and defamation, and by the quondam republicans of the Northern Lakes.' We know he is objecting to their harsh and clumsy style, but he is also speaking of 'tangible eloquence'. Peacock is fond of this kind of sardonic periphrasis. He associates it, we perceive, with the whole group of writers, and he regards as a national peril

the egotistic and mercenary apostacy of [John Bull's] quondam literary champions. Where is now 'the eye that sees, the heart That feels, the voice that in these evil times, Amid these evil tongues, exalts itself, And cries aloud against iniquity'? . . . Where are 'the skirts of the departing year'? Waving, like those of a *Courier's* jacket, in the withering gales of ministerial influence. The antique enemies of 'the monster Pitt' are now the panegyrists of the immaculate Castlereagh. The spell which Armida breathed over her captives was not more magically mighty in the operation of change, than are the golden precepts of the language politic, when presented in a compendious and tangible shape to the 'sons of little men'.[4]

Southey, who met all too zealously the official requirements of his post as Poet Laureate and sang the glories of the regime rather than of the nation, was the most vulnerable target of Peacock's invective. He was the subject of the only worthy strophes – as well as of the most grotesque:

> Here shall Corruption's *laureate wreath*,
> By ancient dulness twined
> With flowers that courtly influence breathe,
> Thy votive temples bind.
> Amid the thick Lethean fen
> The dull dwarf laurel springs
> To bind the brows of venal men,
> The tuneful slaves of Kings.
> Come, then, and join the apostate train
> Of thy poetic stamp
> That vent for gain the loyal strain

> Mid Stygian vapours damp,
> While far below, where Lethe creeps,
> The ghost of Freedom sits and weeps
> O'er Truth's extinguished lamp.[5]

In *Headlong Hall, Melincourt* and *Nightmare Abbey*, the Lake
Poets and their friends and associates not only figure, in different
degrees, among the literary and political targets, but also as
actual characters under the 'revealing disguise' of whimsical and
descriptive names. Tracing such identifications is interesting
only to the extent that they have an immediate and obvious
correspondence to the words and actions represented. It is a
pointless exercise if concerned merely with probabilities. In
*Headlong Hall* Peacock presents Mr Nightshade and Mr Mac
Laurel: 'two very multitudinous versifiers' and 'two senior
lieutenants of a very formidable corps of critics'. Mr Mac Laurel
has a Scottish accent. Does he not then represent John Wilson?
Yet the name itself would more readily fit Southey, the Poet
Laureate. And the words put into the mouth of this character
are clearly devised without much concern to make them representative. Is Mr Nightshade Wordsworth? There is nothing to
demand this identification.[6] And then we have Mr Panscope,
'the chemical, botanical, geological, astronomical, mathematical,
metaphysical, meteorological, anatomical, physiological, galva-
nistical, musical, pictorial, bibliographical, critical philosopher'.
Is this polymath (a veritable Pico della Mirandola) Coleridge?
If it is indeed he, Peacock's depiction is not a close likeness. True,
Panscope speaks a philosophical and learned jargon which at a
pinch could be taken as representing the worst of Coleridge –
as for example :

The authority, sir, of all these great men, whose works, as well as
the whole of the *Encyclopaedia Britannica*, the entire series of the
*Monthly Review*, the complete set of the *Variorum Classics*, and
the Memoirs of the *Academy of Inscriptions*, I have read through
from beginning to end, deposes, with irrefragable refutation, against
your ratiocinative speculations, wherein you seem desirous, by the
futile process of analytical dialectics, to subvert the pyramidal
structure of synthetically deduced opinions, which have withstood

the secular revolutions of physiological disquisition, and which I maintain to be transcendentally self-evident, categorically certain, and syllogistically demonstrable.[7]

We may at least take it that Panscope represents the spirit of German synthetical philosophy embodied in Coleridge and detested by Peacock, who as an analytical empiricist was ever true to the precepts of the Anglo-French enlightenment of the eighteenth century. It is to this synthetical philosophy that he attributes reasonably enough, Coleridge's political development. And yet : Mr Panscope is rich, while Coleridge was poverty-stricken; and it nowhere appears in the novel that Mr Panscope is, or has been, a poet.

Mr Mac Laurel frequently voices the sentiments of his associates and the philosophy of their public position and actions – that is to say, as attributed to them by their enemies; they would have been astonished to hear themselves speak the lines Peacock gives them (this is the Voltairean method at work). Mr Mac Laurel holds the view that good and bad are solely matters of a man's particular views and personal calculation. This prompts Mr Escott to remark : 'Thus, sir, I presume, it suits the particular views of a poet, at one time to take the part of the people against their oppressors, and at another, to take the part of the oppressors against the people.' To which Mac Laurel replies :

Ye mun alloo, sir, that poetry is a sort of ware or commodity, that is brought into the public market wi' a' other descreptions of merchandise, an' that a mon is pairfectly justified in getting the best price he can for his article. Noo, there are three reasons for taking the part o' the people : the first is, when general leeberty an' public happiness are conformable to your ain parteecular feelings o' the moral an' poleetical fetness o' things : the second is, when they happen to be, as it were, in a state of exceetabeelity, an' ye think ye can get a gude price for your commodity, by flingin' in a leetle seasoning o' pheelanthropy an' republican speerit : the third is, when ye think ye can bully the menestry into gieing ye a place or a pansion to hau'd your din, an' in that case, ye point an attack against them within the pale o' the law; an' if they tak nae heed o' ye, ye open a stronger fire; an' the less heed they tak, the mair ye bawl; an' the mair factious ye grow, always within the pale o' the law, till they send a plenipotentiary to treat wi' ye for yoursel, an' then the mair popular ye happen to be, the better price ye fetch.[8]

The satire, one perceives, is still rather vague and crude. The marks of individual identity do not signify much; but the group identity is not in doubt.

There is, moreover, a character in the novel who, while appearing as the crony and partner in iniquity of the 'turncoats', can scarcely be regarded as belonging to their group. This is Geoffrey Gall, ever preoccupied with *The Review*; his name alone would suggest his original in Jeffrey of the *Edinburgh Review*, the great whig periodical. We see him maintaining against Mr Milestone the identical aesthetic theory of 'unexpectedness' advanced by Jeffrey in the *Edinburgh*. *Headlong Hall*, in fact – like *Sir Proteus* before it – conjoins in a single animosity both the political dishonesty (in Peacock's judgement) of the new tories, and also the generality of journalism and of periodical criticism: in particular the two great reviews, the *Edinburgh* and the *Quarterly*. They may seem to be locked in combat, but to Peacock they are twin-offsprings of bad faith, partiality and injustice. The free spirits of the time (the expression does not include the whigs) join Peacock in powerful chorus: Byron, Hazlitt and Shelley himself.[9] The *Edinburgh* crushed Coleridge's *Christabel* as brutally as the *Quarterly* dealt with Keats's poems. Critical canons were all too often tied to political precepts and partisanship. From the political viewpoint, Peacock's animosity is readily explicable as *radical* – in the old English sense of the term – as we shall soon come to see more clearly. Whiggism of the post-1789 era had become a party of opportunism without fixed principles, and the *Edinburgh*, along with the party, engaged in strange oscillations.

*Melincourt* (1817) carries the war to the enemy. Members of the opposing camps meet at Melincourt Castle in Westmorland during a kind of truce – a situation typical of the Peacockian novel. They now wear their labels too prominently for us to fail to recognise them. Not far from Melincourt, at Mainchance Villa, lives Peter Paypaul Paperstamp, whose daughter Celandina is in the marriage market for the first rich suitor. How could this be other than Wordsworth, Distributor of Stamps, bard of the Greater and the Lesser Celandine, and here pilloried as selling his muse? A few months before the novel's publication, Peacock had sent an English celandine to Shelley, then in Switzerland. When the flower reached him faded and withered, Shelley saw in it a symbol of the degeneration of the elder poet:

> A type of that, when I and thou
>   Are thus familiar, Celandine –
> A deathless poet whose young prime
>   Was serene as thine.
> But he is changed and withered now,
>   Fallen on a cold and evil time;
> His heart is gone, his flame is dim,
>   And infamy sits mocking him.[10]

This kind of virulence – so unreal to us today – has to be accepted as inherent in the politico-literary relationships of the period between radicals and reactionaries, especially where the 'turncoats' are concerned.

Mr Feathernest at one time wrote odes on Truth and Liberty; but he has burnt them, and he now spends his mornings in writing odes to all the crowned heads of Europe. He has sold his conscience at a good price: 'It was thought by Mr Feathernest's friends, that he had made a very good bargain' – an example of the satirical phrase in which Peacock is so copious. In his youth the poet drank water, but: 'Now that I can get it for a song, I take my pipe of wine a year:' [an allusion to the Poet Laureate's official allowance of wine] 'and what is the effect? Not cold phlegmatic lamentations over the sufferings of the poor, but high-flown, jovial, reeling dithyrambics "to all the crowned heads in Europe".[11] I had then a vague notion that all was wrong. Persuasion has since appeared to me in a tangible shape, and convinced me that all is right, especially at court.'[12] A little later in the same scenario Feathernest takes up, with augmented cynicism, Mac Laurel's declaration of principles in *Headlong Hall*:

While I was out, Sir, I made a great noise till I was let in. There was a pack of us . . . two or three others got in at the same time: we knew very well that those who were shut out, would raise a hue and cry after us : it was perfectly natural : we should have done the same in their place : mere envy and malice, nothing more. Let them bark on : when they are wanted or troublesome, they will be let in, in their turn. If there be any man, who prefers a crust and water, to venison and sack, I am not of his mind. It is pretty and politic to make a virtue of necessity : but when there is an end of the necessity I am very willing that there should be an end of the virtue. . . . Every man for himself, Sir, and God for us all.[13]

One cannot gainsay the 'key' seeker's association of Feathernest, as here presented, with Southey. But the identification is merely an occasion for a gross and hostile caricature on which to build a brilliant exercise in satirical logic.

In the same way, Mr Vamp 'is' William Gifford of the *Quarterly*. The name is metonymic : Gifford at one point in his very hard early life was apprenticed to a cobbler; Hazlitt, who loathed him, never calls him other than 'Botcher'. Vamp in his study points to a pile of pamphlets, volumes of poetry etc., all of which have, he says, 'only one object; and a most impertinent one it is' :

This object is two-fold : first, to prove the existence, to an immense extent, of what these writers think proper to denominate political corruption; secondly, to convince the public that this corruption ought to be extinguished. Now, we are anxious to do away with the effect of all these incendiary clamours. As to the existence of corruption (it is a villainous word, by the way – we call it *persuasion in a tangible shape*[14] . . . we do not wish to deny it; on the contrary, we have no hesitation in affirming that it is *as notorious as the sun at noonday* : but as to the inference that it ought to be extinguished – that is the point against which we direct the full fire of our critical artillery; we maintain that it ought to exist; and here is the leading article of our next number, in which we confound in one mass all these obnoxious publications, putting the weakest at the head of the list, that if any of our readers should feel inclined to judge for themselves (I must do them the credit to say I do not suspect many of them of such a democratical propensity), they may be stopped in *limine*, by finding very little temptation to proceed.[15]

Vamp goes on to expound the manner of composing a political

article, citing a typical example: 'The political composition of this article is beautiful: it is the production of a gentleman high in office, who is indebted to *persuasion in a tangible shape* for his present income of several thousands per annum; but it wants . . . a little moral seasoning . . . we have some very obstinate and hard-headed readers who will not . . . swallow our politics without a little moral seasoning. . . .' Vamp is representative and type of the periodical journalists and their organs, all of them – even if the question of corruption be set aside – insensible of public good and ill and of general principles, acting as mouthpieces for a class or sectional interest, glorifying everything that belongs to it, and shamelessly attacking and condemning everything that has no part in it.

On to the scene comes Mr Anyside Antijack, 'a very important personage just arrived from abroad on the occasion of a letter from Mr Mystic of Cimmerian Lodge, denouncing an approaching period of public light . . .'. This is Canning, the witty ironist of the *Anti-Jacobin*, whom Peacock links with Coleridge in view of the latter's deploring, in his periodical the *Friend*, the effects of popular education.

These characters forgather at Mainchance Villa to deliberate on the best methods for extinguishing finally and totally the light of human understanding. The framework of the argument is supplied by a caricature of Wordsworthian theories of the simplicity of the common people. A picture in the Villa – possibly 'a family piece' – is described as depicting Mother Goose, surrounded by a bevy of nursery-rhyme children, including Jack Horner at work on his Christmas pie: 'The latter is one of the most splendid examples on record of the admirable practical doctrine of "taking care of number one", and he is therefore in double favour with Mr Paperstamp, for his excellence as a pattern of moral and political wisdom, and for the beauty of the poetry in which his great achievement of extracting a plum from the Christmas pie is celebrated.' Mr Paperstamp and his friends 'are unanimously agreed that the Christmas pie in question is a type and symbol of the public purse'.[16]

A scene preceded and introduced by such heavy humour holds little promise. But the sequel has better to offer.

Mr Forester, who bears a striking resemblance to Shelley, is welcomed and tolerated in his home by Mr Paperstamp as Shelley had been by Southey–Feathernest in 1812. He 'did not much like Mr Forester's modes of thinking; indeed he disliked them the more, from their having once been his own; but a man of large landed property was well worth a little civility, as there was no knowing what turn affairs might take, what party might come into place, and who might have the cutting up of the Christmas pie'.[17]

The scene opens with a post-prandial toast to the scheme for extinguishing the light of human understanding, and Mr Anyside Antijack observes : 'Nothing can be in a more hopeful train. We must set the alarmist at work, as in the days of the Antijacobin war : when, to be sure, we had one or two honest men among our opposers[18] – (*Mr Feathernest and Mr Paperstamp smiled and bowed*) – though they were for the most part ill read in history, and ignorant of human nature.'[19] Feathernest and Paperstamp take exception to this, so Antijack continues :

For the most part, observe me. Of course, I do not include my quondam antagonists, and now very dear friends . . . who have altered their minds, as the sublime Burke altered his mind,[20] from the most disinterested motives.

MR FORESTER :   Yet there are some persons, and those not lowest in the scale of moral philosophy, who have called the sublime Burke a pensioned apostate.

MR VAMP :   Moral philosophy! Every man who talks of moral philosophy is a thief and a rascal, and will never make any scruple of seducing his neighbour's wife, or stealing his neighbour's property.[21]

MR FORESTER :   You can prove that assertion, of course?

MR VAMP :   Prove it! The editor of the Legitimate Review required to prove an assertion !

MR ANYSIDE ANTIJACK :   The church is in danger !

MR FORESTER :   I confess I do not see how the church is endangered by a simple request to prove the asserted necessary connexion between the profession of moral philosophy and the practice of robbery.

MR ANYSIDE ANTIJACK :   For your satisfaction, Sir, and from a disposition to oblige you, as you are a gentleman of family and

fortune, I will prove it. Every moral philosopher discards the creed
and the commandments :[22] the sixth commandment says, Thou shalt
not steal; therefore every moral philosopher is a thief.

MR FEATHERNEST, MR KILLTHEDEAD, MR PAPERSTAMP :   Nothing
can be more logical. The church is in danger! The church is in
danger !

MR VAMP :   Keep up that. It is an infallible tocsin for rallying all
the old women in the country about us, when everything else fails.[23]

The scene has verve; and yet one is tempted to say that the words
put into the mouths of the tory politicans lack credibility. However, at critical points, when the illogicality of the 'reasoning' is
at its height, Peacock refers in footnotes [indicated in our Note
section – Ed.] to number *xx* of the *Quarterly Review* [Peacock
in fact cites number *xxxi* – Ed.]. If the references are verifiable,
this would give fine support to the *vis satirica* of the passage.
Examination of the *Quarterly* article of October 1816 reveals
two things. In the first place, Peacock does himself no service
by sometimes giving an incorrect reference for a genuine citation.
But, secondly, he cannot truly be accused, in most cases, of bad
faith. There was scarcely need for him to palter with this remarkable article in order to distil from it the essence of that illogicality and intellectual dishonesty which angered him, as a firm dialectical rationalist, more than all the other causes of contention
between him and the tories. He triumphantly exposes the
trickeries they deploy, which prove to him how untenable are
their positions in reason – and that means, for him, untenable in
all other respects.

   Let us look at a few examples, Half-knowledge impairs the
judgement, says the *Quarterly* article of October 1816 [pages
226 and 227 – Ed.].

Of all men, the smatterer in philosophy is the most intolerable and
the most dangerous; he begins by unlearning his creed and his
commandments, and in the process of eradicating what it is the
business of all sound education to implant, his duty to God is discarded first and his duty to his neighbour presently afterwards. As
long as he confines himself to private practice, the mischief does
not extend beyond his private circle – his neighbour's wife may be
in some danger and his neighbour's property also, if the distinction

between meum and tuum should be practically inconvenient to a man of free opinions . . .

Peacock has turned 'smatterer in philosophy' into 'moral philopher'. Does the actual text of the *Quarterly* convict him of falsification? Should we not, surely, see the difference between 'smatterer' and 'philosopher' as governed by agreement or disagreement with the philosophical opinions of the journal?

The dinner-table scene at Mainchance Villa is continued with vigour and verve. The people used to be all for the Anti-Jacobin war, declare the companions in reaction. 'They would have been determined on that war if it had been decided by universal suffrage', opines Mr Antijack. Then why the 'Gag Acts'? They look at one another: 'What shall we say to that?' 'Say?!', cries Mr Vamp, inspired: 'The church is in danger! The church is in danger!'

Moreover, observes Mr Antijack, 'Reform . . . is not to be thought of; we have been at war twenty-five years to prevent it; and to have it after all, would be very hard. We have got the national debt instead of it: in my opinion a very pretty substitute.'[24]

This Reform is, of course, electoral reform: the abolition of rotten and pocket boroughs, the introduction of a democratic suffrage. This is the prime objective of the radical reformers. We have already noted that Cobbett, among others, was striving to prove to the people that their economic condition was linked to the political system. Mr Forester, confronted by obscurantists of the Coleridgean type, formulates this point of view clearly:

The people read and think; their eyes are opened; they know that all their grievances arise from the pressure of taxation far beyond their means, from the fictitious circulation of paper-money, and from the corrupt and venal state of popular representation.[25]

We turn to Mr Antijack:

I am happy to reflect that the silly question of reform will have very few supporters in the Honourable House : but few as they are, the number would be lessened, if all who come into Parliament by means which that question attempts to stigmatize, would abstain from voting upon it. Undoubtedly such practices are scandalous, as being legally, and therefore morally wrong : but it is false that any evil to the legislature arises from them.[26]

These superb arguments – including the 'legally and therefore morally wrong' – are taken by Peacock from the text of the *Quarterly*, the editor of which astutely remarks : '. . . why should government be reproached with a corruption which exists wholly and exclusively among the people themselves?' So much the worse for the poor if they are so lacking in moral strength. As for putting an end to corruption – albeit legally, and therefore morally, bad – that is quite another matter. The rotten boroughs, fundamentally, are a fine thing. This time we will quote the *Quarterly* first :

A laudable and useful ambition leads into Parliament the opulent merchant and manufacturer; the lawyer high in his profession; the man who has returned with affluence from the East or West Indies, and is conversant with the customs, wants and interests of our conquests and colonies . . . It is for the advantage of the republic that . . . men liberally educated but more richly endowed with the gifts of nature than of fortune should sometimes prefer the service of the state to that of the army or the navy . . . as an honourable path to distinction. These persons possess no landed or local interests; they owe their seats therefore to someone into whose hands such interests through changes of time and circumstances have devolved, and with whom they coincide in political opinions. Agreeing this upon the general principle, it is not likely that any difference should arise upon a great question; if it should, the member vacates his seat; and whether he who accepts a seat upon this implied condition be not as unshackled, as independent, as conscientious, as honourable a member as the man who keeps away from the discussion of a question upon which his own opinion differs from that of the populace whose favour he courts, is a question which a child may answer. Others there are who have made a direct purchase of their seats, and these may thus far be said to be the most independent men in the House, as the mob-representatives are undoubtedly the least so.[27]

What here outrages an enlightened mind such as Peacock's is not so much the preference for oligarchical over representative

government as the cloaking of this preference in such a phantas-
magoria of sophistry, by which the simple-minded can all too
easily be deceived. It is an outrage to reason and to common
sense. Peacock, as we would expect, makes great play of this mode
of arguing by euphemism and cacophemism :

MR KILLTHEDEAD : The members for rotten boroughs are the
most independent members in the Honourable House, and the
representatives of most constituents the least so.
MR FAX : How will you prove that?
MR KILLTHEDEAD : By calling the former gentlemen, and the
latter, mob-representatives.
MR VAMP : Nothing can be more logical.
MR FAX : Do you call that logic?
MR VAMP : Excellent logic. At least it will pass for such with our
readers.[28]

The main governmental device of English reactionary politics of
this period was alarmism – at all times the strongest weapon in
the armoury of reaction. We are all familiar with the bogey of
the man with a knife between his teeth. Mr Antijack brings forth,
for the salutary terror of his colleagues, 'the great blunderbuss
that is to blow the whole nation to atoms ! the *Spencean* blunderbuss ! (*Saying these words, he produced a pop-gun from his
pocket, and shot off a paper pellet in the ear of Mr Paperstamp . . .*)'.

Peacock comments in a footnote : 'This illustration of the old
fable of the mouse and the mountain, falls short of an exhibition
in the Honourable House, on the 29th of January 1817; when
Mr Canning, amidst a tremendous denunciation of the parliamentary reformers, and a rhetorical chaos of storms, whirlwinds,
rising suns, and twilight assassins, produced in proof of his
charges – *Spence's Plan*.'[29] (Peacock hits off very well the oratori-
cal styles of Canning : see Hazlitt's *Spirit of the Age*.)

'Spence's Plan' was an utopian system of agrarian socialism,
elaborated by an idealistic, poor schoolmaster who drew out of
Scripture, from Moses onward, a kind of Christian communism.
The height of his doctrine's success was its becoming the gospel
of a small sect of 'Spencean philanthropists' which, enwrapped
in nebulous idealism, ran no great risk of growing greater. Its

main tenets – such as 'The profit of the Earth is for all' – easily
became weapons in the hands of unscrupulous opponents. The
*Quarterly*, surveying all the forms of agitation against existing
institutions, concluded: 'What wise man, and what good one,
but must perceive that it is the power of the Democracy which
has increased, is increasing, and ought to be diminished?' The
reformers, it is true, are hardly worth serious intellectual con-
sideration, but – 'The Spenceans are far more respectable than
these, for they have a distinct and intelligible system.' Peacock
puts the phrase into the mouth of Antijack Canning, who then
expounds his strategy to the plaudits of his acolytes: 'I shall set
up the Spencean plan as a more sensible plan than that of the
parliamentary reformers: then knock down the former, and
argue against the latter *a fortiori*.'[30]

It is highly likely that Peacock wrote these pages, not immediately after publication of the *Quarterly* article, but some
months later, on the occasion of a 'great speech' by Canning in
the House of Commons on 29 January 1817. In it, Spence's Plan
was linked with an adventitious occurrence: the throwing of a
stone at the Prince Regent's carriage at the opening of Parliament. The government party did all it could to magnify the incident. As the *Edinburgh Review* was to observe: 'At first it was
confidently alleged, that a bullet had been fired. No smoke, it is
true, had been seen, nor any report heard by the thousands
standing close round the spot: – but then an air gun had been
used ... it dwindled into an air pistol.'[31]

We see that Antijack's 'pop-gun' passage has two points of
resemblance with Canning's speech of late January 1817.
*Melincourt* may have been published in February; if so, it is very
possible that the editor of the *Edinburgh* had seen the novel by
the time he wrote the account of Canning's speech. There are
other curious concurrences. The *Edinburgh*'s editor says that
the speech 'is intended to aid the ministers in sounding an alarm
over the country . . . They appear to expect, that by such means
they can revive the golden days when all jobs were sheltered,
and all opposition disarmed, if not silenced, by the cry of danger
to the Church and the State from Jacobin principles and French
philosophy.'[32]

'We shall make out a very good case', says Paperstamp, 'but you must not forget to call the present public distress an awful dispensation :[33] a little pious cant goes a great way towards turning the thoughts of men from the dangerous and jacobinical propensity of looking into moral and political causes, for moral and political effects.'[34] This 'jacobinical propensity' to seek like causes (or such as are believed to be so) for like effects is the basic tendency of Peacock in all things; such a propensity, at once rational and positive, is of his very nature, and is integral to his strength and to his weakness.

We must leave this very long scene in chapter 39 with much of its matter untouched. It has to be said that, as with many other episodes in *Melincourt*, this scene by now has lost much of its interest. It entirely lacks artistic sobriety. As is proper to a good piece of pamphleteering, it seeks to be all-embracing in scope and to take full account of every aspect. Not a single loophole is overlooked by Peacock in exploring the confusion in which his enemies enmesh themselves. For all his intellectual vigour, his swift exposure of the weak point, the accuracy of his aim and the witty vivacity of his polemic, he piles detail upon detail to an excessive degree. Tireless himself, he wearies us. And yet I run the risk perhaps of overstating this point. For certainly, when he has worked through all the items in his demonstration, he rounds off the chapter with great gusto, presenting the triumph of the gang in a superb, ironic finale :

Mr Feathernest : Sir, I am a wise and good man : mark that, Sir; ay, and an honourable man.
Mr Vamp : 'So are we all, all honourable men !'
Mr Anyside Antijack : And we will stick by one another with heart and hand –
Mr Killthedead : To make a stand against popular encroachment –
Mr Feathernest : To bring back the glorious ignorance of the feudal ages –
Mr Paperstamp : To rebuild the mystic temples of venerable superstition –
Mr Vamp : To extinguish, totally and finally, the light of the human understanding –

Mr Anyside Antijack :   And to get all we can for our trouble!
Mr Feathernest :   So we will all say.
Mr Paperstamp :   And so we will all sing.[35]

And they bellow out, in solo couplets and choral refrains, a song
on the theme of Jack Horner and the 'Christmas pie', the chorus
of which reiterates remorselessly and hammers at the impassioned
greed, the black concupiscence of mercenary politicians :

> And we'll all have a finger, a finger, a finger,
> We'll all have a finger in the CHRISTMAS PIE.

A word should be said on the morality of the scene. Peacock's
unleashing his anger against those he regards as renegades is in
the main prompted by his desire to put above the question of
party a question of public morality. Hence, all the 'personalities'
whereby he pillories the Lake Poets turn on this aspect – as he
sees it – of their public life. The question is of general interest.
The passage from Hazlitt cited earlier clearly shows the part
these conversions played in changing the atmosphere of thought
in the succeeding generation, causing distrust, the fear of being
duped and of fostering illusions, the massive erosion of idealism.
Peacock observes, in the *persona* of Mr Forester : 'If a poet . . .
assume the garb of moral austerity, and pour forth against corruption and oppression the language of moral indignation, there
would at least be some decency if, when he changes sides, he
would let the world see that conversion and promotion have not
gone hand in hand.'[36] And in an earlier passage he has Mr
Forester say :

. . . when it is obviously from mercenary motives, the apostacy of a
public man is a public calamity. It is not his single loss to the cause
he supported, that is alone to be lamented : the deep shade of mistrust which his conduct throws on that of all others, who embark
in the same career, tends to destroy all sympathy with the enthusiasm
of genius, all admiration for the intrepidity of truth, all belief in
the sincerity of zeal for public liberty . . .[37]

For there is no criterion enabling one to distinguish the man who
will remain nobly faithful to his mission from the man who will
use it as a springboard for personal advancement. Mr Fax cites

– ironically – the *Edinburgh Review* of September 1816, whose censure of Swift was solely that he had made a sharp change in his opinions : 'The transition of a young whig into an old tory – the gradual falling off of prudent men from unprofitable virtues, is perhaps too common an occurrence to deserve much notice or justify much reprobation.'[38] Mr Forester replies :

If it were not common, it would not need reprobation. Vices of unfrequent occurrence stand sufficiently self-exposed in the insulation of their own deformity. The vices that call for the scourge of satire, are those which pervade the whole frame of society, and which, under some specious pretence of private duty, or the sanction of custom and precedent, are almost permitted to assume the semblance of virtue, or at least to pass unstigmatized in the crowd of congenial transgressions.[39]

On leaving Mainchance Villa, Mr Fax gives a different expression to the same reflections : 'I no longer wonder . . . that men in general are so much disposed, as I have found them, to look with supreme contempt on the literary character, seeing the abject servility and venality by which it is so commonly debased.'[40] A footnote of Peacock's at this point gives a long quotation from Johnson's *Rambler* (No. 136) on the moral role of the writer and the social crime he commits if he prostitutes his pen or perverts values; and Peacock reproduces the culminating words of the quotation in capital letters :

EVERY OTHER KIND OF ADULTERATION, HOWEVER SHAMEFUL, HOW-EVER MISCHIEVOUS, IS LESS DETESTABLE THAN THE CRIME OF COUNTERFEITING CHARACTERS, AND FIXING THE STAMP OF LITER-ARY SANCTION UPON THE DROSS AND REFUSE OF THE WORLD.

In attacking these turncoat writers, therefore, Peacock believes he is defending the dignity and prestige of literature, and notably of poetry, and the spiritual and intellectual potentiality of letters. We must emphasise that the strictly literary value of their work is not in question.

## II.   General Reflections on Peacock and His Art

1.   Is it necessary once more to indicate Peacock's limits? He
belongs to a human type which, on the whole, only rarely makes
its voice heard : the type of the sage. Not the philosopher or the
lover of wisdom, but 'the sage'. Without doubt, this type at its
highest level is the richest and most comprehensive of all. The
most precious and rare wisdom is that which, far from avoiding
life, involves itself in life in its most various and intense aspects.
Such is the wisdom of certain great poets – of Goethe, for
example; and (though I dare to say it is less evident) of
Shakespeare. As all wisdom consists of mastering an experience,
the supreme form of wisdom is that which masters, or is capable
of mastering, all experience. The wisdom of Peacock is of another
sort. It consists of surveying the possibilities of experience, of
measuring it. Its natural and preferred milieu is calm and com-
posure; it does not master the storm. It is Epicureanism.

Epicureanism – and we discount here the vulgar notion of it –
is far from always achieving wisdom. A doctrine solely and of itself never makes for wisdom; this is the outcome of a combination of a doctrine with a temperament. Now a many-sided temperament – and there are plenty such – chooses its doctrine, I
venture to say, by adhering to the predominant trait. Those tendencies which are not incorporated take their revenge. The life
of Sainte-Beuve, to cite only one example, presents the curious
spectacle of an Epicureanism painstakingly built on the dangerous
and false basis of his natural hedonism (it is a mistake to confuse
hedonism with Epicureanism) and hence of a repression of the
strength of the will. His Epicureanism is a mongrel of weak constitution, vulnerable to the sharp and painful pricks of life. For
all that he may be one of the most fervent pupils of the school,
an Epicurean so readily given to perfidy and venom as the
worthy Sainte-Beuve is remote from the master Epicurus and
from the true disciples, such as Montaigne.

A modern Epicureanism, drawing strength from the ancient
original, which it perhaps purifies and certainly enriches, has
about it, as an effect of the long perspective of time, a kind of
Romanticism. One calls to mind the Romantic outlook so deli-

cately formulated by Pater and attributed to his Marius. That of Peacock is also partly blended with what we may term (in an admittedly arbitrary identification) the Hellenic conception of life : a harmonious individualism, governed by the appreciation of beauty in things, in acts, in thinking, and by a religious feeling about the real and material world.

Peacock exhibits the links between Utilitarianism and Epicureanism : the endeavour to rationalise pleasure and to create, out of rational enquiry into pleasure, a personal and social morality. Reason imposes on the individual an awareness of the universal, and it impels Peacock towards democratic doctrines, the logic of which is immediately apparent if one is convinced both of the universality of egoism and of the universal legitimacy of pleasure – that is, if one is at once a Hobbesean and a rational Epicurean.

2. Peacock's development can be summarised fairly briefly. There are two periods – the first combative, the second defensive – in the lives of almost all thoughtful men, though these periods are sometimes disguised by insincerity or, most frequently, by illusion. In the first they conceive, and tend to believe achievable, a world fashioned to their tastes and inclinations; in the second they are concerned with protecting their tastes and inclinations from the world as it actually is or as it threatens to become.

By nature sceptical and wary, delighting in the game of dialectics, but perceiving beyond this the individualism of the human intellect and the wholly relative character of its conclusions, Peacock nevertheless found in the Utilitarianism of Bentham a doctrine to sustain him. This is his first period. But soon enough the anarchism which Benthamism encourages makes for something quite different from the position of Bentham himself, who was ever preoccupied with absolute verities and smitten at not finding them in human affairs. Peacock, in compensation, begins to strike out his own comic and philosophic path in pursuit of imposture and the Proteus of illusion. At the same time he perceives that to rationalise the world requires the world's co-operation. The world reveals itself as incapable of emerging

from an anarchic confusion of values – anarchic and also oppressive. From this point Peacock's development is logical. As
he turns away from the attempt to rationalise individualisms or
to justify social oppression on grounds of Utility, he recovers his
own individuality which, at the outset of his Utilitarian phase,
he had bravely thrown into the common stock in the interests
of social-contact theory. The artist in him, his sensibility to beauty
and to the good things of body and mind, reawaken. He had
earlier proclaimed the downfall of the poet who voluntarily
departed from the city, but he now feels increasingly ill at ease
in face of the choice of values presented by the city, and he con-
fronts in his own terms, implicitly, our contemporary problem
of the day-to-day position of the intellectual and his culture in
the modern city. To the value systems suited to unpretentious
and ordinary individualities, the numerical majority, there is opposed a system, aristocratic in character, which sustains the
notion of a hierarchy of intellect, and does not regard numbers
as of prime importance – indeed, on the contrary, is apprehen-
sive of their hostile pressure. Isolated by circumstance, Peacock
chooses to increase the isolation by renouncing the city and with-
drawing to his own version of Thélème. It is the conclusion of a
curious endeavour.

Generally speaking, Peacock's evolution corresponds to the
trend of his epoch – or, more precisely, to a fairly broad revulsion from the trend. The subjective causes of his development
– the principal one being, as he himself realises, the simple elapse
of time together with the withdrawal into himself – are mingled
with objective causes, among which the main one is a pessimistic,
or at least bitter, reaction against materialism and the mechanistic notion of progress. There is about Peacock something of a
nineteenth-century Montaigne : an intellect critical, ironic,
pyrrhonian, applied to the gradual liquidation of the idea of
progress.

3.   In seeking wisdom in the modern world, Peacock's path
needs must follow mechanistic progress or Romantic escapism,
or some systematisation which runs counter to these two routes.
It is fascinating to observe his relationship with Romanticism,

for what it has to tell us concerns not only Peacock.

In poetry and prose he deploys many of the Romantic themes; in the main these are the most obvious, 'exterior' themes, the prime catch-all categories which captivate the Romantic mind : Nature, Solitude etc. Peacock comes soon enough – after *Melincourt* – to have a sage's view of *wild* nature, to master it and to counter the sublime terrors of Burke by a brave pantheism. As for Solitude : it is throughout his life the regulator of his thoughts and his feelings – albeit far remote from him is the wilderness where the passions swell. Can he have had more than a hazy notion of the true solitude, he who thought to find it by leaving London for the English countryside?

There is only one Romantic theme for which this friend of Shelley (here wavering in his allegiance to Epicurus) has a full appreciation, if not a deep feeling : the theme of Absolute Love; for he was, in this respect at least, a Platonist. It figures prominently in his work, right up to that moving culmination in the autumn of his life, *Gryll Grange*. Even so, he is for ever striving to make even Platonism rational.

Admittedly, it is only in *Nightmare Abbey* that Peacock makes a frontal attack on Romanticism, as being unwholesome. But in all his writings he is campaigning against the subtle disguises, the metamorphoses, of Romanticism. For unbridled individualism, that is Romanticism. The passionately held system of thought and action, the grand personal idea offered to others for their salvation or well-being, and the huge endeavour to convert men – these also are elements in Romanticism. The idea of progress itself – so absurdly debased into the reign of the machine, the frenzy for production, for speed and so on – is for him the collective and, so to say, organic Super-Romanticism of modern times. Confronting it, Peacock becomes one of the first of a paradoxical race (though well established by our day) : that of the Rousseauan rationalists.

And even in regard to material progress his position is not a simple one, for his rational, reasonable mind and his sense of proportion modify the Rousseauan critique. He is far from being a remote and ineffectual desk-bound censurer; he designs and successfully builds steam-engines, to show he knows what

he is talking about when depreciating steam-power and seeking
to keep it in its place.

4. The two stages of Peacock's thought are translated into
comedy, and thereby is revealed, under this transformation, the
profound and substantial unity of his spirit. Within all his
comedy – *Gryll Grange* excepted – there is an individualism
making mock of individualism. It is an individualism moderated
and self-aware, accepting the conditions necessary for universa-
lising itself; and it ridicules the individualism of the immoderate,
encroaching and proselytising kind, seeing in this nothing other
than the desire for power masked by illusions.

We find in Peacock a strong sense of comedy – of the comic
spirit even – and very little of the satiric spirit. The things he
mocked at most often were those close to himself, the frenzies
or disorders of a kind of individualism which clearly fascinated
him: the individualism of the eccentric the deviser of theories,
the discoverer of panaceas, the enthusiast, the man with a saving
mission – in short, the 'crank'. (This English word is the only
exact designation of the type for, despite the example of Fourier
and others, it is a type essentially English.) The crank, the individual who has attained certitude, is borne along by a Romanticism of the brain. It is among seekers after the Absolute that our
author found his favourite subjects, and it is with such materials
that his dialectical mind fashioned what I would term his intellectual comedies. And yet, for all the derision with which he ex-
plores the fantastic by-ways of the Idea, we feel that he loves it
for itself, as one may love a woman without any need to possess
her.

He makes jest of the unconscious alliances between thinking
and private fantasy (we say fantasy, not imagination, for this
latter merits respect as the supreme faculty of mind; and be it
noted that Peacock prefers as a subject the second-rate system-
builder, the proponent of the preposterous). But these he
replaces by a conscious alliance. If he decks thinking with cap
and bells, it is to enable him to frisk about more freely, more
gaily. The originality of Peacock lies in his setting up a post in
the frontier zone of thought, imagination and fantasy, and in

helping to bring a rather arid terrain into the demesne of the literary art. He animates, with the charms of an amateur's naïveté and awkwardness, some very bizarre puppets. And yet, as this or that one performs, not a few of us will say, smilingly (for it is all in the mind only): 'Mon semblable, mon frère'.

In the strong maturity of his intellectual life, Peacock was much mistrustful of poetry, which most of us would regard as the highest form of literature. As a good Epicurean and an optimist by temperament, he put life itself in first place. This characterises all his writing.

5. Peacock's comic spirit shows itself at many points in the concurrence of a cathartic, secondary function (a little akin to the symbolic function of a poem or a drama) with a form of fantasy which is directly expressive and jocund. This, I believe, is the essential characteristic of the role of wine at his fictional dinner-parties. Wine makes for joy in a wholly different manner from the other sources of sensuous pleasure. The mutual bottle goes round the table; it is the visible, tangible and collective source of personal feelings which are not only happy but quasi-fraternal. Hence wine – together with good food, of course – is not only the symbol of all the vivid, yet not extreme, pleasures of the life of the body; it is also the type of a communion in these pleasures, opposing to the solitude of the mind and spirit the sociability of the body. For Peacock – by intention – is the most sociable of individualists; and it is perhaps this touch of contradiction that imparts such sureness to his aim and such success to his humorous critique of individualism.

The bottle always stands, even if some see it waveringly double, as a figure of objective reality among the table-companions – more real than the lucubrations of more temperate, but solitary, moments (let us remember that it is all a matter of symbols). With the admirable exception of Seithenyn in *The Misfortunes of Elphin*, Peacock chooses to ignore drunkenness and its unreality.

6. The well-known epigram of Horace Walpole tells us that the world is a comedy to those that think, a tragedy to those that

feel. This is at the least a gross simplification; it is all a question of a difference of proportion. The remarkable thing about Peacock, the thing which keeps him away from the highest peaks of comedy, is not that his head overrules his heart, but that head and heart are so blithely separate in their functioning. The greatness and profundity of Molière's comedy come from their interaction. When the critical and comic spirit is quiescent in Peacock, he sentimentalises; thus it is with his heroines, and with his Nature.

7.  Stendhal remarks somewhere: 'We say that a man has genius when he has invented his *genre*.' Dialectical comedy, such as is blended with a fantasy so diverse and subtle, is pretty well Peacock's invention.

A classicist by temperament, he displays nothing of the sad sense of imperfection, though he almost always evinces a great concern for formal finish. This makes him appear, in the broad day of the nineteenth century, a remotely classical spirit. Herein Peacock is an anomaly, and this has governed his literary reputation right up to our own day. A disillusioned imagination such as Peacock's receives worthy appreciation only in an age of disillusionment.

8.  His life, personality and character are compounded of greatness and littleness. Beneath the gaiety and the jesting we discern a massive and compact strength; and we watch him over the years in proud pursuit of his solitary course. But shall we call it grand or petty, this olympian, non-comic mask which he wears as a protection from fully human experience?

Judgement of Shelley has often been based on the Shelleyans, the lanky young men with high-pitched voices and missionary zeal for their idol. It would be quite as unfair to judge Peacock by the Peacockians who cherish him solely as he was in his old age: the quizzical man of letters, the Hellenistic gourmet, the squat and staid Epicurean.

SOURCE: extracts from *Un Epicurien Anglais* (Paris, 1932) pp. 143–60, 613–20; translated by D. Mirfin.

### NOTES

1. [Ed. – *Letters of P. B. Shelley*, ed. F. L. Jones (1964); letter to Elizabeth Hitchener, 2 January 1812 : vol. 1, pp. 218–19.]

2. William Hazlitt, 'On the Jealousy and Spleen of Party', in *The Plain-Speaker* (1826). [Ed. – reprinted in *The Complete Works of William Hazlitt*, ed. P. P. Howe (1931), vol XII, pp. 372, 373, 374.]

3. Peacock, *Poems*, Halliford edn. vol. VI, p. 285 [verse citations are from the Halliford facsimile edition of *The Works of Thomas Love Peacock*, ed. H. F. B. Brett-Smith and C. E. Jones, 10 vols (London, 1924–34; repr. 1967)].

4. Ibid. p. 289.

5. Ibid. p. 312.

6. [Ed. – The generally accepted identification is with the poet Campbell.]

7. *Headlong Hall*, ch. 5, p. 46 [text cited here is that of the Pan Classics four-novel compendium, *Novels of Thomas Love Peacock* (1967)].

8. Ibid. p. 43.

9. Cf. Byron's *English Bards and Scotch Reviewers* (1809), and Hazlitt's essay, 'Mr Jeffrey', in *The Spirit of the Age* (1825).

10. Poem rediscovered by W. Peck : see his *Shelley, His Life and Work* (1927), 1 476.

11. Here, as elsewhere, Peacock harps on Southey's *Carmen Triumphale* of 1814.

12. *Melincourt*, ch. 16, p. 176 [text cited here is that in vol. II of the Halliford edition – see note 3 above].

13. Ibid. p. 179. Cf. a very similar passage in Voltaire's *Jeannot and Colin*.

14. Similar – indeed, almost identical – euphemisms are to be found in the *Quarterly Review*, treating in an easy-going and playful manner these peccadillos of the *ancien régime*, if we may so term it, in England. *Melincourt* is crammed with them. [Ed. – Cf. Peacock's footnote reference (p. 408) to No. *xxxi* of the *Quarterly*, 'from which I have borrowed so many exquisite passages'.]

15. *Melincourt*, ch. 13, pp. 135–6.

16. Ibid. ch. 39, pp. 396–7.

17. Ibid, p. 398.

18. [Ed. – Peacock's footnote here cites *Quarterly Review*, No.

*xxxi*, 237. The full reference is 'Parliamentary Reform', *Quarterly Review*, October 1816 : Vol. XVI, No. *xxxi*, 225–78.]

19. [Ibid. 237, footnote.]

20. [Ibid, 252. footnote.]

21. [Ibid. 227, footnote.]

22. [Ibid. 227, footnote.]

23. *Melincourt*, ch. 39, pp. 400–3.

24. Ibid. pp. 406–7.

25. Ibid. p. 403.

26. Ibid. p. 407. [Peacock's footnote here cites *Quarterly R.*, op. cit. 258.]

27. *Quarterly R.*, op. cit., 258 [subsequently cited in Peacock's own footnote]

28. Melincourt, ch. 39, pp. 412–13.

29. Ibid. p. 410.

30. Ibid. pp. 411–12.

31. 'History of the Alarms', *Edinburgh Review*, March 1817 : Vol. XXVII, No. *lv*, 63.

32. Ibid. 61. Cf. ibid. 73 for an example of Canning's style : 'France is the standing example of perils too lightly estimated in their beginning, and not resisted until they had grown to a strength which at once alarmed and overpowered resistance. The projects of innovation do not stop with Parliaments and Governments; the projectors would, in the end, shear property to the quick. This is no conjecture of mine. . . .'

33. [Peacock's footnote here cites *Quarterly R.*, op. cit., 276]

34. *Melincourt*, ch. 39, pp. 413–14.

35. Ibid. pp. 416–17.

36. Ibid. p. 416.

37. Ibid., ch. 6, p. 177.

38. *Edinburgh R.*, September 1816, p. 10. This is the same issue as that in which Thomas Moore tore to shreds Coleridge's *Christabel*.

39. *Melincourt*, ch. 16, pp. 178–9.

40. Ibid. ch. 40, p. 420.

*Olwen W. Campbell*

# *MELINCOURT* AND THE PEACOCK HEROINE (1953)

In March 1817 appeared *Melincourt*. It was well reviewed, and Shelley thought much more highly of it than of *Headlong Hall*; but it was not republished till 1856, and it is often held to be less good than the other novels. Mr. Brett-Smith complains that in this novel, 'the author allowed himself to take sides, and resigned his attitude of impartial mockery.' But Peacock was not an impartial mocker, and in *Melincourt* he added an ingredient which was lacking in *Headlong Hall* and which came from his own serious idealism and natural warmth of heart. Impartial mockery is never funny for very long, from sheer lack of contrast, and because the finest humour depends on a distinct *partiality* for human nature; and on a half-rueful sense of the pitifulness as well as the comicality of its efforts to be effective and wise. In *Melincourt* there are quite a number of lovable characters, however lightly sketched, and the heroine, for whom her creator devised the exquisite name of Anthelia Melincourt, is one of those women with cultivated and independent minds whom Peacock seems to have put for the first time into English fiction.

This was a more original achievement than has been realised. It is true that the heroines of eighteenth-century romances were often, unlike the usual Victorian type, possessed of character and courage, but they were represented as exclusively interested in love and marriage. In 1817 Scott was already filling his novels with heroines who had often nothing to them beyond colourless virtues of an accepted pattern. Jane Austen's novels were only beginning to be known, and there is nothing to indicate that Peacock ever read them; although there are some minor points of similarity in style and sentiment between his novels and hers.

This can be seen from the opening paragraph of *Melincourt*, which has just Jane Austen's roguish and ironical flavour.

Anthelia Melincourt, at the age of twenty-one, was mistress of herself and of ten thousand a year, and of a very ancient and venerable castle in one of the wildest valleys in Westmorland. It follows, of course, without reference to her personal qualifications, that she had a very numerous list of admirers, and equally of course that there were both Irishmen and clergymen among them. The young lady nevertheless possessed sufficient attractions to kindle the flame of disinterested passion; and accordingly we shall venture to suppose that there was at least one in the number of her sighing swains with whom her rent roll and her castle were secondary considerations; and if the candid reader should esteem this supposition too violent for the probabilities of daily experience, he will at least concede it to that degree of poetical licence which is invariably accorded to a tale founded on fact.

Jane Austen, however, fought very shy of the learned woman – Mary Bennet is the measure of her respect for such, and if she on her side could have read Peacock (she died the year *Melincourt* was published) she would certainly have agreed with many critics of the book, that Anthelia is a prig and a blue-stocking.

It is true that Anthelia expresses herself on serious matters in a rather pompous manner – but so do most of the male characters in the novels, and Peacock had the originality to believe that a woman and a man talking on serious matters might speak with equal authority and earnestness. There is a very good example of this in *Melincourt*, where at the Anti-saccharine festival Mr. Sarcastic has delivered himself of a clever and devastating attack on the selfishness of human beings. It is Anthelia who puts him right, and winds up the discussion by protesting that most acts of selfishness come from ignorance rather than cruelty, and that it is not by persuading misguided people that all the world is as bad as themselves, that they can be given clearer views and better feelings : 'if the general condition of man is ever to be ameliorated, it can only be through the medium of *belief in human virtue.*' Anthelia has no use for impartial mockery.

Peacock rarely lavished so much care on any character as he did on Anthelia. The effects are built up with an unusual subtlety. How much her uncle, old Mr. Hippy the hypochondriac, loves her is shown early in the book when he leaps up from his blue devils and his gout on the receipt of a letter from his niece inviting him to Melincourt Castle. It is insisted that Anthelia (like Peacock) cares for nature quite as much for literature; and she wanders alone and fearlessly among the wild valleys near her home. When she is trapped on a rocky island by a rising flood she is not frightened: 'she had always looked with calmness on the course of necessity: she felt she was always in the order of nature.' The progress of her romance with Mr. Sylvan Forester, an unworldly and philanthropic young gentleman who lives in an old abbey one time known as *Rednose* Abbey, but altered by him to *Redrose*, is through the discovery of genuine affinities. Mr. Forester first comes on proofs of her sympathy and generosity to her tenants; next, when they meet in her library, he finds that they read and enjoy the same books; that she reads Latin and would like to read Greek – an ambition of which he warmly approves; and finally – an irresistible touch – he discovers that she, like himself (and again like Peacock) refuses to have sugar used in her house because it was the product of slave labour.

Anthelia 'did not wish to condemn herself to celibacy', but she was quite sure that it was far preferable to an ill-assorted or loveless marriage, and she had formed for herself an ideal which she hardly hoped ever to meet. On this subject her friend Mrs. Pinmoney is very discouraging. The widow Pinmoney is one of Peacocks liveliest caricatures. She has come to Melincourt to try to persuade Anthelia to take an interest in her own nephew, Sir Telegraph Paxarett – a foolish but well-meaning and very honest young man who becomes in the end quite a sympathetic personage. Mrs. Pinmoney protests at Anthelia's lonely way of life; and her daughter Danaretta (whose name it is explained means *danaro contante* or *ready money*, and is an intimation to all fashionable Strephons of the only terms on which she is to be had), Miss Danaretta remarks that the solitude would be all right for a time if there were a *preux chevalier* outside the castle pining for the lady and declaring he had been seven years dying for her favours. Mrs Pinmoney bursts forth: 'Heaven defend me from such hypocritical fops! Seven years indeed! It did not take as many weeks to bring me and poor dear dead Mr. Pinmoney together.'

ANTHELIA : I should have been afraid that so short an acquaintance would scarcely have been sufficient to acquire that mutual knowledge of each other's tastes, feelings, and character, which I should think the only sure basis of matrimonial happiness.

THE HON. MRS. PINMONEY : Tastes, feelings, and character! Why, my love, you really do seem to believe yourself in the age of chivalry, when those words certainly signified very essential differences. But now the matter is, very happily, simplified. Tastes : – they depend on the fashion. There is always a fashionable taste : a taste for driving the mail – a taste for acting Hamlet – a taste for philosophical lectures – a taste for the marvellous – a taste for the simple – a taste for the brilliant – a taste for the sombre – a taste for the tender – a taste for the grim – a taste for banditti – a taste for ghosts – a taste for the devil – a taste for French dancers and Italian singers, and German whiskers and tragedies – a taste for enjoying the country in November, and wintering in London till the end of the dog-days – a taste for making shoes – a taste for picturesque tours – a taste for taste itself, or for essays on taste : – but no gentleman would be so rash as have a taste of his own, or his last winter's taste, or any taste, my love, but the fashionable taste. Poor dear Mr. Pinmoney was reckoned a man of exquisite taste among all his acquaintance; for the new taste, let it be what it would, always fitted him as well as his new coat, and he was the very pink and mirror of fashion, as much in the one as the other. So much for tastes, my dear.

ANTHELIA : I am afraid I shall always be a very unfashionable creature; for I do not think I should have sympathised with any one of the tastes you have just enumerated.

THE HON. MRS. PINMONEY : You are so contumacious, such a romantic heretic from the orthodox supremacy of fashion. Now, as for feelings, my dear, you know there are no such things in the fashionable world; therefore that difficulty vanishes even more easily than the first.

ANTHELIA : I am sorry for it.

Anthelia's unfashionable attitude has an immediate appeal to Sylvan Forester. At their first meeting they soon arrive at one of Peacock's strongest convictions, the right of women to be educated. Anthelia agrees, but says rather sadly : 'To think is one of the most unpardonable errors a woman can commit in the eye of society. In our sex a taste for intellectual pleasures is almost equivalent to taking the veil.' She goes on to admit that too much reading of poetry may unfit a woman for the real world. 'The ideal beauty which she studies will make her fastidious, too fastidious perhaps.' But Mr. Forester has been shown to be equally fastidious – they are obviously made for one another.

Aware that the romance was running a little too smoothly, or it may be because his publisher wanted a longer book, Peacock introduced, about half way through, the kidnapping of Anthelia by a disappointed suitor, Lord Anophel Achthar. Forester and his friend set off, on what proves to be for the most part only one of Peacock's talkative walking tours, in pursuit of her. Emotionally this part is very irrelevant; but the kidnapping allows one more glimpse of the independence of Anthelia, for when Lord Anophel, having failed to move her, threatens violence and remarks that after that she will be glad enough to hush all up and go to church with him, she astounds him by saying that she would hush nothing up, and that his threats are due to his supposition that 'your wickedness would be my disgrace, and that false shame would induce me to conceal what both truth and justice would command me to make known.'

I have dwelt at length on the character of Anthelia because Peacock's attitude to women played such an important part in his novels. It is one of the established pillars in and out of which his fantastical jigs are woven. You can never tell whether he will be appearing on the right or left, with the tories or revolutionaries, whether he will be decrying or praising the advances of science; whether he will be always looking backward over his shoulder towards the good old days or being moved to throw a glance of hope into the future, but you can be quite sure that his enthusiasm for intelligent and courageous women, his hatred of mercenary marriage, his contempt for the feminine affectations encouraged by society, will never be shaken – they are as firmly founded as his love of natural scenery and his passion for 'ancient books'. His treatment of his female characters is refreshingly lacking in preconceptions and prejudices; he is as ready to be charmingly sentimental about an old maid, like Miss Ever-

green of *Gryll Grange*, as to turn against some other female, like
Miss Philomela Poppyseed of *Headlong Hall*, a kind of mockery
which, as van Doren has pointed out, was usually reserved for
men.

His heroines need of course heroes to match them. It has
sometimes been supposed that Mr. Forester and Mr. Falconer
of *Gryll Grange* – those very poetical young men – are based
upon Shelley. They certainly have something of Shelley about
them – in their uncompromising idealism, their philosophic
humanism, their rejection of the world. But for all their oddities
they are essentially sober young men; and Peacock knew as well
as anyone that a sobered Shelley would be a contradiction in
terms. These heroes have fine qualities of heart and high principle, but they are permeated by an Epicurean spirit of moderation and self-control, sometimes to a disturbing degree (as when
Forester mixes his search for the lost Anthelia with so much
general philosophic discourse). They worship and constantly
quote classical and Italian literature, and are in some cases
interested in precisely the same things as Peacock – the May
Queen for example, and St. Catherine. They do not belong in
the world of mere opinion, where the voice may or may not be
Peacock's own: they are, in the main, expressions of his own
romantic, eccentric and enduringly youthful personality. A
different side of that personality appears in the warm-hearted
worldliness and common sense of Drs. Folliott and Opimian.

SOURCE: extract from *Thomas Love Peacock* (London,
1953) pp. 37–44.

*Mario Praz*

# THE BOURGEOIS QUALITY OF
# PEACOCK (1956)

But perhaps the ultimate depth of Peacock's philosophy is to be found in a passage in *Crotchet Castle*, another dialectical novel in the spirit of Aristophanes that appeared at the beginning of 1831, where one of the characters says, of the controversy between the economist and the medievalist: 'Gentlemen, you will never settle this controversy, till you have first settled what is good for man in this world; the great question, *de finibus*, which has puzzled all philosophers.' The Peacock of *Crotchet Castle* insists upon the fundamental individualism of man. But whereas the utilitarians who, in the economic field, clung to individualistic and liberal doctrines – free competition, free negotiation between capital and labour – believed at the same time in the coercive force of good political institutions to secure the happiness of man, Peacock displayed an opposite contradiction. An individualist both by temperament and by profound conviction, Peacock never tired of hurling sarcasms at political, legal, and all kinds of institutions, whether ancient or modern, and felt the need of legislation precisely in that economic sphere in which individuals, thanks to capitalist policy, no longer encountered each other as such, and in which some people, in face of the weakness of the subordinate masses, found themselves invested with a power monstrous in itself and yet, often, unrelated to their personal worth.

The bourgeois quality of Peacock is well illustrated by his attitude towards the masses, as revealed in *Crotchet Castle*. Incendiarism [which Praz has previously discussed in relation to Lamb] provoked, in Peacock, a reaction similar to that of the conservative Lamb; he makes use, ironically, of the same expression – the 'march of mind' – which the Conservatives used to stigma-

tize the revolutionary spirit. One of the characters in *Crotchet
Castle* says : 'The march of mind . . . has marched into my rick-
yard, and set my stacks on fire, with chemical materials, most
scientifically compounded.' Also : 'The policemen, who was sent
down to examine, says my house has been broken open on the
most scientific principles. All this comes of education.' And,
whereas Peacock had already reproved Burke for using the expression 'swinish multitude', he now himself starts talking about
the 'rabble-rout'.

But *Crochet Castle* already presents us with a Peacock who
has become at the same time both dense and dried-up : he had,
in the meantime, come under the influence of the French
'romans gais' – Pigault-Lebrun, Paul de Kock (no less than 144
volumes by this novelist were found in Peacock's library at his
death !), and even *Le Compère Mathieu* by that sinister character, the rebel priest Henri Joseph Du Laurens, a nihilistic and
scabrous novel which, in accordance with the custom in vogue
during those years in France to find an excuse for the most suspect works, concluded by pretending that its intention had been
to make fun of the nihilistic principles paraded throughout the
book, and by holding up, as its true philosophy, the ideal of a
quiet life in accordance with the dictates of self-respect, justice,
and moderation. Peacock's article *On French Comic Romances,*
which appeared in the *London Review* of 1835–6, throws light
on the conception he had formed of the function of the 'roman
gai' : an intense love and a clear apprehension of the truth, he
says, are both of them essential in comic compositions of the first
rank. So that Peacock's own work, outwardly comic, is evidently
serious in intention : the eternal *ridendo dicere verum.* His mission
is the search for truth, without fear, without reserve, almost without concern for anybody. Nevertheless, while Peacock gives free
play to his satirical and destructive vein in order to pull down
everything that appears to be superstructure, he still fails to find
the ultimate truth which alone could justify such devastation;
and, as Professor Mayoux observes, the psycho-analysis of social
communities has its dangers, for the most useful and solid con-
structions can rest on rotten foundations, provided nobody knows
it.

In a nerveless work such as *Crotchet Castle* we witness the breaking of the precarious balance between heart and brain which had still persisted in *The Misfortunes of Elphin*. This balance was replaced by a double figure : on one side a positive Peacock for whom reality is without veils, or even worse than it really is, on the other, a Peacock becoming more and more sentimental with age, and contenting himself with a facile idealism well protected from all hazardous tests. The two bourgeois figures – the eighteenth-century one who produced the philosophic novels *à la* Voltaire, and the nineteenth-century one who is already coloured with sentimentalism and easy Victorian optimism – meet together in that singular transitional figure which is Peacock.

In 1836 James Mill died, and Peacock succeeded him in the important position of Examiner at India House; he busied himself, with recognized competence, in public works, especially in the application of steam navigation to the communications of India, as we have already said. One of Peacock's daughters, Mary Ellen, having been left a widow in 1844 by the death of her husband Edward Nicolls, a naval lieutenant, in 1849 met and agreed to marry Meredith – a union which was destined to come to a dramatic end. In 1862 Peacock finished his last, very slight work, a translation of a famous Italian Cinquecento comedy, *Gl'Ingannati*. Tended, till his very last years, by an adopted daughter, he died at the height of the Victorian period; as Professor Mayoux says, 'il cultive son jardin, il grogne, il sentimentalise, il hellénise, il relit Dickens et s'attendrit, il préside à des fêtes d'enfants le premier jour de mai . . .'.

With regard to Peacock's poetry, its formula, as Professor Mayoux has well observed, was the opposite of Wordsworth's : it was not 'emotion recollected in tranquillity', but 'tranquillity recollected with emotion'. And in this reversal lies the whole meaning of the literary revolution that was in process of being accomplished : on the far side, Romanticism, on this side Biedermeier. Poe praised Peacock's poem *Rhododaphne* as being 'brimful of music'. Peacock, however, as a poet, lacks truly intimate experience of the beauty that is his constant aim, and the sensuous appeal of this musical poetry is indirect, reflected, as it were, not gushing naturally from an image-generating sensation; it is, in fact, the poetical exercise of an intellectual.

The most notable part of Peacock's work is the tales, which form a link in the development of English literature between Ben Jonson's comedy of humour, Restoration comedy, and Voltaire's novels on the one hand (with, in the background, Rabelais), and, on the other, the modern intellectual novels of Meredith, and, in an even more obvious way, of Norman Douglas and Aldous Huxley. The style of Peacock's novels is descriptive rather than suggestive, with a tendency towards the exploiting of pedantry for comic effect, and towards Rabelaisian redundancy (for an example of pedantry: 'Mr. Cranium being utterly destitute of natatorial skill was in immediate danger of final submersion'). It is a style which, even when it achieves beauty, at the same time reveals a flaw – the omnipresent feeling of an illusory charm. The rhythm of this style is not spontaneous, but is, rather, of an architectonic order, as carefully controlled as a dance-figure, very different from Voltaire's rhythm, which is elastic and boundlessly free. Amongst the expedients for achieving comic effect, the least convincing is perhaps the very ancient one of giving the characters names which crystallize the characteristics that the author intends to parody. Peacock, in this field, attains subtleties which might well have made him the subject of a comic portrait by Proust (of the type of the philologist in *Sodome et Gomorrhe*). For instance, the name of Lord Anophel Achthar in *Melincourt* means: 'terrae pondus inutile,' ἀνωφελ(ὲs) ἄχθ(οs) ἀρ(ούρης). The most successful comic effects are obtained by means of encounters between the manifold typical characters: theories and theorists, manias and maniacs, cranks of every kind butt into each other on almost every page of Peacock with automatic regularity – that automatic quality in which, according to Bergson, the essence of laughter consists. This may become monotonous, but it may sometimes produce an irresistibly comic result, as in the description of Lord Littlebrain's garden in *Headlong Hall*, and in the suggestion of an atmosphere of complete idiocy which is given forth by the refrain: 'And there is Lord Littlebrain, rowing in an elegant boat . . . and there is Lord Littlebrain walking under it . . . and there you see Lord Littlebrain, on the top of the pavilion, enjoying the prospect with a telescope . . . and there you see Lord Littlebrain looking out of the window . . .' (ch. 6). But Peacock's taste for suddenly upsetting the balance, for turning somersaults, for the reduction of the human body to its material and geometrical elements, belongs to a far coarser type of humour : this is a taste which Professor Mayoux sets alongside that other taste for Rabelaisian enumerations, for avalanches of words, helter-skelter.

The architectonic tendency dominates not only the style but also the choice of characters; especially in *Headlong Hall*, which displays all Peacock's salient characteristics. There, the central group is of a perfect symmetry : Foster on one side, Escot opposite him, Jenkison in the middle : thesis, antithesis, synthesis personified, as in a popular print. Creator of the 'novel of talk', Peacock, with his elegant distorting mirror, gives an oblique reflection of modes and manners and opinions, reducing the vast Romantic heaven, torn by a hundred blasts, to a storm in a teacup : there rises again in him, beneath a superficial Romantic patina which soon flakes away, a kind of eighteenth-century spirit, which, however, has coarsened and grown bourgeois.

S O U R C E : extract from *The Hero in Eclipse in Victorian Fiction* (London, New York and Toronto, 1956; repr. 1969) pp. 97–101.

*Northrop Frye*

# A MENIPPEAN SATIRIST (1957)

. . . most people would call *Gulliver's Travels* fiction but not a novel. It must then be another form of fiction, as it certainly has a form, and we feel that we are turning from the novel to this form, whatever it is, when we turn from Rousseau's *Emile* to Voltaire's *Candide*, or from Butler's *The Way of All Flesh* to the Erewhon books, or from Huxley's *Point Counter Point* to *Brave New World*. The form thus has its own traditions, and, as the examples of Butler and Huxley show, has preserved some integrity even under the ascendancy of the novel. Its existence is easy enough to demonstrate, and no one will challenge the statement that the literary ancestry of *Gulliver's Travels* and *Candide* runs through Rabelais and Erasmus to Lucian. But while much has been said about the style and thought of Rabelais, Swift, and Voltaire, very little has been made of them as craftsmen working in a specific medium, a point no one dealing with a novelist would ignore. Another great writer in this tradition, Huxley's master Peacock, has fared even worse, for, his form not being understood, a general impression has grown up that his status in the development of prose fiction is that of a slapdash eccentric. Actually, he is as exquisite and precise an artist in his medium as Jane Austen is in hers.

The form used by these authors is the Menippean satire, also more rarely called the Varronian satire, allegedly invented by a Greek cynic named Menippus. His works are lost, but he had two great disciples, the Greek Lucian and the Roman Varro, and the tradition of Varro, who has not survived either except in fragments, was carried on by Petronius and Apuleius. The Menippean satire appears to have developed out of verse satire through the practice of adding prose interludes, but we know it only as a prose form, though one of its recurrent features (seen in Peacock) is the use of incidental verse.

The Menippean satire deals less with people as such than with mental attitudes. Pedants, bigots, cranks, parvenus, virtuosi, enthusiasts, rapacious and incompetent professional men of all kinds, are handled in terms of their occupational approach to life as distinct from their social behavior. The Menippean satire thus resembles the confession in its ability to handle abstract ideas and theories, and differs from the novel in its characterization, which is stylized rather than naturalistic, and presents people as mouthpieces of the ideas they represent. Here again no sharp boundary lines can or should be drawn, but if we compare a character in Jane Austen with a similar character in Peacock we can immediately feel the difference between the two forms. Squire Western belongs to the novel, but Thwackum and Square have Menippean blood in them. A constant theme in the tradition is the ridicule of the *philosophus gloriosus*, already discussed. The novelist sees evil and folly as social diseases, but the Menippean satirist sees them as diseases of the intellect, as a kind of maddened pedantry which the *philosophus gloriosus* at once symbolizes and defines. . . .

SOURCE: extract from *The Anatomy of Criticism* (Princeton, 1957) pp. 308–9.

# A. E. Dyson

## THE PROBLEM OF SERIOUSNESS
(1965)

### I

Peacock's frivolity is central . . . to these works; but is it incompatible with the serious ironic intention which we sometimes discern? The problem is forced upon us by the very nature of Peacock's method, which is to collect a number of individuals with interesting hobby-horses, and to race them against one another in a kind of caucus-race of the mind. The detached amusement with which this race is commented upon suggests a certain superior reasonableness in the author; whose pose may be less Olympian than Gibbon's, yet has an urbane self-assurance of its own. What we appear to be offered is the reassertion of common-sense over wild intellectualism, a two-sides-to-every-question geniality, steering all sharp exchanges towards the safety of sport. The very setting is attuned to this kind of resolution. In *Headlong Hall* Squire Headlong drinks his Burgundy in rural intactness, his Horatian well-being an ambience where all crankiness is baptised and absorbed. In *Crotchet Castle* the 'schemes for the world's regeneration' evaporate 'in a tumult of voices', as Mr Crotchet's 'matchless claret' has its destined effect.

All of which is abundantly pleasant; and surely too pleasant to be intruded upon by any morose reflections which the sober moralist may entertain? Yet the moralist has his right to be heard, and indeed must be heard, if the right kind of claim for Peacock is in the end to be made. The 'wand of enchantment' which Mr Milestone flourishes is Peacock's also; he creates a world for our pleasure, more idyllic, for all its irony, than the world as it actually is. We submit to his spell as we read, and are properly grateful; yet if we submit too completely, we may overlook how much is surrendered by the admirably genial tone. The mental sharpness which any totally satisfying irony must have is surrendered; and so is the radicalism from which this irony, in particular, often pretends to spring. Peacock's characters are not 'good' or 'bad' in any serious sense, as I have already noted; they are morally neutral in themselves, whatever the implications for good or ill in their ideas. They are more-or-less eccentric, more-or-less loveable cranks; or alternatively, more-or-less eccentric, more-or-less loveable cynics, resisting crankiness in the name of common sense, good humour and port. Peacock's own *persona* veers in different novels between the two: in Mr Hilary of *Nightmare Abbey* he puts himself in the latter camp, but in Dr Folliott of *Crotchet Castle* and the Reverend Dr Opimian of *Gryll Grange* (both part *personae*) he moves somewhat the other way. A revealing remark about Dr Folliott is made by Lady Clarinda: 'He is of an admirable temper, and says rude things in a pleasant, half earnest manner, that no-body can take offense with.' This 'manner' is one which Peacock clearly admired; yet how much complacency, how much insensitivity, how much intransigent reaction, must it have sanctioned in its time?

The setting is attuned, then, to Peacock's temperament; and so is his characteristic handling of ideas. He hardens ideas towards absurdity, as politicans harden one another's policies in election year. There is little regard for truth, and none for fairness. To make the ideas amusing, and therefore impossible, is the sole intent.

The damage sustained by the ideas has already been touched on; they are made to sound like part of a Christmas game. They need, for Peacock's purpose, to be both simplified and arrested: simplified so that original notions sound wildly eccentric; and arrested so that one simplified idea can clash with its opposite to the greatest effect. The result falls far short, one need scarcely add, of synthesis; and still further short of the point where any meaningful action might occur. It guarantees that no synthesis or action will ever be possible – not, that is to say, while Peacock's geniality can keep its hold.

In itself, the technique can be amusing, and not unsubtle – as in this exchange in *Nightmare Abbey*, when Scythrop and his father clash over a choice of bride (Mr Glowry speaks first).

'Sir, I have pledged my honour to the contract – the honour of the Glowries of Nightmare Abbey : and now, sir, what is to be done?'

'Indeed, sir, I cannot say. I claim, on this occasion, that liberty of action which is the co-natal prerogative of every rational being.'

'Liberty of action, sir? there is no such thing as liberty of action. We are all slaves and puppets of a blind and unpathetic necessity.'

'Very true, sir; but liberty of action, between individuals, consists in their being differently influenced, or modified, by the same universal necessity; so that the results are unconsentaneous, and their respective necessitated volitions clash and fly off in a tangent.'

'Your logic is good, sir; but you are aware, too, that one individual may be a medium of adhibiting to another a mode or form of necessity, which may have more or less influence in the production of consentaneity; and, therefore, sir, if you do not comply with my wishes in this instance (you have had your own way in everything else), I shall be under the necessity of disinheriting you, though I shall do it with tears in my eyes.' Having said these words, he vanished suddenly, in the dread of Scythrop's logic.

Ostensibly, this is an intellectual discussion depending on logic; obliquely, it is a clash of wills, conveyed to us precisely through the exuberant irrelevance of the ideas. The fun is beautifully managed, with Peacock's usual side-glances at transcendental long-windedness, yet the ideas are totally sacrificed to the humour of the situation itself. And why not, when Peacock writes as amusingly as this? – except that one would like to be sure that the author realises the limits, as well as the possibilities, of his technique. Our suspicion is that he does not realise the limits; that he mistakes his skill in having fun with ideas for serious satire against the ideas themselves. He misunderstands, it sometimes seems, his actual target – which is not a variety of ideas, but one kind of person : the person who talks rather than acts, and is superficial in his talk. The various incarnations by which Shelley and Coleridge are pursued through his writings are always amusing; but does he realise that they are not Shelley and Coleridge? Does he see that they are, rather, undergraduates talking Shelley and Coleridge? – talking fluently and pretentiously, and with all the major ideas just slightly askew?

Did Peacock realise, in fact, that Shelley really was an exceptional man, for all his absurdities, and that Coleridge (to use

Mill's tribute) was one of the two great seminal minds of his age? This matter is clearly important, for though there is nothing objectionable in caricature recognised as caricature, there is certainly something objectionable in caricature parading as satiric truth. And Peacock himself may not have known this; there is no evidence that he understood the nature of a truly original or speculative mind. He had little understanding of which questions were really worth asking, or of which kinds of enquiry might lead towards truth. He had no insight into which kinds of originality might be productive. The charlatan and the scientist, to him, were entirely the same.

Mr Cranium in *Headlong Hall* is an interesting instance; Mr Cranium's theory, it will be remembered, is that our behaviour is largely determined by bumps. He lectures on this theme with amusing pedantry, and what he says, one agrees, is almost self-evidently absurd. Yet *is* it as absurd as we think it? – or is it the kind of absurdity which might be a growing pain for truth? Mr Cranium was wrong about bumps, and human behaviour cannot be related to them; it can, however, be related to genes, though Mr Cranium was naturally in no position to know about these. His search for some physical link was, however, inherently plausible. Might we not see him in retrospect as a transitional figure between magic and science – a necessary link, even, between the astrologer, and the molecular biologist of today?

My contention is not that there are no Mr Craniums in the world we live in, for clearly there are, and every bit as silly as Peacock makes out. It is, rather, that there are also geniuses who superficially resemble Mr Cranium, and that Peacock makes no distinction whatever between the two. In *Nightmare Abbey* the scientific butt is Mr Asterias; and of course Mr Asterias *is* very funny, with his theory that all life evolved from the water, and his search for mermaids and tritons as a missing link. But would Peacock have seen a Mr Asterias in Darwin? It is virtually certain that he would. In *Crotchet Castle* Mr Firedamp's remedy for malaria is remarkably funny, and it is no doubt unfortunate, for Peacock at least, that it also turned out to be true. And Mr Toogood's political theories are 'the strangest of the lot', as Captain Fitzchrome points out: 'He wants to parcel out the world into squares like a chess-board, with a community on each, raising every thing for one another.'

If Peacock had lived in the twentieth century, Freud would have been a godsend to him, while Professor Fleming's early experiments with penicillin would have exhibited just the kind of absurdity he relished most. And this, really, is why a moral point about him cannot be evaded : he makes his cranks representative of the men who shape destiny, as cosy reactionaries nearly always do.

## II

I have suggested that Peacock failed to distinguish between genius and crankiness. He failed also, from his own point of view more disastrously, to distinguish between complacency and common sense. You have only to compare him with Johnson, whom he sometimes paraphrased and obviously admired, to make this failure almost embarrassingly clear. In the writings of Johnson there is always a vital distinction between ills such as death, which we must learn to accept, however painfully, and ills such as poverty, against which we must never cease to campaign. From the former we can learn fortitude, from the latter justice; and the two together form part of a true 'commonsense'. Common sense, as Johnson conceives it, is a kind of wisdom : a distillation of human experience over the ages, a codification of all that is fine. To turn from this concept to Peacock's is to turn from human greatness to the smug complacency which 'commonsense' usually is. Peacock sees little difference, as facts that must be accepted, between death and poverty; since both are part of the world we live in, to protest against either would be somewhat absurd. His acceptance of class distinctions is everywhere apparent, in the early and more 'radical' works like *Melincourt*, as well as in *Crotchet Castle* and *Gryll Grange*, where resistance to social change has turned into a major theme. And with the acceptance of class distinctions, there is acceptance of the social *status quo*. In *Melincourt*, it is true, a corrupt clergyman is satirised for his attacks on education, but in *Crotchet Castle* the pendulum has swung the other way. This time it is Lord

Brougham who is satirised, for his efforts to spread education to the workers. It has dawned upon Peacock that if you educate people they might get ideas above their station. They might even be disruptive to the people who have educated them : and this, Peacock's brand of radicalism cannot be expected to endorse.

Exactly here, I think, we have a clue to our ambivalence about Peacock : I speak for myself, of course, but I fancy that many modern readers might feel the same. The more realistic he is, the less we like him; for the more realistic he is, the more conscious we become of basic assumptions with which it is impossible to agree. The nearer he moves, however, to idyll and fantasy, the greater his hold on our imagination, and indeed on our affection, becomes. As a realist he is reactionary, and his tone, when it fails to be genial, can sound harsh and false. As a writer of idyll and fantasy, he is a great entertainer; and the entertainment has its own pleasantness, its own validity, its own proper tone.

### III

I want in conclusion to develop this distinction, and to suggest that Peacock is a reactionary writer whom his greatest opponents can still, however, enjoy. Even in *Melincourt*, reactionary habits of mind proliferate, despite the attack on slavery, which Peacock vigorously and honestly launched. The Anti-Saccarine Fête, it will be remembered, is part of a boycott; sugar is a West Indian product, and Mr Forester sees the boycott as a means of resisting slavery from home. But the Fête, though launched as a boycott, turns into a feast; and the manner in which even Mr Forester thinks of it suggests something less than wholehearted commitment to a cause. When ills nearer home are mentioned, the radical impulses appear to have expended themselves. The chapters on Desmond and his family are a *locus classicus* for anyone wishing to assimilate benevolence to the political right. Desmond is driven by poverty nearly to desperation, but is rescued by the private charity of a benefactress – in this case, by the heroine of the book. The payment for charity is, of course, heartfelt gratitude; and this Desmond offers, in company with the wife and children who have been rescued along with himself.

Mr Forester's approval of the whole episode is also Peacock's, and his words are worth quoting in full.

I am no revolutionist. I am no advocate for violent and arbitrary changes in the state of society. I care not in what proportions property is divided (though I think there are certain limits which it ought never to pass, and approve the wisdom of the American laws in restricting the fortune of a private citizen to twenty thousand a year), provided the rich can be made to know that they are but stewards of the poor, that they are not to be the monopolisers of solitary spoil, but the distributors of general possession; that they are responsible for that distribution to every principle of general justice, to every tie of moral obligation, to every feeling of human sympathy : that they are bound to cultivate simple habits in themselves, and to encourage most such arts of industry and peace, as are most compatible with the health and liberty of others.

How, one wonders, can this not be ironic? But in Peacock no irony is intended, not even, I think (though I am less sure of this) in the very peculiar parenthesis about 'the wisdom of the American laws'. Mr Forester is no revolutionist, certainly, as he admits : he is, rather, the exponent of that brand of optimistic Toryism which can afford to be good-humoured and genial, as long as 'simple habits' are not interpreted in too austere a sense. A radical's irony would be certain to be at the opposite pole to this with Oscar Wilde : 'the virtues of the poor may be readily admitted, and are much to be regretted'. Has any radical ever been able to consider the gratitude of the poor without dismay?

*Crotchet Castle* is altogether the harshest and least pleasing of Peacock's novels, no doubt because here the threat to benevolent Toryism is most pressingly felt. 'I am out of all patience with this march of the mind,' announces Dr Folliott. 'My cook must read his rubbish in bed; and as might naturally be expected, she dropped suddenly fast asleep, overturned the candle, and set the curtains in a blaze.' 'His rubbish' is Lord Brougham's *Observations on Education of the People*, and the effect on the cook ('naturally to be expected,' says Mr Folliott) combines the literal and symbolic dangers of education in one. Lady Clarinda, the heroine of *Crochet Castle*, is strangely egotistical and cynical;

her wit has the glitter and hardness of Restoration Comedy, yet Peacock seems to endorse it in the course of the tale. The element of farce in this novel becomes more violent. For once, someone is actually killed in the course of a brawl, but since he is only a robber, and a lower-class robber at that, we are made to feel that his death hardly counts. The attack on America, moreover, is surprisingly lacking in the urbanity we have come to expect. We are reminded, naturally enough, of *Martin Chuzzlewit*, but the similar content merely underlines the dissimilar tone. Dickens's satire originated in disappointed idealism; Peacock's is more like the stay-at-home's 'I told you so'.

In the early novels Peacock's serenity rested in the unchanging pattern of English life; given this, radicalism was a luxury he could well afford. Only later, when social change turned out to be in full flood, did he see the threat contained in it to all that he valued most. The ideas he had played with so amusingly seemed somehow less funny; they had taken hold – or some of them had – and the very world where one could laugh at them was being destroyed. In *Crotchet Castle* Peacock seems just to have made this discovery, and there is a corresponding rawness in his tone. But by the time *Gryll Grange* was written, much later in his life, he had assimilated the change, and was able to wave his wand of enchantment once again. This last novel is both his mellowest and his most purely delightful, even though his reactionary sympathies are here most openly displayed. And this, if I am right, is because he has returned from realism, or near realism, to fantasy. Once more, the mood of idyllic seclusion is fully established; the mood of Dr Opimian, indulging in his country retreat the four tastes which were so much Peacock's own: 'a good library, a good dinner, a pleasant garden, and rural walks'. Dr Opimian is not so much a benevolent Tory as a reconciled Canute; confronting the incoming tide which cannot be halted, he enjoys present good fortune all the more fully in such time as is left. His views on science are famous, and one hundred years later sound less eccentric, perhaps, than they may have done at the time:

Science is one thing, and wisdom is another. Science is an edged tool, with which men play like children, and cut their own fingers.

If you look at the results which science has brought in its train, you will find them to consist almost wholly in elements of mischief. See how much belongs to the word Explosion alone, of which the ancients knew nothing. . . . See collisions and wrecks and every mode of disaster by land and by sea, resulting chiefly from the insanity for speed, in those who for the most part have nothing to do at the end of the race, which they run as if they were so many Mercuries speeding with messages from Jupiter. . . . Look at our scientific machinery, which has destroyed domestic manufacture, which has substituted rottenness for strength in the thing made, and physical degradation in crowded towns for healthy and comfortable country life in the makers. The day would fail, if I should attempt to enumerate the evils which science has inflicted on mankind. I almost think it is the ultimate destiny of science to exterminate the human race.

Whereas the doctrine of regress was once, for Peacock, one eccentric extreme to be played off against its opposite, it now speaks fairly directly for himself. And there are other interestingly prophetic passages in this last of the novels: Dr Opimian already foresees the pattern of Britain's declining influence in a changing world: '. . . the time will come when by mere force of numbers, the black race will predominate, and exterminate the white'.

But alas for radicalism – and alas for the hope that Peacock's England might submit gracefully to the drift of world events. In the face of the threat, all Dr Opimian's reactionary prejudices float to the surface: the inferiority of foreigners (especially coloured foreigners) and the inferiority of peasants, both self-contained categories, whose emergence from obscurity can be expected to cause nothing but harm.

Yet geniality in *Gryll Grange* has re-established itself; and not least in the plot, with its total defiance of these gloomy forebodings about the great world outside. In the plot, nothing is changed: the old order is arrested at its most idyllic point, and celebrated in strains of high romance. The main frame of the novel presents us, in fact, with a choice of two idylls; the Horatian contentment of Dr Opimian in his rural seclusion, and the fairy-tale contentment of Mr Falconer, secure and studious in his 'enchanted palace', with seven chaste young ladies to order his life. The idyll of Mr Falconer, longingly though Peacock toys with it, is the one that has to yield. Peacock will believe, himself, in the bare possibility, but he knows that it is 'too good for this world'. The world will disbelieve in Mr Falconer's purity; and Mr Falconer's seven virgins *are* lower class, despite the superior education they have had. This 'superior education' is, at a more realistic level, the problem: it has unfitted the seven young ladies for their normal station, so what is a novelist responsible for them to do? If they are not to devote themselves chastely to Mr Falconer they must find other employment; but Peacock finds it hard to see what this could possibly be. Fortunately, when realism is powerless, idyll comes to the rescue. Seven virtuous young men of the virgins' own class appear, rugged and healthy, admiring and true. These young men know that the young ladies are too good for them, but are prepared to marry and cherish them just the same. 'They are so like young ladies,' as one of them puts it, 'they daze us, like.' Any italics that a modern reader is tempted to insert here are entirely his own.

With the intervention of the seven providential peasants, the other complications of personal relationship are also solved. The novel can move to its last major statement in the Aristophanic Comedy, a showing forth of the truth that for nearly two thousand years nothing has changed but for the worse. Modern music, modern cities, modern inventions, all conspire against us, in a shadowy regress which only mirth and present laughter can hold at bay.

And is this not a fitting apotheosis for Peacock himself, as well as for the last of his works? If irony cannot stop ideas and customs from changing, at least it can extract humour from them in the present that we have. To enjoy the present, to swallow up foreboding in geniality, to feast and to celebrate – these are Peacock's gifts as a writer, the wand of enchantment which he, like his own Mr Milestone, has. And in his hands, too, the wand is a genuine magic, whether we respond to its owner's vision or not. For why should we not respond, even though our own vision may be a different one? If a man has reasonable taste and reasonable wealth; if he loves the good things of life, yet is by temperament reclusive; if he enjoys the play of ideas, but mistrusts their meanings; if he can forget the encroachments of change, and lay social conscience by : is this not a possible way for him to live, even today ?

If, like Peacock, he can also amuse and entertain us, making some part of his good fortune vicariously ours, there seems every reason to accept unchurlishly what he gives.

SOURCE: extract from *The Crazy Fabric* (London, 1965) pp. 61–71.

# Lionel Madden

# HEADLONG HALL (1967)

## THE PHILOSOPHERS

. . . The majority of Peacock's characters in the conversation novels exist chiefly as mouthpieces for the expression of ideas. The most important clash of opinion in *Headlong Hall* occurs over the question whether mankind is progressing or degenerating. The three main characters are described as 'Mr. Foster, the perfectibilian; Mr. Escot, the deteriorationist; Mr. Jenkison, the statu-quo-ite'. Foster and Escot hold diametrically opposed views about the past and present states of mankind.

Foster's first utterance proclaims his philosophy : '. . . every thing we look on attests the progress of mankind in all the arts of life, and demonstrates their gradual advancement towards a state of unlimited perfection'. Escot immediately dissents from this view : '. . . these improvements, as you call them, appear to me only so many links in the great chain of corruption, which will soon fetter the whole human race in irreparable slavery and incurable wretchedness . . .'. In this, as in all future debates, Jenkison adopts a middle position : '. . . there is not in the human race a tendency either to moral perfectibility or deterioration . . .'. The speeches of these three characters throughout the whole novel are merely variations on the themes here stated. No one is convinced by any opposing argument and there is no conclusion to the debate.

It is natural to question whether Peacock was merely interested in the conflict of opinion for its own sake or whether his own attitude can be discerned through the conversations. The author's opinions never obtrude and he never explicitly supports any of the characters against the others. The arguments seem to be partly derived from opinions expressed by Shelley, Peacock

and Hogg, but they are all pushed to such extreme lengths that it
would be wrong to attempt to attribute them specifically to any
living people. There is, of course, a comic element in the ex-
tremism of the opinions but the question remains whether the
debate is intended to be taken at all seriously by the reader. There
is no doubt that the subject itself is fundamentally serious. The
conversations echo ideas found in important philosophical writings of the period. Foster's argument that intellectual and
material progress would inevitably lead to moral progress
resembles the doctrines of Joseph Priestley (1733–1804) and
William Godwin (1756–1836). In his *Political Justice* (1793)
Godwin, following Priestley, asserted that 'Perfectibility is one of
the most unequivocal characteristics of the human species'. His
creed of perfectibility through the development of human reason
and his doctrine of Necessitarianism – the belief that all actions
are due to the working of inevitable laws of nature – exercised a
strong influence on Shelley. Like Godwin, Foster seems to believe in the necessary progress of the human race. Thus in
Chapter 10 he declares : 'There are many things that may, and
therefore will, be changed for the better.' Escot's attack upon
civilisation because it encourages the growth of luxury and corruption is reminiscent of the arguments of those Romantics who
advocated a return to the simple life of nature. Like Rousseau,
Escot adopts the noble savage as his ideal.

There is some justification for thinking that Peacock was inclined to favour the opinions expressed by Escot. Although both
characters speak with passionate enthusiasm, Escot's words seem
to carry more weight than Foster's. His praise of the life lived
close to nature receives support from Peacock's romantic descriptions of scenery. On many occasions he is given the last word,
as at the end of the arguments in Chapters 2, 4, 7 and 10. The
last chapter in the book is almost wholly devoted to a monologue
by Escot, although here Jenkison is allowed to speak after him,
closing the work on a note of sobriety. Escot is the only character
among the three who emerges as more than a mere voice. His
love story is the most important in the book and he gains personal
individuality by the conflict between his actions as a lover and
his philosophic theories. It is significant, too, that many of

Escot's opinions reappear in Peacock's next novel, *Melincourt*, in the mouth of Mr. Forester, where there is no doubt that he is intended as a sympathetic figure, expressing many of Peacock's own ideas and attitudes at the time. It is therefore natural to suppose that in *Headlong Hall* Peacock was experimenting with the expression of ideas which he was himself coming to hold, although there is no evidence that at this time he was prepared to maintain them so strongly as he was to do during the next few years.

In assessing Peacock's attitude to the philosophic questions discussed in the book it is necessary to note that the quotation from Swift's *Cademus and Vanessa* which appears on the title-page of *Headlong Hall* is fundamentally satiric :

> All philosophers, who find
> Some favourite system to their mind,
> In every point to make it fit,
> Will force all nature to submit.

The implication is that Peacock was more amused by the extreme expression of opinions than an advocate of any of them.


LANDSCAPE GARDENING

The discussion of landscape gardening in *Headlong Hall* is an interesting example of the way in which Peacock used a current controversy for comic purposes. During the eighteenth and early nineteenth centuries frequent attempts were made to define the qualities of and the relations between 'sublime', 'beautiful' and 'picturesque' scenery. It is not necessary here to examine in detail the various ways in which these difficult terms were defined. It is sufficient for the appreciation of the book to note that Peacock based his discussions of landscape gardening on the controversies which had taken place during the early nineteenth century between Humphrey Repton, Sir Uvedale Price and Richard Payne Knight. Each of these writers attacked the others' theories.

Repton upheld more formal principles than Price, who appealed
to the example of the great landscape painters. Price attempted,
too, to distinguish between beautiful and picturesque scenery.
Knight joined with Price in criticising Repton but attacked
Price's distinction between the beautiful and the picturesque,
claiming that the picturesque was not a quality in a scene but a
way of looking at it. His viewpoint is summarised in his *Analytical
Inquiry into the Principles of Taste* (1805) where he criticises
Price's theories : '. . . the great fundamental error, which prevails
throughout the otherwise able and elegant *Essays on the Picturesque*, is seeking for distinctions in external objects, which only
exist in the modes and habits of viewing and considering them.'

Peacock had been interested in the controversy for some years.
In a letter to Edward Hookham, dated 1809, he requests information about the progress of the controversy. His own sympathies
seem to have lain with Knight. In *An Essay on Fashionable
Literature* he describes Knight's *Analytical Inquiry into the
Principles of Taste* as 'one of the most admirable pieces of philosophical criticism that has appeared in any language'.

In *Headlong Hall* the figure of Marmaduke Milestone seems
to have been chiefly intended as a satiric portrait of Repton.
Humphrey Repton (1752–1818) was the most influential landscape gardener of the day. He is mentioned in Jane Austen's
*Mansfield Park*, published a year before *Headlong Hall*, when
Rushworth says : 'Smith's place is the admiration of all the
country; and it was a mere nothing before Repton took it in
hand.' As Milestone he appears as a rather pompous figure, un-
able to appreciate the beauties of natural scenery. In Chapter
6 he discusses with Squire Headlong, Miss Tenorina and Miss
Graziosa his plans for Lord Littlebrain's park. The nobleman's
name is sufficient to indicate Peacock's contempt for the scheme
and it is evident throughout the conversation that his sympathies
are with Miss Tenorina in her delight in the romantic character
of the unimproved landscape. Milestone's speeches are deliberately cast in a form which ensures that his descriptions of the
objects of his condemnation make the reader approve of them.
Thus he alludes to 'a little stream, dashing from stone to stone,
and over-shadowed with these untrimmed boughs'. Against this

he pictures the scene after its reformation : 'The stream, you see, is become a canal: the banks are perfectly smooth and green, sloping to the water's edge : and there is Lord Littlebrain, rowing in an elegant boat.' Similarly, he describes 'a large rock, with the mountain-ash rooted in its fissures, overgrown, as you see, with ivy and moss; and from this part of it bursts a little fountain, that runs bubbling down its rugged sides'. In the improved state, the rock is 'cut into the shape of a giant. In one hand he holds a horn, through which that little fountain is thrown to a prodigious elevation. In the other is a ponderous stone, so exactly balanced as to be apparently ready to fall on the head of any person who may happen to be beneath : and there is Lord Littlebrain walking under it.' The constant reference to Lord Littlebrain emphasises Peacock's ridicule of the improvements, while Milestone's blindness to the beauties of unimproved nature shows his fundamental lack of taste.

In his poem, *The Landscape* (1794), Knight included two engravings, depicting the same scene of a country house and its grounds as it might look first in its wild natural state and then after it had been landscaped by Capability Brown or Humphrey Repton. The illustrations . . . show clearly the sort of 'improvements' Mr. Milestone hoped to effect in Squire Headlong's grounds. There is no doubt that Peacock, like Knight, would have admired the wild luxuriance of the first scene and disliked the artificial neatness and order of the second.

Milestone's oppenent, Sir Patrick O'Prism, is based partly on Price and partly on Knight, both of whom had criticised Repton's theories. In the early paragraphs of Chapter 4, however, Peacock presents ideas from the writings of Repton, Price and Knight without attempting to make any character consistently express the views of any one theorist. This seems to imply that he depicted the controversy primarily because it provided a good basis for comic dialogue. In so far as he takes sides on the question he seems to attack the whole concept of landscape gardening. His own affection for wild and 'untamed' scenery has already been mentioned. His descriptions of the landscape of the Welsh countryside carry an implicit condemnation of formal landscaping. The criticism of Repton's methods is most overt in the discussion of Milestone's plans for Lord Littlebrain's park, and the identification of Repton with Milestone is most complete in this scene.

It is important to note the difference of tone in the descriptions of wild scenery in *Headlong Hall* and *Melincourt*. In *Headlong Hall* Peacock does not attribute any moral influence to nature and the scenery is described in merely pictorial terms. In *Melincourt*, however, the heroine's whole outlook has been coloured by her upbringing amidst majestic and awe-inspiring scenery. In *Headlong Hall* comparisons between the 'improvements' of Milestone and the natural state of the landscape are wholly based upon their visual effect. Thus Peacock, although he found the controversy interesting, was not yet committed to a theory of the moral influence of nature and could therefore regard the discussion primarily from an aesthetic standpoint, preferring to emphasise its comic aspect rather than the moral and philosophical issues which lay behind it.

## LESSER CHARACTERS

The other characters in *Headlong Hall* are of much less significance and may be briefly discussed. Mr. Cranium represents the current enthusiasm for phrenology, a pseudo-science based on the belief that the physical shape of a person's head indicates his character and intelligence. In Gall, Treacle, Mac Laurel and Nightshade, Peacock attacks the reviewers who judged not according to merit but according to selfish or party interest. It has been claimed that Gall is based on Jeffrey, the first editor of *The Edinburgh Review*, and Nightshade on Southey. The identifications are not very important, however. The satire of these characters is significant because it demonstrates Peacock's hostility to corruption in the practice of literary criticism. Miss Philomela Poppyseed is based on Mrs. Amelia Opie, a popular contemporary novelist.

Mr. Chromatic is the first of a line of musicians in the novels.

Peacock's knowledge of music was considerable but in his fiction he devotes relatively little space to its discussion. His most frequent criticism is of the habit of judging a performance by virtuosity of execution rather than by depth of feeling; thus he notes ironically: '. . . our readers are of course aware that rapidity of execution, not delicacy of expression, constitutes the scientific perfection of modern music . . .'.

Mr. Panscope is a first and unsuccessful attempt at satire of Coleridge. This conception of Coleridge is developed in the character of Mr. Mystic in *Melincourt*. The Reverend Doctor Gaster, an unintelligent glutton, totally devoid of taste and breeding, is the first of Peacock's hostile depictions of Church of England clergymen. Peacock's early clergymen form a sharp contrast with those of the later novels. Although his scepticism about Christianity itself never faded, his attitude to the clergy became more sympathetic. The only similarity between the intelligent and well-read clergymen of the later novels and their predecessors in *Headlong Hall* and *Melincourt* lies in their love of a good dinner. . . .

SOURCE: extract from *Thomas Love Peacock* (London, 1967) pp. 75–81.

· *Howard W. Mills*

## *NIGHTMARE ABBEY* (1968)

'The object of *Nightmare Abbey*', Peacock wrote to Shelley, was 'to bring to a sort of philosophical focus a few of the morbidities of modern literature.'[1] And in May 1818 he told him : 'I have almost finished *Nightmare Abbey*. I think it necessary to "make a stand" against the "encroachments" of black bile. The fourth canto of *Childe Harold* is really too bad. I cannot consent to be *auditor tantum* of this systematical "poisoning" of the "mind" of the "reading public".'[2]

Shelley characteristically leapt to the conclusion that Peacock was fighting the same battle he had fought in *The revolt of Islam* and its Preface, against what he termed the 'gloom and misanthropy' caused largely by the disappointment of the French Revolution. He wrote back : 'You tell me that you have finished *Nightmare Abbey*. I hope that you have given the enemy no quarter. Remember, it is a sacred war.'[3] But the centre of the novel turned out to be Scythrop, a character satirically based on Shelley himself.

Shelley reacted to the book with generous praise but with a significant qualification : 'I am delighted with *Nightmare Abbey*. I think Scythrop a character admirably conceived and executed, and I know not how to praise sufficiently the lightness, chastity and strength of the language of the whole. It perhaps exceeds all your works in this. I suppose the moral is contained in what Falstaff says – *"For God's sake talk like a man of this world;"* and yet looking deeper into it, is not the misdirected enthusiasm of Scythrop what JC calls the salt of the earth?'[4]

This balance of admiration and dissent perfectly conveys the response of genuine friendship – the response that was suppressed or distorted on both sides over *Melincourt*. Shelley here shows towards Peacock what Peacock (through Scythrop) shows

towards Shelley; appreciation with an awareness of difference –
perhaps we can simply say appreciation of difference.

Shelley defended Scythrop's 'misdirected enthusiam'. But he
found nothing offensive or cruel in the parody of himself, and
enjoyed the art and wit of the whole novel. The two qualities
go together. Whereas *Melincourt* moves only fitfully, tied down
by too close reference to its various 'sources' in the life of 1817,
*Nightmare Abbey* is a self-propelled and fully airborne construction. Scythrop and Flosky get off the ground with a life independent of control by sources. While they offer by analogy and implication many insights into Shelley and Byron (which this
chapter will largely treat in the notes rather than the text), they
are not slavish transcriptions. As Humphry House puts it, Peacock 'took elements from the Shelley situation and explored the
thoughts that accrued around them'.[5]


The accepted account of the novel, and its difference from (say)
a comparable one by Jane Austen, is that 'In *Northanger Abbey*
the characters are individuals, whereas in *Nightmare Abbey* the
characters are abstractions and it is their opinions which form
"the main matter of the work". Unlike Jane Austen, Peacock
is more interested in ideas than in people.'[6] On the relation of
Peacock's characters to his 'originals' it is, therefore, usually considered enough to say that 'The views of Mr. Flosky the Kantian
satirize those of Coleridge: the views of Mr. Toobad, the mani-
chaean Millenarian, satirize those of J. F. Newton: while those
of Mr. Cypress satirize Byron . . . Scythrop's opinions caricature
those of Shelley at a certain point in his life.'[7]

*Nightmare Abbey* is the shakiest of grounds on which to base
a generalisation that Peacock is 'more interested in ideas than
in people'. In the earlier two novels he uses the *views, opinions*
or *ideas* of Shelley and others, either satirically or seriously: the
characters opinionate at length. One rarely catches Scythrop
passing an opinion. In the discussion-scenes he keeps quiet, except for the occasional aside to Marionetta and the brief exchange
with Mr. Cypress. He makes occasional speeches to his father
and his girls, but more often to himself. He much prefers the

silence of mystery, brooding and inward fantasy.

When Scythrop does burst into speech, Peacock dwells on the underground connections of opinions with character. Such an outburst comes at the climax of chapter 3. He is chasing Marionetta, whom he has frightened by proposing a blood-drinking pact, 'when, at an ill-omened corner, where two corridors ended in an angle, at the head of a staircase, he came into sudden and violent contact with Mr. Toobad, and they both plunged together to the foot of the stairs, like two billiard-balls into one pocket'.[8] To Mr. Toobad this is 'one of the innumerable proofs of the temporary supremacy of the devil'. He is a survival from *Headlong Hall*, a crotchet who opinionates, and is always of the same opinion. But there is more to Scythrop's reply: '. . . you are perfectly in the right, Mr. Toobad. Evil and mischief, and misery, and confusion, and vanity, and vexation of spirit, and death, and disease, and assassination, and war, and poverty, and pestilence, and famine, and avarice, and selfishness, and rancour, and jealousy, and spleen, and malevolence, and the disappointments of philanthropy, and the faithlessness of friendship, and the crosses of love – all prove the accuracy of your views . . .'.[9]

There is nothing here worth considering as an *idea*. What matter are the particular and personal motives behind the generalisations about the Triumph of Evil : the list leads from the universal (death, war) to Scythrop's own grudges in the background of his mind ('the disappointments of philanthropy') to 'the crosses of love' in the immediate foreground. The whole breathless paragraph conveys to us Scythrop's temperament and nervous system, with his overflowing pity and self-pity, that are inseparable from his emotional fluctuations and violence in the preceding scene with Marionetta, and his physical volatility in the headlong chase. The words that come to mind about Scythrop are 'headlong', 'erratic', 'impetuous', 'self-preoccupied'. They are terms that characterise the individual centre of personality from which radiate all the particular facets of voice, movements, physical appearance, actions – and ideas.[10]

The outburst on the stairs is a rarity, for Scythrop usually retreats into his inner world where his emotionalism and violence gnaw away in silence.

How this character developed is told in an ironical case-history in chapter 2.

He had some taste for romance reading before he went to the university, where, we must confess, in justice to his college, he was cured of the love of reading in all its shapes; and the cure would have been radical, if disappointment in love, and total solitude, had not conspired to bring on a relapse. He began to devour romances and German tragedies, and, by the recommendation of Mr. Flosky, to pore over ponderous tomes of transcendental philosophy, which reconciled him to the labour of studying them by their mystical jargon and necromantic imagery. In the congenial solitude of Nightmare Abbey, the distempered ideas of metaphysical romance and romantic metaphysics had ample time and space to germinate into a fertile crop of chimeras, which rapidly shot up into vigorous and abundant vegetation.[11]

In so far as this is true of Shelley's youth, it is (so far) a criticism which Shelley himself could make. It will be recalled that in his second letter to Godwin he wrote: 'I was haunted with a passion for the wildest and most extravagant romances: ancient books of Chemistry and Magic were perused with an enthusiasim of wonder, almost amounting to belief ... From a reader, I became a writer of romances; before the age of seventeen I had published two, "St. Irvyne" and "Zastrozzi" . . .'.[12] Shelley, however, claimed that reading *Political Justice* made him 'a wiser and better man. I was no longer a votary of Romance; till then I had existed in an ideal world – now I found that in this universe of ours was enough to excite the interest of the heart ... I beheld, in short, that I had duties to perform ... My plan is that of resolving to lose no opportunity to disseminate truth and happiness.'[13]

But Scythrop's *passion for reforming the world* only extends his private fantasy-world. 'He built many castles in the air, and peopled them with secret tribunals, and bands of illuminati, who were always the imaginary instruments of his projected regeneration of the human species.'[14] The world of Godwin is submerged in that of Schiller's *Robbers*.[15] In this fantasy he has a flattering rôle: 'As he intended to institute a perfect republic, he invested himself with absolute sovereignty over these mystical dispensers of liberty.'[16] His self-importance grows: he 'foresaw that a great leader of human regeneration would be involved in fearful dilemmas, and determined, for the benefit of mankind in general, to adopt all possible precautions for the preservation of himself'.[17] His only practical act is to publish a treatise called *Philosophical gas; or, a project for a general illumination of the human mind*, which he expects to 'set the whole nation in a ferment' but which sells only seven copies. The validity of this portrait does not depend on its fitting Shelley: but in fact all these characteristics of Scythrop's *passion for reforming the world* can be detected either in Shelley's first letters to Godwin or in his subsequent writings and actions.[18]

Into this same fantasy-world Scythrop tries to assimilate the two girls. Marionetta is a poor choice for this purpose:

Being a compound of the *Allegro Vivace* of the O'Carrolls, and of the *Andante Doloroso* of the Glowries, she exhibited in her own character all the diversities of an April sky. Her hair was light-brown; her eyes hazel, and sparkling with mild but fluctuating light; her features regular; her lips full, and of equal size; and her person surpassingly graceful. She was a proficient in music. Her conversation was sprightly, but always on subjects light in their nature and limited in their interest: for moral sympathies, in any general sense, had no place in her mind. She had some coquetry, and more caprice, liking and disliking almost in the same moment; pursuing an object with earnestness while it seemed unattainable, and rejecting it when in her power as not worth the trouble of possession.[19]

For several reasons this should be compared with the description of Harriet in the 'Memoirs of Shelley':

She had a good figure, light, active, and graceful. Her features were regular and well-proportioned. Her hair was light brown, and dressed with taste and simplicity. In her dress she was truly *simplex munditiis*. Her complexion was beautifully transparent; the tint of the blush rose shining through the lily. The tone of her voice was pleasant; her speech the essence of frankness and cordiality; her spirits always cheerful; her laugh spontaneous, hearty, and joyous. She was well educated. She read agreeably and intelligently. She wrote only letters, but she wrote them well. Her manners were good, and her whole aspect and demeanour such manifest emanations of pure and truthful nature, that to be once in her company was to know her thoroughly. She was fond of her husband, and accommodated herself in every way to his tastes. If they mixed in society, she adorned it; if they lived in retirement, she was satisfied; if they travelled, she enjoyed the change of scene.[20]

There are resemblances between Marionetta and Harriet, with great differences. But the main resemblance is that both passages are real and serious descriptions of character. The passage from the novel is not a skit or caricature : if anything, the livelier style makes it a less conventional reading of character than that of Harriet. In fact the temperament read through Marionetta's appearance and manner is more complicated and interesting than Harriet's. Here and through the novel she is perverse and capricious, both *allegra vivace* and *andante dolorosa*. The description, as different from a skit as from the conventional admirabilities of Anthelia Melincourt, is something new in the novels.

Scythrop falls in love with Marionetta, although she does not realise his '*pure anticipated cognitions* of combinations of beauty and intelligence'.[21] When she suddenly turns cold, he does not argue or plead with her but, characteristically, retreats into his tower and his fantasy, 'muffled himself in his nightcap, seated himself in the president's chair of his imaginary secret tribunal, summoned Marionetta with all terrible formalities, frightened her out of her wits, disclosed himself, and clasped the beautiful penitent to his bosom'.[22] Caught in the act by the real Marionetta, he tries to co-opt her to the council as 'the auxiliary of my great designs for the emancipation of mankind' – and manages to frighten her too out of her wits. The pattern of cross-purposes in this scene – his fantasy, breast-beating violence and 'passionate language of romance' against her archness, puzzlement and alarm – continues through the novel.

Marionetta cannot fit into the fantasy-world, but Stella seems to spring from it. She appears like a ghost in the tower, a mysterious fugitive from 'atrocious persecution' and, as a reader of *Philosophical gas*, emphatically an enemy to every shape of tyranny and superstitious imposture.

Stella, in her conversations with Scythrop displayed a highly culti-
vated and energetic mind, full of impassioned schemes of liberty,
and impatience of masculine usurpation. She had a lively sense of
all the oppressions that are done under the sun; and the vivid pictures which her imagination presented to her of the numberless
scenes of injustice and misery which are being acted at every
moment in every part of the inhabited world, gave an habitual
seriousness to her physiognomy, that made it seem as if a smile had
never once hovered on her lips.[23]

It is usual to compare this with the description of Mary Shelley
given in Peacock's 'Memoirs of Shelley', or to speculate whether
Claire Clairmont, rather than Mary, was the model.[24] But the
critic is concerned not with Peacock's historical model but with
his human subject. A more useful comparison will therefore be
with a character from another novelist whom nobody would
suggest was 'more interested in ideas than in people'.

a smile of exceeding faintness played about her lips – it was just per-
ceptible enough to light up the native gravity of her face. It might
have been likened to a thin ray of moonlight resting upon the wall
of a prison ...
   The unhappiness of women! The voice of their silent suffering
was always in her ears, the ocean of tears that they had shed from
the beginning of time seemed to pour through her own eyes. Ages
of oppression had rolled over them ...[25]

Admittedly the description of Stella is brief, and little is subse-
quently shown of her, whereas the description of Olive Chancel-
lor merely indicates what is to be fully conveyed in the drama
of the novel. But Peacock and James are here interested in the
same thing : not in ideas, but in the emotional nature that makes
both women take on the burden of the world's evils – 'ages of
oppression', 'all the oppressions ... under the sun' – and the way
this burden is registered in their faces.
   Scythrop's ensuing dilemma is comic :

Passing and repassing several times a day from the company of the
one to that of the other, he was like a shuttlecock between two
battledores, changing its direction as rapidly as the oscillations of
a pendulum, receiving many a hard knock on the cork of a sensi-

tive heart, and flying from point to point on the feathers of a super-sublimated head . . . The old proverb concerning two strings to a bow gave him some gleams of comfort; but that concerning two stools occurred to him more frequently, and covered his forehead with a cold perspiration.[26]

But he is not the deflated figure of fun that Dr Jack suggests in saying that his situation 'recalls that of a hypocritical rake in Goldsmith or Sheridan'.[27] The dilemma is serious in the sense that we understand it as we understand Shelley's dilemma in the 'Memoirs' and the corresponding letters: the novel has created the *données*, Scythrop's temperament and the qualities of the two girls that fit his various needs.

For a solution he first turns to Romance, hoping that Stella approves the ideal of Goethe's play which bears her name, and will agree to set up a *ménage à trois*. Failing this, he adopts the ultimate Romantic role from *The sorrows of Werther* and orders for dinner

> A pint of port and a pistol.
> [*Raven the butler:*] A pistol!
> [*Scythrop:*] And a pint of port.[28]

All of Scythrop's words and attitudes reek of second-rate fashionable literature which has 'blended itself with the interior structure of his mind'.[29]

'The views of Mr. Flosky', runs the common account, 'satirize those of Coleridge.'[30] On the basis of this common account stands the commonest criticism of Peacock, that he fails to do justice to Coleridge's ideas. 'It is a serious failure,' says Humphry House, 'and points plainly to Peacock's limitations. He did not really understand or care about philosophy; he never dealt with the deeper and more exacting struggles of thought but only with thought as it emerged into opinion or emotional attitude.'[31]

This sweeping account and charge can be undermined by a number of general caveats to be supported by close illustration. First, Peacock has no one view of Coleridge. We must balance against his caricatures his appreciation of the poet in the *Essay*

*on fashionable literature.* Among the caricatures, Panscope in
*Headlong Hall* and Mystic in *Melincourt* never spring to life as
persons as Flosky does. There is nothing more to them than their
intellectual labels imply – Panscope the Polymath, Mystic the
Kantian. No such label attaches itself to Flosky. He reminds us
of many sides of Coleridge's mind. More important, whereas
Panscope and Mystic are eager to expound their views, the only
common factor in Flosky's ideas is his almost pathological difficulty in communicating them. A second reply to Humphry House
is that a study of 'thought as it emerged into [or *from*] . . . emo-
motional attitude' need not be trivial. The underground connections between temperament and ideas which Peacock also studies
in Scythrop, Coleridge was himself ready to dwell on in his note-
book introspections.

Unlike Panscope and Mystic, Flosky grows through the novel.
Different scenes focus on different aspects. Flosky, like most of
*Nightmare Abbey's* characters, is introduced by an ironical life-
history :

He had been in his youth an enthusiast for liberty, and had hailed
the dawn of the French Revolution as the promise of a day that
was to banish war and slavery, and every form of vice and misery,
from the face of the earth. Because all this was not done, he deduced that nothing was done; and from this deduction, according
to his system of logic, he drew a conclusion that worse than nothing
was done; that the overthrow of the feudal fortresses of tyranny and
superstition was the greatest calamity that had ever befallen mankind; and that their only hope now was to rake the rubbish together, and rebuild it without any of those loopholes by which the
light had originally crept in. To qualify himself for a coadjutor in
this laudible task, he plunged into the central opacity of Kantian
metaphysics, and lay *perdu* several years in transcendental darkness, till the common daylight of common-sense became intolerable
to his eyes. He called the sun an *ignis fatuus* and exhorted all who
would listen to his friendly voice, which were about as many as
called 'God save King Richard', to shelter themselves from its
delusive radiance in the obscure haunt of Old Philosophy. This word
Old had great charms for him.[32]

This is clearly a History of Ideas, and of Coleridge's ideas too.

It attributes to Coleridge in exaggerated form the reactions to the French Revolution which Shelley described in his Preface to *The revolt of Islam* :

The sympathies connected with that event extended to every bosom. The most generous and amiable natures were those which participated the most extensively in these sympathies. But such a degree of unmingled good was expected, as it was impossible to realise . . . The revulsion occasioned by the atrocities of the demagogues and the re-establishment of successive tyrannies in France was terrible . . . many of the most tender-hearted of the worshippers of the public good have been morally ruined by what a partial glimpse of the events they deplored, appeared to show as the melancholy desolation of all their cherished hopes. Hence gloom and misanthropy have become the characteristics of the age in which we live, the solace of a disappointment that unconsciously finds relief only in the wilful exaggeration of its own despair. This influence has tainted the literature of the age with the hopelessness of the minds from which it flows. Metaphysics,[33] and inquiries into moral and political science, have become little else than vain attempts to revive exploded superstitions, or sophisms like those of Mr. Malthus, calculated to lull the oppressors of mankind into a security of everlasting triumph.[34]

Here is Shelley's 'sacred war', and the sketch of Flosky's life puts Peacock for the moment among the holy Crusaders. Yet (putting aside the rights and wrongs of the Cause) what a sharper swordsman Peacock is! One might even worry the metaphor further and say that, while Peacock is out on the field engaged in close fighting, Shelley is still at home speechifying and moralising. His exposition of the Cause (which I have cut severely in my quotation) is painfully slow, pompous and unspecific, overflowing with melodramatic Scythropian jargon and imagery. Peacock is specific, pinning the abstract reactions on a concrete character.

The introduction of Flosky, then, gives his mental case-history, tracing what made him what he is. Yet as the resulting character acts and speaks we are little aware of specific ideas. What comes across is a voice, wandering through an uncertain sequence of logic. The obscurity of Flosky's style is in harmony with his ob-

scure meaning. There is no brisk Kantian self-justification such
as Moly Mystic offers, but more of gnomic and biblical tones,
the tangle of arrogance and false humility, the coy hints and
startling connections, that often characterised Coleridge's awk-
ward flirtations with 'the reading public' in *The friend* and the
*Lay sermons*. The reader stumbling along behind is never quite
sure who is fooling whom. Is Flosky (to use his own idiom)
guiding us over complicated terrain with the torch of truth? Or
is it an *ignis fatuus*? Does *he* know where we are heading for?
Is he perhaps trying to shake us off the trail? Flosky is always
ready to confirm our worst suspicions. Poor Mr Listless, struggling
with Flosky's proposition that 'Tea, late dinners, and the French
Revolution, have played the devil, Mr. Listless, and brought the
devil into play', murmurs politely that he 'cannot exactly see the
connection of ideas'. Flosky replies that 'I should be sorry if you
could; I pity the man who can see the connection of his own
ideas. Still more do I pity him, the connection of whose ideas
any other person can see. Sir, the great evil is, that there is too
much commonplace light in our moral and political literature.'[35]

What follows is a long defence of 'abstract truth' and 'synthetical reasoning'. It happens to parallel very closely a self-
defence that Coleridge once wrote, in reply to a criticism of
Southey's. By comparing the relevant passages of Southey, Coleridge and Peacock, we can be more specific in judging the validity
of Peacock's parody, and its difference from the stock conservative reaction to Coleridge.

The criticism which Southey expressed to Coleridge in conversation is also recorded for the modern reader in a letter to a
third party, Miss Barker :

It is not a little extraordinary that Coleridge, who is fond of logic,
and who has an actual love and passion for close, hard thinking,
should write in so rambling and inconclusive a manner; while I,
who am utterly incapable of that toil of thought in which he
delights, never fail to express myself perspicuously, and to the
point . . . Coleridge requested me to write him such a letter upon
the faults of the 'Friend' as he might insert and reply to . . . It described the fault you have remarked as existing in Burke, and having
prevented him from ever persuading anybody to his opinions . . .

You read his book, and saw what his opinions were; but they were given in such a way, evolving the causes of everything, and involving the consequences, that you never knew from whence he set out, nor where he was going. So it is with C.; he goes to work like a hound, nosing his way, turning, and twisting, and winding, and doubling, till you get weary with following the mazy movements. My way is, when I see my object, to dart at it like a greyhound.[36]

Southey makes a common enough criticism of Coleridge.[37] Yet one is here reluctant to accept its standpoint, for it stems from habits of mental conservatism. The strong tones of complacency indicate a mind tending to inertia, in the sense of conserving itself from being disturbed by different mental habits. Least of all does it want to be disturbed by Coleridge's example of activity, curiosity, exploration. It might be argued that Southey's concern here is not with those positive aspects of Coleridge, only with his weaknesses. Yet he cannot criticise those weaknesses with any authority because he cannot see the positive aims which are their context and their cause. Southey criticises Coleridge's mind as if it were only attempting the same things as his own. Of course perspicuity and directness come easier to Southey because for him they are ends in themselves, and because they take account of less. The pattern of his logic, and ultimately of his wisdom from experience, is simpler because of what it excludes and ignores for the *sake* of simplicity.

So Southey has no standing as a critic of Coleridge, because he does not comprehend him. I mean 'comprehend' in both senses, which are in fact linked at their deepest. He does not understand Coleridge's mind; nor does he encompass it and look further and wider. Quite the reverse; it is fitting that Coleridge's defence follows Southey in time and encompasses it:

There is no way of arriving at any sciental End but by finding it at every step. The End is in the Means; or the adequacy of each Mean is already its End. Southey once said to me: You are nosing every nettle along the Hedge, while the Greyhound (meaning himself, I presume) wants only to get sight of the Hare, and Flash – strait as a line! he has it in his mouth! – Even so, I replied, might a Cannibal say to an Anatomist, whom he had watched dissecting a body. But the fact is – I do not care two pence for the Hare; but

I value most highly the excellencies of scent, patience, discrimination, free Activity; and find a Hare in every Nettle I make myself
acquainted with. I follow the Chamois-Hunters, and seem to set
out with the same Object. But I am no Hunter of *that* Chamois
Goat; but avail myself of the Chace in order to [pursue] a nobler
purpose – that of making a road across the Mountain in which
Common Sense may hereafter pass backward and forward, without
desperate Leaps or Balloons that soar indeed but do not improve
the chance of getting onward.[38]

Happily this reply represents Coleridge very favourably in the
present discussion. It describes very persuasively his conception
of true thinking. At the same time it is Coleridge at his most
lively. He picks up with alacrity the metaphor Southey had used
smugly, and makes it telling and vivid. It allows him to be
humorous – self-directed humour in the context of self-justification, and humour at Southey's smugness. It allows the meta-
phorical expression of the virtues of what Arnold called 'free
play of mind' : 'scent, patience, discrimination, free Activity'.
True, as Coleridge continues to hunt and nose out the metaphor,
it becomes more complicated and fanciful : but it is entirely acceptable because it develops so informally and spontaneously. It
demonstrates that free play of mind which Coleridge is defending. And it ends happily in the image of the explorative mind
opening up new intellectual territory – 'making a road across the
Mountain in which Common Sense may hereafter pass backward
and forward'.

Yet one may admire the passage and still feel uneasy. Certainly it drowns Southey's criticism : but isn't it a rashly extreme
reaction? 'I do not care two pence for the Hare'; '[I] find a Hare
in every nettle' – these provide sufficient footholds for Peacock's
parody. Mr Flosky is table-talking :

Now the enthusiasm for abstract truth is an exceedingly fine thing,
as long as the truth, which is the object of the enthusiasm, is so
completely abstract as to be altogether out of the reach of the
human faculties; and, in that sense, I have myself an enthusiasm
for truth, but in no other, for the pleasure of metaphysical investigation lies in the means, not in the end; and if the end could be
found, the pleasure of the means would cease. The mind, to be kept

in health, must be kept in exercise. The proper exercise of the mind is elaborate reasoning. Analytical reasoning is a base and mechanical process, which takes to pieces and examines, bit by bit, the rude material of knowledge, and extracts therefrom a few hard and obstinate things called facts, every thing in the shape of which I cordially hate. But synthetical reasoning, setting up as its goal some unattainable abstraction, like an imaginary quantity in algebra, and commencing its course with taking for granted some two assertions which cannot be proved, from the union of these two assumed truths produces a third assumption, and so on in infinite series, to the unspeakable benefit of the human intellect. The beauty of this process is, that at every step it strikes out into two branches, in a compound ratio of ramification; so that you are perfectly sure of losing your way, and keeping your mind in perfect health, by the perpetual exercise of an interminable quest; and for these reasons I have christened my eldest son Emanuel Kant Flosky.[39]

The parody is valid because Peacock, unlike Southey, first entertains Coleridge's idea, enters into its spirit before criticising it. Peacock works by keeping close to Coleridge's imagery and train of reasoning, then edging it gradually more and more off course to an absurd conclusion. The passage does not drown Coleridge for us as Coleridge drowns Southey, but establishes itself as an unavoidable partial truth. If Coleridge's passage describes the ideal, Peacock's exposes the attendant dangers and temptations. If the Coleridgean ideal demands extraordinary powers of mind, it can also encourage and camouflage extraordinary weaknesses.

The surprise is that Peacock did not have as his model that particular passage of Coleridge, which comes from an unpublished manuscript. It is uncanny how often, in reading Coleridge or Shelley, one is pulled up by passages that Peacock could not have read but which he seems to echo directly, so well he catches their voice. Perhaps with Mr Flosky's blessing we may call them *pure anticipated cognitions.* In that manifesto-speech of Flosky's, the weaknesses exposed are intellectual ones. But as the novel develops they come home to us, like Scythrop's, as failings of personality and of human contact.

Not that Peacock dwells on the human *causes* of Flosky's mental habits – that is, on the sense we have with Scythrop that whatever the philosophical justifications imported from Königs-

berg, the real motives can be found nearer home. There is little
hint of the analysis which Coleridge himself made in the
*Dejection Ode* –

> For not to think of what I needs must feel,
>  But to be still and patient, all I can;
> And haply by abstruse research to steal
>  From my own nature all the natural Man
>  This was my sole resource, my only plan:
> Till that which suits the part infects the whole,
> And now is grown the habit of my Soul.[40]

– and which he frequently elaborated in private to De Quincey
and others. There is no hint at all in *Nightmare Abbey* of such
specific causes as Coleridge's wife and his opium-addiction. This
omission is, I think, a fine example of Peacock's 'good taste' in
two solid senses of that phrase – in human tact and artistic judgement. With Shelley he could draw on intimate knowledge so as,
paradoxically, to be able to make Scythrop an authentic but independent creation. Knowing Shelley intimately also meant that
he could judge where and where not the creation would hurt
Shelley personally (Shelley's response in letters shows that Peacock's judgement on this point was perfect). On the other hand
with the private life of Coleridge whom he did not know, Peacock could neither get more to work on than hearsay (gossip or
slander), nor gauge the effect of a portrait on Coleridge. What
touches he did take from Coleridge's private life, he transferred
to the creation of Mr Glowry, the glorifier of gloom in the after-
math of a dismal marriage.

But if Peacock does not look back for human causes, he is always
anticipating human effects. Even the most respectful reader of
*The friend*, the *Lay sermons* or reports of the less coherent lectures, might find himself entertaining the comic possibilities of
such a mind engaged in everyday human intercourse. These are
just the possibilities Peacock seizes on. Not that he is measuring
Coleridge's complex mind by 'the impudent footrule of his own
common sense' (Leslie Stephen's phrase for Hazlitt). He does
not fall foul of De Quincey's accusation: 'Coleridge, to many
people, and often I have heard the complaint, seemed to wander;

and he seemed then to wander the most when, in fact, his resistance to the wandering instinct was greatest – viz., when the compass and huge circuit by which his illustrations moved travelled furthest into remote regions before they began to revolve. Long before this coming round commenced most people had lost him, and naturally enough supposed that he had lost himself.'[41]

Peacock would, I think, have acknowledged this defence of Coleridge when the subjects under discussion demanded intricate paths of thought linking remote areas of knowledge. In this context he would have enjoyed the frustration of Carlyle at Highgate, wanting a simple answer to a complex problem – '[I] tried hard to get something about *Kant* and Co. from him, about "reason" *versus* "understanding", and the like; but in vain',[42] 'you put some question to him . . . instead of answering this, or decidedly setting out towards answer of it, he would accumulate formidable apparatus, logical swim-bladders, transcendental life-preservers and other precautionary and vehiculatory gear, for setting out'.[43] For, whatever he later became, Carlyle appears here the cut-and-dried intellectual wanting, like Mr McCrotchet, the experts to 'settle' the big topics of the day. But, for even the subtlest genius, there are occasions that demand a simple answer to a simple question. There comes the time when the author of *The golden bowl* has to ask his way to the King's Road, or say a kindly word or two to some children on the beach.[44] And so – Peacock's mind must have speculated – what happens when the transcendental philosopher is asked to 'condescend to talk to a simple girl in intelligible terms'[45] on a factual matter? The speculation leads straight to the encounter between Flosky and Marionetta.

Worried by Scythrop's extreme air of mystery, Marionetta goes to Flosky's apartment to ask for clues. She breaks in upon him rather like the Person from Porlock, for he is sitting with curtains and shutters drawn against the noonday sun 'engaged in the composition of a dismal ballad'.

He sate with 'his eye in a fine frenzy rolling,' and turned his inspired gaze on Marionetta as if she had been the ghastly ladie of a

magical vision; then placed his hand before his eyes, with an appearance of manifest pain – shook his head – withdrew his hand –
rubbed his eyes, like a waking man – and said, in a tone or rueful-
ness most jeremitalorically pathetic, 'To what am I to attribute this
very unexpected pleasure, my dear Miss O'Carroll?'

MARIONETTA :    I must apologise for intruding on you, Mr. Flosky;
but the interest which I – you – take in my cousin Scythrop –

MR FLOSKY :    Pardon me, Miss O'Carroll; I do not take any
interest in any person or thing on the face of the earth; which sentiment, if you analyse it, you will find to be the quintessence of the
most refined philanthropy.

MARIONETTA :    I will take it for granted that this is so, Mr.
Flosky; I am not conversant with metaphysical subtleties, but –

MR FLOSKY :    Subtleties! my dear Miss O'Carroll. I am sorry to
find you participating in the vulgar error of the *reading public*, to
whom an unusual collocation of words, involving a juxtaposition
of antiperistatical ideas, immediately suggests the notion of hyper-
oxysophistical paradoxology.

MARIONETTA :    Indeed, Mr. Flosky, it suggests no such idea to me.
I have sought you for the purpose of obtaining information.

MR FLOSKY (shaking his head) :    No one has ever sought me for
such a purpose before.[46]

As Marionetta's questions get more fretful and frustrated, so
Flosky's manner becomes more abstract and abstracted :

MARIONETTA :    Will you oblige me, Mr. Flosky, by giving me a
plain answer to a plain question?

MR FLOSKY :    It is imposible, my dear Miss O'Carroll. I never
gave a plain answer to a question in my life.

MARIONETTA :    Do you, or do you not, know what is the matter
with my cousin?

MR FLOSKY :    To say that I do not, would be to say that I am ignorant of something; and God forbid, that a transcendental meta-
physician, who had pure anticipated cognitions of everything, and
carries the whole science of geometry in his head without ever
having looked into Euclid, should fall into so empirical an error
as to declare himself ignorant of anything : to say that I do know,
would be to pretend to positive and circumstantial knowledge
touching present matter of fact, which, when you consider the
nature of evidence, and the various lights in which the same thing
may be seen –

MARIONETTA :    I see, Mr. Flosky, that either you have no information, or are determined not to impart it, and I beg your pardon
for having given you this unnecessary trouble.
MR FLOSKY :    My dear Miss O'Carroll, it would have given me
great pleasure to have said anything that would have given you
pleasure; but if any person living could make report of having obtained any information on any subject from Ferdinando Flosky,
my transcendental reputation would be ruined for ever.[47]

This is a *tour de force* as a comic episode bringing to fruition the
comic creation of Flosky. Yet its force arises from comedy and
criticism reinforcing one another; for personal contact is to Peacock the significant area in which to criticise Flosky.

However, Peacock's focus is not narrowed to one character :
he brings home Flosky's harmful connections with others, especially with his 'dearest friend' Scythrop. Scythrop 'had a strong
tendency to the love of mystery, for its own sake, that is to say,
he would employ mystery to serve a purpose, but would first
choose his purpose by its capability of mystery'.[48] In this he has
clearly been encouraged by Flosky, who tells Marionetta that
'Mystery is the very key-stone of all that is beautiful in poetry,
all that is sacred in faith, and all that is recondite in transcendental psychology.'[49] Flosky also offers Marionetta choric comments
in the spirit of the age that encourages the affectation of gloom
by Scythrop as well as by Mr Glowry. 'It is the fashion to be unhappy. To have a reason for being so would be exceedingly
commonplace; to be so without any is the province of genius :
the art of being miserable for misery's sake, has been brought to
great perfection in our days.'[50]

This discussion has tried to establish what different aspects of
Flosky interest Peacock, and what relation they have to aspects
of Coleridge. But many readers impatiently return the discussion
to Square One : 'Why didn't he take Coleridge's ideas seriously?'
It is all 'abundantly pleasant', sometimes even 'splendidly funny',
admits Mr Dyson : but 'Did Peacock realise, in fact, that . .
Coleridge (to use Mill's phrase) was one of the two great
seminal minds of his age?' The tone and spirit of this can be
countered by a number of other stern rhetorical questions. Can

we hope for any free enquiry or intellectual progress if we dogmatically mark every dissenting opinion of Coleridge by an un-
questioned standard? Can our age's estimate of Coleridge be the
Victorian one? In particular, are we to be intellectually bound
and gagged by Mill's essay? Does not that essay lack the qualities
that distinguish the earlier essay on Bentham – the balance of
appreciation with criticism, the sense of humour, the quick feeling for the pretentious or ludicrous, and the constant reference
of specialist fields of study to what Arnold called 'a central, a
truly human point of view'? If we agree with Arnold that the
function of criticism is to cultivate 'a free disinterested play of
mind', 'a current of true and *fresh* ideas', 'a more free speculative
treatment of things', then there is something wanting in Mill's
essay and even more so in our exaggerated respect for it. On the
other hand, those evocative phrases of Arnold do fit the spirit of
Peacock, which is not to lay down a dogmatic and complete account of Coleridge, but a provocative 'partial portrait'. It is a
sign of our times that by 'provocative' we tend to mean gratuit-
ously irritating, rather than fruitfully stimulating – calling forth
free play of mind by boldly setting out one of the many possible
views. It is wrong to say that Peacock's portrait was an under-
standable one given that it was written in 1818 but that it was
quickly superseded. We should not be patronising Peacock but
using him. In fact, whereas the literary world of 1818 badly
needed a sympathetic account of Coleridge to keep its mind in
free play, modern Coleridge studies badly need to entertain Peacock's irreverent view.

Although irreverent, his view was far from frivolous. It engaged with as much in Coleridge as did Mill's view. Here in con-
firmation is a passage from a modern critic which sums up
Flosky's clumsy failure to communicate with 'the reading public'.
It traces that failure through precisely the vicious circle of impo-
tence, wilfulness and arrogance that interested Peacock :

A serious psychological maladjustment towards his public can be
detected . . . An awareness of the probable unpopularity of his ideas
and a certain sense of conscious superiority over his readers made
it impossible to address them as intellectual equals. The consciousness that he was in possession of truths denied to others produced

the characteristic note of pontification which is evident in early and late works alike. It led to the creation of an air of mystery through the use of out-of-the-way allusions, erudite quotations, unfamiliar words, and technical terms; and to his paying a too 'willing homage to the illustrious obscure'. It led also to the fairly frequent examples of proud self-defence against attacks that had not been and never were to be delivered . . . An additional hazard was his almost pathologigal fear of popularity. As long as he was sure that his words were unlikely to be fully understood he could convince himself that they contained invaluable truths. The use of a less complex style might well have attracted more readers; it would certainly have exposed him to the embarrassment of being generally understood.

The point of quoting that passage is that, while it reads like a perceptive analysis of Flosky, it is in fact the conclusion that Mr J. Colmer draws from his close and sympathetic reading of *Coleridge, critic of society*.[51]

Flosky not only illustrates in himself the spirit of the age, but also takes part in general discussions on it. In these he is, like his fellow-guests, the subject of Peacock's great art in altering at will the focus of the novel. Characters who elsewhere stand out in bold idiosyncratic isolation, fit into a chorus where they retain their individuality but the reader is led to attend as much to what is said as *who* says it. With the same skill Peacock can momentarily draw an individual out of the chorus to speak as a particular case – and then sink back into relative impersonality. All this management of voices in a chorus can surely be credited to Peacock's appreciation of opera, and underlines the point made earlier that a writer may learn profoundly from art-forms other than his own, and that real influence is not traceable merely in surface signs (*opera buffa* stage-business, or explicit references to Rossini and Mozart). The art of the chorus is that which Lord Mount Edgcumbe described in a passage Peacock marked in his copy and quoted in his review. Whereas in the time of Metastasio choruses were rare and solo arias the rule : 'In an opera we now require more frequent duos and trios, and a *crashing* finale. In fact, the most difficult problem for the opera poet is the mixing the complicated voices of conflicting passions in one common harmony, without injuring their essence.'[52] In the central chorus

of discussion scenes (chapters 5, 6, 7 and 11), this art lets Peacock's account of the Regency move unobtrusively between the
particular symptoms and a general diagnosis.

The subject is briefly introduced – and illustrated – in chapter
5, by Mr Flosky and the Honourable Mr Listless. Listless is the
average bored and indolent gentleman who rarely laughs because
'the exertion is too much for me'; and who is so mentally lazy
that his butler thinks for him : 'Fatout ! When did I think of
going to Cheltenham, and did not go ?'[53] He is no great reader :
'I hope you do not suspect me of being studious. I have finished
my education.' Beneath this facetious tone is a real anxiety, for
being studious would be then as now a suspicious matter, likely
to spread alarm and despondency in any polite gathering by the
threat of 'heavy conversation'. Yet the same conversational eti-
quette directs that 'there are some fashionable books that one
must read, because they are the ingredients of the talk of the day'.
And so he receives an express parcel of the latest publications,
full of heroic villainy and misanthropy. 'MR. FLOSKY (*turning
over the leaves*) : "Devilman, a novel." Hm. Hatred – revenge
– misanthropy – and quotations from the Bible. Hm. This is the
morbid anatomy of black bile. "Paul Jones, a poem". Hm. I see
how it is. Paul Jones, an amiable enthusiast – disappointed in
his affections – turns pirate from ennui and magnanimity. . . '.[54]

Peacock acutely points out that works like Godwin's novels
and Byron's tales flatter men like Listless, who confesses that
'modern books are very consolatory and congenial to my feelings.
There is, as it were, a delightful north-east wind, an intellectual
blight breathing through them; a delicious misanthropy and discontent, that demonstrates the nullity of virtue and energy, and
puts me in good humour with myself and my sofa.'[55]

This reminds us of the vicious circle of literature, taste and
manners which is discussed in the contemporary 'Essay on
fashionable literature'. When Mr Cypress appears later in the
novel, we realise that it is only one step from Listless's fashionable apathy to the spirit of *Childe Harold's pilgrimage*, although
there is a contradictory gusto to Cypress's nihilism.

Even Flosky is conditioned by the spirit of the age and the
state of the reading public. There is something perversely rigid

about his anti-fashionable stance: 'This rage for novelty is the
bane of literature. Except my works and those of my particular
friends, nothing is good that is not as old as Jeremy Taylor.'[56]
Here is one seed of his obscurity and difficulty in communicating,
which we have already studied.

The next chapter skilfully leads into the general theme from
the particular story of Scythrop and Marionetta. The link is made
through Dante, which Scythrop pretends to read while jealous
of Listless, with whom Marionetta flirts: 'Marionetta . . . peeped
into his book, and said to him, "I see you are in the middle of
Purgatory." – "I am in the middle of hell," said Scythrop
furiously . . . "and I", said the Honourable Mr. Listless, "am
not reading Dante, and am just now in Paradise," bowing to
Marionetta.'[57]

The effect of Listless's inane compliment is to mock Scythrop,
whose ostentatious anti-sociable manner is only the reverse side
of Listless's social conventionality (as Flosky's anti-popularity is
only the perverse reverse of Listless's fashionable taste). This
small incident is symptomatic of the rest of Scythrop's behaviour,
just as Byron's behaviour at his famous first dinner with Rogers
gives a good clue about the psychology of the Byronic hero.[58]

Listless has not read Dante, 'But I find he is growing fashionable, and I am afraid I must read him some wet morning.'[59] He
is in fashion, it is decided, because he appeals to modern blue
devils: and this leads Flosky, after his parenthetical defence
of 'synthetical reasoning', to analyse modern fashionable literature: 'the French Revolution has made us shrink from the name
of philosophy, and has destroyed . . . all enthusiasm for political
liberty. That part of the *reading public* which shuns the solid
food of reason for the light diet of fiction, requires a perpetual
adhibition of *sauce piquante* to the palate of its depraved imagination.'[60]

So far this echoes Coleridge's and Wordsworth's attacks on
the reading public; but Peacock implicates Coleridge himself:
'[The reading public] lived upon ghosts, goblins, and skeletons
(I and my friend Mr. Sackbut served up a few of the best).'[61]
Flosky follows with a sketch of the successive literary rages from
1798 to 1818. The market for the supernatural becoming flooded,

'now the delight of our spirits is to dwell on all the vices and blackest passions of our nature, tricked out in the masquerade dress of heroism and benevolence'.[62] The point was often to be made by critics of the Byronic hero.

The only threat to Peacock's sharp but playful diagnosis occurs when Mr Hilary breaks in: 'If we go on this way, we shall have a new art of poetry, of which one of the first rules will be: To remember to forget that there are such things as sunshine and music in the world.'[63] But Listless gracefully averts the danger: 'It seems to be the case with us at present, or we should not have interrupted Miss O'Carroll's music with this exceedingly dry conversation.'[64] And the scene ends with a song, very relevant to Scythrop –

> Why are thy looks so blank, grey friar? . . .
> But couldst thou think my heart to move
>     With that pale and silent scowl?[65]

which reconciles the lovers.

The next discussion, in chapter 7, is led by a new arrival, Mr Asterias the ichthyologist, hot on the trail of a mermaid (who like Flosky's ghost turns out to be Mr Toobad's missing daughter, alias Stella . . .). He justifies his belief in mermaids by a threadbare and *recherché* catalogue of precedents. But, provoked by Listless's Byronic question as to 'the *cui bono* of all the pains and expense you have incurred',[66] Asterias takes up the position of a genuine scientist-explorer, an amateur in the best sense rather than a blundering eighteenth-century virtuoso-crank, who 'enjoys the disinterested pleasure of enlarging the intellect and increasing the comforts of society'.[67] Only 'the more humane pursuits of philosophy and science . . . keep alive the better feelings and more valuable energies of our nature',[68] for: 'A gloomy brow and a tragical voice seem to have been of late the characteristics of fashionable manners: and a morbid, withering, deadly, anti-social sirocco, loaded with moral and political despair, breathes through all the groves and valleys of the modern Parnassus; while science moves on in the calm dignity of its course.'[69]

This was to be repeated almost verbatim in 'The four ages of poetry'. Yet the similarity brings home the advantages the novel's dramatic discussion-form has over the expository essay. However fruitfully provocative, 'The four ages' can argue in only one direction, dogmatically establish one point of view. In *Nightmare Abbey* the effect is of a 'free play of minds' on the same subject, which is kept in the air bouncing between a range of voices and attitudes of which Asterias's is only one. The subject never comes to rest in one attitude, nor is any one character unqualifiedly endorsed by Peacock. We are never quite sure, for instance, how seriously we can take Asterias's love of science. Doesn't it rest too much on an appetite for experience and action in themselves? 'I have made many voyages, Mr. Listless, to remote and barren shores : I have travelled over desert and inhospitable lands : I have defied danger – I have submitted to privation. In the midst of these I have experienced pleasures which I would not at any time have changed for that of existing and doing nothing.'[70]

This is not Peacock's voice, but has a fanatical note probably intended to mock a similar passage in the Preface to *The revolt of Islam*.[71] Peacock's only clumsy touch in this scene is the closing speech by Mr Hilary to the effect that 'a happy disposition finds materials of enjoyment everywhere'.[72] It is too long and pompous, and receives too much prominence and endorsement. It deadens the 'free speculative treatment' of the subject by pulling it down to a single attitude. It conveys a naïve or complacent idea of 'a happy disposition' – enjoying 'a theatre . . . crowded with elegance and beauty' and 'gliding at sunset over the bosom of a lonely lake' – which makes Hilary himself a conventional emanation of the spirit of the age. Luckily the scene does not quite rest there, but concludes with Scythrop's complaint that 'these remarks are rather uncharitable' – these are hard times for 'ardent spirits'.

The fourth discussion-scene (chapter 11) centres on Mr Cypress, calling to say farewell on his way to the Continent. The subject of foreign travel provokes characteristic responses. Cypress asks the Philistine Mr Glowry if he feels 'No wish to wander among the venerable remains of the greatness that has passed for ever? Mr. GLOWRY: Not a grain.'[73] Nor has Scythrop any wish to 'wander among a few mouldy ruins . . . and meet at every step the more melancholy ruins of human nature – a degenerate race of stupid and shrivelled slaves, grovelling in the lowest depths of servility and superstition'.[74] Besides, a peer and a genius like Byron has duties in the fight for liberty at home.[75] It is no use Flosky denying all hope of political progress 'after what we have seen in France', for 'a Frenchman is born in harness, ready saddled, bitted and bridled, for any tyrant to ride', while Englishmen are born free.[76] Cypress brushes aside this moral earnestness with supercilious egotism: 'Sir, I have quarrelled with my wife; and a man who has quarrelled with his wife is absolved from all duty to his country. I have written an ode to tell the people as much, and they may take it as they list.'[77] This logical link once asserted, the way is open to blow up one's personal dissatisfactions and failures into a general pessimism, an indictment of life itself. 'I have no hope for myself or for others. Our life is a false nature; it is not in the harmony of things; it is an all-blasting upas . . .'[78] The phrases and images from *Childe Harold's pilgrimage* are made to sound even more extravagant when strung together in the prose of Cypress's succeeding speeches.

Hilary attacks this pessimism as the offspring of false expectations: 'To expect too much is a disease in the expectant, for which human nature is not responsible.'[79] On love, Hilary says: 'You talk like a Rosicrucian, who will love nothing, but a sylph, who does not believe in the existence of a sylph, and who yet quarrels with the whole universe for not containing a sylph.'[80] Of this, which applies strongly to Scythrop, Humphry House says that 'A whole long chapter of Professor Irving Babbitt says little more.'[81]

Hilary's protest that 'the highest wisdom and the highest genius have been invariably accompanied with cheerfulness' is greeted by variations on the theme, 'How can we be cheerful . . .?' and calls for 'a nice tragical ballad', which is provided by Cypress's *There is a fever of the spirit*.[82] In this and the preceding prose parodies of Byron, Peacock exposes the cant and also the perverse pleasure in Byron's nihilism, together with the cliché and confusion of his imagery. It is a sign of Peacock's quickness and insight that he seized on *Childe Harold's pilgrimage* (particularly canto IV, which had only recently appeared) as the work that both focused and exploited one of the spirits of the age; and that he made about it the central criticisms that most later critics have made.

These scenes give the impression of a comprehensive survey of 'modern gloom' as one of the prevailing spirits of the age. It is comprehensive in that, although a suggestive sketch rather than a survey thick with detail, it characterises convincingly all the relevant areas and representative figures, together with their connections by which the mechanism of fashion and production, supply and demand, is kept in motion. By that vicious circle also studied in the 'Essay on fashionable literature', modern manners and spirits help determine modern literature, which in turn influences manners. Peacock also connects developments in different areas of life and intellectual activity, each with its representative speaker: Flosky prophesies that 'let society only give fair play at one and the same time . . . to your Cypress' system of morals, and my system of metaphysics, and Scythrop's system of politics, and Mr. Listless' system of manners, and Mr. Toobad's system of religion, and the result will be as fine a mental chaos as even the immortal Kant himself could ever have hoped to see.'[83]

Above all, in tracing a common spirit of the age Peacock distinguishes the different levels on which that spirit existed. He distinguishes, for instance, the merely fashionable (in Listless) from the intensely personal (Scythrop, who reads the same rubbish as Listless but absorbs it into his personality, his 'interior structure'). It will be objected that he does not distinguish clearly enough from these the authentically creative – what in the period was represented by the best of Coleridge. But this lies outside Peacock's terms of reference. It is sufficient that, in his dealings with Coleridge as with Byron, he can diagnose the qualities that bind them to the limitations of their age, despite their efforts to stand apart from it. This means that Peacock himself could stand above the period, and have the insight into it which we can normally expect only from the vantage-point of a later period.

There is a superficial resemblance between the two novels published in 1818, *Northanger Abbey* and *Nightmare Abbey*, as satires on different forms of romanticism. Dr Jack believes the difference to be that, 'unlike Jane Austen, Peacock is more interested in ideas than in people'. This chapter has tried to show that this is not true, and the real differences lie where Dr Jack finds similarities.

Both novels, says Dr Jack, satirise 'the excesses of modern literature as exemplified in the work of Mrs Radcliffe and the "German" drama of the day'.[84] Mrs Radcliffe and German drama are strongly in the background at Nightmare Abbey, but in the foreground are *Childe Harold's pilgrimage*, *Mandeville* and *Biographia literaria*. As Flosky points out, ghosts, goblins and skeletons have been out of fashion for years. 'Modern literature' in Peacock's novel is the literature and taste of 1818, not (as with Jane Austen's novel) the turn of the century.

Dr Jack adds that 'in Jane Austen's book a young woman discovers the difference between life in books and life in fact: in Peacock's a young man makes the same discovery'.[85] But in *Northanger Abbey* romance or romanticism belongs only to 'life in books', and an extraordinarily ordinary girl merely confuses it with prosaic if sometimes inhospitable 'real life'. Peacock on the other hand diagnoses inside Scythrop romanticism as it fuses with individual character and directs one's life. To feel the pulse of such a personality, of what might be called lived romanticism, needed more intimate and sympathetic insight than to make fun of 'the excesses of modern literature'. It needed much more than what Dr Jack claims Jane Austen and Peacock share in these two novels, 'a conservative and "eighteenth century" attitude'.[86]

SOURCE: extract from *Peacock, His Circle and His Age* (Cambridge, 1968) pp. 135–64.

NOTES

1. 15 September 1818 : 'Halliford edition', ed. H. F. B. Brett-Smith and C. E. Jones, 10 vols (London, 1924–34, repr. 1967), VIII 204. [This edition hereafter referred to as 'Halliford' – Ed.]

2. 30 May 1818 : ibid. 193.

3. 25 July 1818 : *Letters*, ed. F. L. Jones, 2 vols (Oxford, 1964), II 27.

4. *Letters*, ed. Jones, II 98.

5. The *Listener*, XLII (8 December 1949) 997.

6. This conveniently succinct version of the widespread view is from Ian Jack's *English Literature, 1815–32* (Oxford, 1963) p. 213.

7. Ibid. p. 217.

8. Halliford, III 25.

9. Ibid.

10. It would be necessary to apologise for making so much use of that accident on the stairs, had not other readers made so much fuss about Peacock making (they claim) so little of it. 'This is splendidly funny,' says Mr Dyson, 'and entirely in keeping with all that has led up to it, but do we even begin to wonder whether Scythrop or Mr. Toobad has been hurt? The precipitation of each into his gloomiest philosophising strikes us, rather, as a festive comic release. Everything depends upon the timing, as in a Laurel and Hardy film. Peacock sets out to entertain us, and any moral lessons are very much on the way.' (*The Crazy Fabric: Essays in Irony* (London, 1965) p. 61.)

11. Halliford, III 13–14.

12. 10 January 1812 : *Letters*, ed. Jones, I 227.

13. Ibid. 227–9.

14. Halliford, III 14.

15. In the 'Memoirs of Shelley', Peacock notes that 'Brown's four novels, Schiller's *Robbers*, and Goethe's *Faust*, were, of all the works with which he was familiar, those which took the deepest root in his mind, and had the strongest influence in the formation of his character' (Halliford, VIII 78). For the sketch of Scythrop's political fantasy, Peacock owed something to the eleutherarchs of Hogg's *Prince Alexy Haimatoff*.

16. Halliford, III 14.

17. Ibid. 17.

18. For self-importance, cf. Scythrop's determination, 'for the benefit of mankind in general, to adopt all possible precautions for the preservation of himself', with Shelley at the end of his second letter to Godwin : 'My plan is that of resolving to lose no opportunity to disseminate truth and happiness' (10 January 1812 : *Letters*, ed. Jones, I 229), or his invitation to Elizabeth Hitchener to join his pamphlet campaign in Ireland : 'you would share with me the high delight of awakening a whole nation from the lethargy of its bondage' (27 February 1812 : ibid. 263).

K. N. Cameron complains that the reception of the Irish pamphlets, and even of those launched by balloon and bottle in Devon, is not fairly represented by the reception of Scythrop's pamphlet.

But Peacock's main target is the self-importance and visionary optimism of both ventures.

19. Ch. 3 : Halliford, III 20–1.

20. Ibid. VIII 95.

21. Ch. 3 : ibid, III 21.

22. Ibid. 22.

23. Ch. 10 : Halliford, III 93–4.

24. Among several critics, N. I. White (*Shelley*, 2 vols (London,
1947) I 705 n. 47) argues for Claire Clairmont, who first presented
herself to Byron as Stella presents herself to Scythrop. J.-J. Mayoux
(*Un Epicurien anglais: Thomas Love Peacock* (Paris, 1932,
p. 269) gives further evidence in favour of Claire.

25. Henry James, *The Bostonians* (London, 1886) I 10–11, 55.

26. Ch. 10 : Halliford, III 95–6.

27. *English Literature, 1815–32*.

28. Ch. 14 : Halliford, III 137.

29. The phrase is from the 'Memoirs of Shelley' : Halliford, VIII 78.

30. Ian Jack, *English Literature, 1815–32*, p. 217.

31. The *Listener*, XLII (8 December 1949) 998.

32. Ch. 1 : Halliford, III 10–11.

33. 'I ought to except Sir W. Drummond's "Academical Questions"; a volume of very acute and powerful metaphysical criticism.' (Shelley's footnote.)

34. *Poetical Works*, ed. Mary Shelley, 4 vols (London, 1839) I
147–8.

35. Ch. 6 : Halliford, III 48–9.

36. 29 January 1810 : *Selections from the Letters of Southey*, ed.
J. W. Warter (London, 1856) II 188–9.

37. Hazlitt, among others, echoed Southey by saying that
Coleridge was an 'excellent talker, very – if you let him start from
no premises and come to no conclusion' (a remark reported by
Carlyle, *Life of Sterling* (London, 1851) p. 74).

38. From the unpublished MS. Egerton 2801, fo. 126 : watermark
1822. Printed in *Inquiring spirit: A new presentation of Coleridge*,
ed. K. Coburn (London, 1951) pp. 143–4.

39. Ch. 6 : Halliford, III 49–50. The final allusion is to the naming
of Hartley and Berkeley Coleridge.

40. In *Sibylline leaves* (London, 1817) p. 241. It is worth noting
that the *Ode* first appeared in book form while Peacock was plan-
ning the novel.

41. 'Coleridge', in *Collected writings*, ed. D. Masson (Edinburgh,
1889) II 152–3.

42. *Reminiscences*, ed. C. E. Norton (London, 1887) II 131.

43. *Life of Sterling* (London, 1851) p. 73.

44. Edith Wharton's report of the first incident is too well known to need quoting here. The second incident is described in Jessie Conrad's *Joseph Conrad and his circle* (London, 1935) p. 115 : 'Some three or four little girls caught his attention and in his most ingratiating manner he stopped to talk to them. He began by presenting each with some pence and then proceeded to harangue them far above their understanding. The kiddies at last flung the coins on the ground and burst into loud sobbing before they ran away.'

45. Marionetta's own phrase : ch. 8 : Halliford, III 75.

46. Ibid. 72–4.

47. Ibid. 78–9.

48. Ibid. 71.

49. Ibid. 75–6.

50. Ibid. 78.

51. (Oxford, 1959) p. 173.

52. The Earl of Mount Edgcumbe, *Musical reminiscences* (London, 1834) p. 235.

53. This draws, of course, on the well-known Windermere anecdote of Beau Brummell.

54. Halliford, III 39. Devilman alludes to Godwin's *Mandeville*, which Shelley said 'shakes the deepest soul' (*Letters*, ed. Jones, I 523–4).

55. Halliford, III 41.

56. Ibid.

57. Ibid. 45.

58. Refusing each course in turn and being asked by the desperate host what he *did* eat and drink, Byron replied, 'Nothing but hard bisquits and soda-water.' [Rogers continues] 'Some days after, meeting Hobhouse, I said to him, "How long will Lord Byron persevere in his present diet?" He replied, "Just as long as you continue to notice it." – I did not know then, what I now know to be a fact – that Byron, after leaving my house, had gone to a Club in St. James's Street, and eaten a hearty meat-supper.' (A. Dyce, *Recollections of the Table-talk of Samuel Rogers*, ed. M. Bishop (London, 1952) p. 189.)

59. Halliford, III 45–6.

60. Ibid. 50–1.

61. Ibid. 51.

62. Ibid.

63. Ibid. 53.

64. Ibid.

65. Ibid. 54.

66. Ibid. 64. The weary question *Cui bono?* forms the title of the Smith brothers' parody of Byron, in their *Rejected addresses*.

67. Ibid. 66.

68. Ibid. 65

69. Ibid. 65–6.

70. Ibid. 64–5.

71. Shelley is claiming to have the 'education peculiarly fitted for a Poet' : 'I have been familiar from boyhood with mountains and lakes, and the sea, and the solitude of forests : Danger, which sports upon the brink of precipices, has been my playmate. I have trodden the glaciers of the Alps, and lived under the eye of Mount Blanc . . .' (*Poetical Works*, ed. Mary Shelley, p. 149).

72. Halliford, III 68.

73. Ibid. 101–2.

74. Ibid. 102. Peacock is transcribing verbatim a letter from Shelley : 'The people here, though inoffensive enough, seem both in body and soul a miserable race. The men are hardly men, they look like a tribe of stupid and shrivelled slaves.' (20 April 1818 : *Letters*, II 9.) This is a common note in Shelley's Italian letters.

75. Cf. Shelley : 'The number of English who pass through this town [Milan] is very great. They ought to be in their own country at the present crisis. Their conduct is wholly inexcusable' (from the letter quoted above). Shelley was abroad, he claimed, for health reasons.

76. Halliford, III 103–4. Cf. again the central argument of the Preface to *The revolt of Islam*.

77. Ibid. 103.

78. Ibid. 104.

79. Ibid. 107–8.

80. Ibid. 108.

81. 'The novels of Thomas Love Peacock', the *Listener*, XLII (8 December 1949) 998.

82. Ch. 11 : Halliford, III 109–11.

83. Ibid. 105.

84. *English Literature, 1815–32*, p. 213.

85. Ibid.

86. Ibid.

# Carl Dawson

# *GRYLL GRANGE* (1970)

During the thirty years that elapsed before Peacock completed another novel, England found a whole generation of novelists. Scott and Jane Austen gave way to Dickens, to the Brontës, to Thackeray, to Trollope, to George Eliot. In view of Peacock's penchant for assimilating, it would seem reasonable for him to have drawn on the younger writers, especially on Dickens, whom he read and admired. Yet his reported comment on Dickens, the tenor of which is predictable, makes clear that the provenance of the last novel differs little, if at all, from that of the earlier stories. 'Dickens,' he is supposed to have said, 'is very comic, but – not *so* comic as Aristophanes.'[1] The phrasing here is probably not Peacock's, but the sentiment clearly is. The scenario for 'Aristophanes in London', a play produced by the guests at Gryll Grange, occurs towards the high point in the story. But of Dickens there is neither mention nor echo. Excepting its satiric references, *Gryll Grange* deferred to its times only by appearing serially in *Fraser's Magazine*.

Peacock may be said to have borrowed for this novel from his own earlier works. The characters and setting are new, the targets of his censure are in part also new, yet 'the author of *Headlong Hall*' is as readily identifiable in this his final novel as in his first, written over forty years before. *Gryll Grange* and *Headlong Hall* actually share qualities that are to a degree absent from the intervening novels. Although *Gryll Grange* comes close to *Melincourt* in its size and in its type of story and registers, like *Crotchet Castle*, some grave doubts about the Victorian temper, it approximates more nearly the other-worldly quality of *Headlong Hall*. Squire Gryll proves a less impetuous host than Squire Headlong; Dr. Opimian emerges a far more rational, if equally conservative, clergyman than Dr. Gaster; acute apologists for rural retreat supplant diverse philosophers; still, there is a familiar atmosphere with the same detached and stylized comedy of ideas.

Except for the official side of his life, most of what had occupied Peacock during his seventy years emerges in one way or another in *Gryll Grange*, so that the novel becomes a kind of last manifesto. It treats of good fellowship, good food and wine, and of classical literature. Opimian receives an invitation to visit Mr. Falconer only because, on stopping to admire 'The Folly' – Falconer's residence – he mutters to himself some lines from Homer, which Falconer overhears. Elsewhere Opimian says: 'Consider how much instruction has been conveyed to us in the form of conversations at banquets, by Plato and Xenophon and Plutarch. I read nothing with more pleasure than their *Symposia*: to say nothing of Athenaeus, whose work is one long banquet' (v 197). This is the usual provision of Peacock's works; but he also yokes together comments on land enclosure, vestal virgins, St. Catherine, competitive examinations, America, public lectures, ice-skating, and knighthoods.

Thackeray, who met Peacock at Erle Stoke, home of Lord Broughton (John Cam Hobhouse), in 1850, described the 'small select party' gathered together by the host, 'a most polite and good natured [man], with a very winning simplicity of manner'. Not knowing that Peacock was still to write *Gryll Grange* and continued to write poems, Thackeray says: '. . . a charming lyrical poet and Horatian satirist he was when a writer; now he is a white-headed jolly old worldling . . .'.[2]

The narrator of *Gryll Grange* speaks like 'a jolly old worldling' and, excepting India, seems to introduce the range of information that had impressed Thackeray. The *Saturday Review*, delighting in Peacock's learning, also praised his 'quaint, hearty, unostentatious Paganism'. 'The volume reads', they suggested, 'like a few numbers of *Notes and Queries* jumbled up with a funny love story, and pervaded by a fine Pagan morality. The greatest tribute to its merits that can be paid is to say – what may be said with perfect truth – that all this queer mixture flows easily along, and that we never feel we have been delivered over to a learned bore.'[3]

Goethe, who himself wrote far into old age, remarked that the
greatest of the arts was that of self-limitation. And, tacitly, Peacock seems to have worked by a similar maxim. The queer mixture or medley – which somehow, as the *Saturday Review*
pointed out, manages to move along without difficulties in the
narrative or without the notes and queries seeming like the intrusion of pedantry – offers a description that is as true of the
earlier works as much as of *Gryll Grange* itself. To say that the
book deserved all of the *Saturday Review*'s praise is not, then, to
imply that Peacock as an old man became an inventive novelist,
striking out in a new direction. This is not the case at all. But
the novel seldom flags from limited incident or meagre story. It
repeats, but it is not redundant, while offering the wisdom that
too rarely comes with age and the wit that all too often dis-
appears.

As in *Melincourt*, Peacock once again builds two neighbouring
estates, the one conveniently housing the hero, the other the
heroine. Algernon Falconer and Morgana Gryll are less
Rousseauistic and less priggish versions of Forester and Anthelia.
They are also more fully presented as people. Of the various
characters who visit the country estate of Squire Gryll, few
resemble the crotcheteers of the earlier works. Unlike Squire
Crotchet, Gryll is a relaxed gentleman, particular about his
guests. The guests include such people as Miss Ilex, Peacock's
one pleasant old lady, and Miss Niphet and Lord Curryfin, who,
while not complex characters, have a certain emotional range –
and a capacity to listen. Curryfin, Peacock's first portrait of a
lord that is not damning – and who perhaps reflects his later
friendship with Lord Broughton – actually develops during the
course of the story by learning something about himself and by
acting according to the knowledge. He begins as a fashionable
public lecturer, telling fishermen about fish, but at the close of
the story he puts aside childish things and deserves the inscrutable
Miss Niphet. In short, Peacock seems to make amends here for
the not very agreeable family of the Crotchets and for their sometimes poor taste in guests. The people in *Gryll Grange* spout
opinions and disagree, but Peacock clearly approves of host and
guests alike.

Entitled 'Misnomers' – it might have been called 'Farrago' in
Juvenal's sense – the first chapter of *Gryll Grange* not only introduces the work and three of its important characters, it reveals
Peacock's entire method in miniature. Consider Dr. Opimian's
opening conversational gambit :

'Palestine soup !' said the Reverend Dr. Opimian, dining with his
friend Squire Gryll; 'a curiously complicated misnomer. We have
an excellent old vegetable, the artichoke, of which we eat the head;
we have another of subsequent introduction, of which we eat the
root, and which we also call artichoke, because it resembles the first
in flavour, although, *me judice*, a very inferior affair. This last is a
species of helianthus, or sunflower genus of the *Syngenesia frustranea*
class of plants. It is therefore a girasol, or turn-to-the-sun. From
this girasol we have made Jerusalem, and from the Jerusalem artichoke we make Palestine Soup.'

Apart from offering a witty gastronomic *jeu d'esprit* and a text-
book example of chiasmus, the doctor's words serve as a cue to
Squire Gryll. He replies, 'A very good thing, Doctor'; and when
Opimian responds that it is 'A very good thing; but a palpable
misnomer', Squire Gryll can launch into an almost equally epigrammatic and well-turned speech on 'a world of misnomers'.
Each provides the other with a mounting-block; each is ready
to discuss any subject. For when the squire closes his polished
tirade, he invites the Doctor to continue : 'While we are on the
subject of misnomers, what say you to the wisdom of Parliament?'
And Opimian, needing but the slightest prompt, bounds after
the new topic. He then accedes to the Squire's contention that
'Palestine soup is not more remote from the true Jerusalem than
many an honourable friend from public honesty', and cheer-
fully agrees to a glass of Madeira.

At this point Morgana Gryll, lovely niece of the Squire, enters
the conversation and epitomizes what has transpired : 'You and
my uncle, Doctor, get up a discussion on everything that presents
itself; dealing with your theme like a series of variations in music.'
She both speaks to the point, and prompts the talk once more :
'You have run half round the world *àpropos* of the soup. What
say you to the fish?' Dr. Opimian, like Athenaeus's characters,
is an authority on fish, and speaks accordingly. After a list of

various species and their merits – Opimian prefers the taste of
the fish with one-syllabic names – the subject moves to Lord
Curryfin, a lecturer on fish, to lectures in general, to *tensons* and
their possible use in conversation, and finally to the desirability
of producing an Aristophanic comedy – for passing judgment on
the times. Miss Gryll suggests that the comedy be presented at
Christmas, and that suitable roles might include 'Homer, and
Dante, and Shakespeare, and Richard the First, and Oliver
Cromwell' – in addition to the original and ancestral Gryllus,
who, the narrator says, 'maintained against Ulysses the superior
happiness of the life of other animals' (v 1–12), specifically that
of pigs.[4] The narrator finally interrupts the conversation: 'Before
we proceed further, we will give some account of our interlocutors', and the chapter closes (v 1–12).

Several things become clear from this chapter. Every sentence
is at once carefully developed and seemingly spontaneous. Because of their turns of phrase, many of the sentences are self-
contained, standing as prose epigrams. Miss Gryll's desire for a
formal *tenson* is, as the narrator implies, gratuitous, since the
kind of *tenson* she envisions is taking place as she speaks. The
'series of variations in music', as she describes it, is a matter of
balance and interplay between the speakers and their themes.[5]
Just as each sentence is complete in itself, so is the whole episode.
The pause to give 'account of our interlocutors' offers the same
sort of cue that Opimian gives to Gryll, for the chapters, discreet
like the sentences, proceed from one conversational episode to
another.

In range of subject the chapter is broad indeed: a few pages
treat of many topics. Yet this is the lightest of conversation, delicate, mannered, and intellectual. It takes place, after all, over
the span of two courses at dinner: and the dinner provides the
stimulus for the talk. Whatever will arise in the next chapter,
it is clear that the characters will return to table before long, and
that whatever thunderclouds may develop within the course of
the story, such an opening calls for such an end.

The story itself follows the pattern of the earlier novels, though
it presents a new complication. Morgana Gryll, only relative of
the Squire, remains unmarried, not having encountered her

ideal young man. Through the quaintly Pandaric activities of
Dr. Opimian, she is introduced to the Gryll's reclusive neighbour, Algernon Falconer. Falconer resembles Molière's Alceste,
except that he has a little self-knowledge. Peacock laughs at him,
sympathizes with him, reforms him. Unfortunately for Morgana,
as the story opens, Algernon has committed himself to a life of
retirement, boasting the service of a group of seven sisters, 'seven
vestals', who look after his household while he occupies his mind
with Homer and his spirit with St. Catherine. Unlikely as all this
seems – and Mrs. Opimian's comment is : 'I don't trust young
men' – the story nonetheless depends upon it. For Morgana, an
emancipated young lady, admits her love for Falconer by leaving
open a revealing page of the poet Boiardo, so that the resolution
of the novel depends upon his descent from a tower, in which
he actually does live. Falconer, then, plays his own *senex* in this
comedy, and of course his younger self finally triumphs.

Falconer has a temporary rival in Lord Curryfin, who veers
towards Morgana before falling in love with the quieter and, it
turns out, more suitable Miss Niphet. But all is finally resolved.
Algernon asks for Morgana, thereby giving Squire Gryll hope
for an heir. The seven 'vestals' marry seven fortuitously suitable
local farmers, and Lord Curryfin asks for Miss Niphet. There
is a mathematical coupling, outstripping even that of *Headlong
Hall*. After performing the Aristophanic comedy, everyone joins
in celebrations, which, like those of *Headlong Hall* and *Crotchet
Castle*, take place at Christmas.

Peacock introduces few songs in *Gryll Grange*. One guest sings
a gentle song of 'Love and Age' :

> I played with you 'mid cowslips blowing,
> When I was six and you were four;
> When garlands weaving, flower-balls throwing,
> Were pleasures soon to please no more.
> Through groves and meads, o'er grass and heather,
> With little playmates, to and fro,
> We wandered hand in hand together;
> But that was sixty years ago . . . (v 146)

and Dr. Opimian recites a rather cantankerous poem called 'A

New Order of Chivalry' (probably written earlier and inserted
into the novel). But the songs are proportionately fewer and
usually weaker than those in the earlier novels. Instead of songs,
Peacock offers the play within a play, 'Aristophanes in London'.
As might be imagined, Aristophanes, with Circe and Gryll as
his main characters, finds even more to condemn in modern
England than he had in ancient Athens. He speaks, as a matter
of fact, with a distinctly English intonation. Circe can sum up
his indictment in a few lines :

> Three thousand years ago,
> This land was forest, and a bright pure river
> Ran through it to and from the Ocean stream.
> Now, through a wilderness of human forms,
> And human dwellings, a polluted flood
> Rolls up and down, charged with all earthly poisons.
>
> Houses, and ships,
> And boats, and chimneys vomiting black smoke,
> Horses, and carriages of every form,
> And restless bipeds, rushing here and there
> For profit or for pleasure, as they phrase it. (v 279)

Industry is, in short, the major villain. But Peacock also levels
some of the traditional charges of Aristophanes, indicting political
demagoguery, misleading rhetoric, and idle theoretical speculation.

Peacock suggests by his play, and by the conversation generally, that in an age given over to absurdities, when people travel
without purpose and live without enjoyment, some things may
be offered as fingers for the dike. What one cannot change, one
can by music, conviviality, and natural surroundings avoid.
Falconer says to Opimian shortly after they meet : 'The world
will never suppose a good motive, where it can suppose a bad
one. I would not willingly offend any of its prejudices. I would
not affect eccentricity. At the same time, I do not feel disposed
to be put out of my way because it is not the way of the world . . .'
(v 30). So he, like the other characters, does go his own way,
and the world may go to the devil.

Such an attitude necessarily reflects on the Aristophanic comedy, which is really more of a tribute to Aristophanes than a re-creation of his method; it is, to use the phrase of Meredith, 'a breath of Aristophanes'. Carl Van Doren has called *Gryll Grange* 'New Comedy', as opposed to the 'Old Comedy' of *Maid Marian*, and though the distinction is useful, it is not wholly apt, for even *Maid Marian* has little of Aristophanes – and its plot, like that of the other stories, is essentially 'new comedy'.[6] Van Doren's point calls attention, however, to some differences between *Gryll Grange* and the earlier novels. Peacock has dispensed in his final novel with characters who are merely 'embodied classifications'; he has substituted more or less normal movements for the farcical tumbling of, say, *Headlong Hall*; he has become less harsh in his censure of humours, and somewhat more preoccupied with effecting the traditional happy ending.

In *Melincourt* Peacock had spoken of the type of writer convinced of his powers to set the world right, perhaps with his earlier self in mind. The course of his novels, slight as the changes may be, culminates in *Gryll Grange*, for, aware and acute as he is, Peacock has accepted another role. One way to appreciate his attitude is to consider the author's note preceding the novel, where he says : 'In the following pages, the New Forest is always mentioned as if it were still unenclosed. This is the only state in which the author has been acquainted with it. Since its enclosure, he has never seen it, and purposes never to do so.' The 'as if it were' epitomizes the underlying attitude of the work. Not bitterly muttering his *vanitas vanitatum*, or bemoaning everything like his own Mr. Toobad, Peacock is rather talking eloquently in the world's despite.

In addition to Aristophanes, Peacock pays tribute in *Gryll Grange* to Petronius, whom he quotes extensively and cites with approval. Dr. Opimian owes his name, ultimately, to the famous wine produced during the rule of Opimian, but Peacock no doubt borrows the name directly from Petronius. In the *Satyricon* Trimalchio serves his guests 'Opimian wine 100 years old' – and therefore, presumably, unpalatable. Peacock has often referred to Petronius, often laughed with him. He delights in the anecdote about the German scholar who, informed that a 'complete

Petronius' had been discovered, raced down to Italy to find the mere corporeal remains of the Catholic saint (IX 361). In Petronius, as in Lucian, he found an enviable blend : here was a satirist, a versifier, and a man, like himself, with antipathy towards his age. The *Satyricon*, mixing prose and verse, and revolving around Trimalchio's incredible feast, understandably became one of Peacock's favourite works. His own fiction, similarly oriented around dinner tables, similarly mixing prose and verse – a practice already waning in the late-eighteenth-century novel – might be considered a modern equivalent for Petronius's type of Menippean satire. What qualifies such a view is Peacock's restraint. There is little in his novels, and particularly little in *Gryll Grange*, of Petronius's gross burlesque of social customs, certainly none of the explorations of sexual oddities. If Peacock could admire Petronius's energetic descriptions and the range of his comments – unlike Smollett, who found the *Satyricon* unfit reading for an English gentleman, but whose 'realism' seems occasionally indebted to Petronius – Peacock borrows only a general method of narrative. He has been said to have the amused curiosity of Lucian rather than the fierce mockery of Swift. Petronius substituted for Swift would affect the justice of the observation little. But it might be better to say, as Thackeray did, that he has the tolerant laughter of Horace rather than the – partly assumed – anger of Juvenal. And Dr. Opimian, that broad-ranging student of classics, devotee of Athenaeus, and connoisseur of lobster, Dr. Opimian himself embodies Peacock's amiable satiric tone. His name stems from a Falernian wine, but his real genesis is the good-humoured eighteenth-century eccentric, in Addison, Fielding, or Sterne.

The qualities of Peacock's comedy are reflected throughout in the various houses and country settings, wherein he creates 'all this queer mixture' of 'funny love story', 'Pagan morality', and talk. Peacock began at least one story after *Gryll Grange*, but he completed none;[7] and the Gryll mansion is the last of his comic settings. It is worth a few more comments.

Houses, of course, play an important part in so much mid-nineteenth-century fiction. One has only to think of such titles as *Bleak House* and *Wuthering Heights*; or to remember the drama enacted in the Casaubon library in *Middlemarch*, in Miss Haversham's unlit room, where Pip enters upon his illusions as well as his expectations, and in Mowbray Castle, in Disraeli's *Sybil*, where 'the two nations' finally meet in symbolic battle.[8] Thackeray, in *Vanity Fair*, creates an entire satiric stage in Becky and Rawdon's house in Curzon Street and in 'the house on Russell Square'. Wilkie Collins makes Blackwater Park, its name suggestive enough, into a place of villainy and intrigue in *The Woman in White*.

Peacock's houses, by comparison, suggest another muse and another world, with entirely different rules and possibilities. As in those of Jane Austen, there is no hunger in his houses, no echo of guns; there is also no treachery, no lasting affliction, no real pathos. Whereas the Brontës, Dickens, and George Eliot use their houses as emblems of a world in emotional or social turmoil, Peacock's remain at an apparently safe remove. Even Meredith, in the houses of the Feverils and Sir Willoughby Patterne, describes places of dark corners, and his comic spirit, whatever its indebtedness to Peacock, casts intermittent shadows down below. In *Melincourt,* Peacock moved briefly in the direction of the great Victorian realists; but in that novel, too, comedy raises its voice at the expense of pathos. More usual in Peacock is the situation of Headlong Hall and Nightmare Abbey, separated from 'civilization' by narrow and almost impassable roads.

The final novelistic setting, Gryll Grange, epitomizes these isolated and carefree houses; it is as enclosed and self-contained as Windsor Forest itself. There can be no doubt, I think, that the Gryll residence reflects a more genial comedy than that in *Crotchet Castle* and the earlier novels. More genial because more isolated, more consciously separated from satanic mills, dark city streets, and the conditions that Marx and Owen, Carlyle and Mill had been crying out against.

And hence the houses of Peacock's younger novelistic contemporaries seem not only more involved with contemporary life, but also more committed to life itself. In our own time, when literature is often associated with political ends, when realism has become the accepted norm for fiction, when a writer's sincerity seems more important than his artifice, when 'serious' grappling with moral issues has been offered as the hallmark of the *real* English novel, of the great tradition, works like Peacock's may seem like unimportant escapism. The charge has occasionally been made, and it is one that ought to be met.

Let me begin by twisting the meaning of a comment by Northrop Frye, who argues – with a view to the ritual elements of comedy – that comedy contains within itself potential tragedy.[9] This is evidently true of *Measure for Measure*, say, or *Volpone*, as it was of the more immediately ritualistic comedies of Aristophanes, Menander, or Plautus. Is it also perhaps true of Peacock's comedy? My point throughout has been that Peacock places his characters in an intact world, where they have little to do but talk; and that, whatever the import of their talk, the characters enact traditional comic roles. In *Melincourt* and in parts of *Crotchet Castle*, Peacock draws in the outside world, either by extensive allusion, or by letting his characters confront suffering. Elsewhere his characters are remote from suffering. And they seem especially remote in *Gryll Grange*.

The point to be made about *Gryll Grange* is not that the book contains potential tragedy; rather that tragedy is the assumed daily condition – beyond the bounds of Gryll's estate. The more isolated Peacock makes his setting, the more he suggests tragedy by implication. For the setting, the intact social world, is as precarious as it is desirable. There is the same sort of parallel at work in *Gryll Grange* as in Shakespeare's *As You Like It*. However idyllic the forest and unscathed the foresters, we know that Arden is a good, a green or 'golden' world only by inverse reflection on the usurped dukedom. (Some of Peacock's characters, Scythrop and Toobad among them, sound like Jacques: professional malcontents in idyllic surroundings.) To speak about 'romantic comedy' may be a way of calling Peacock's books anachronistic modes in an age of literary realism, a way of saying that they are, after all, escapist literature. The question to be asked is whether such description automatically implies censure or whether it merely offers a useful means of classification.

To Mario Praz, among the harshest but most persuasive of

Peacock's commentators, and normally one of the acutest critics, Peacock's retreats, and generally his type of fiction, represent stagnant eddies in the nineteenth-century mainstream. I have mentioned before Mr. Praz's dislike of Peacock's songs. To such an opinion he is clearly entitled; it matters little whether one critic likes a song and another does not. But arguing on the basis of a thorough misconception of Peacock's art, Mr. Praz allows himself almost incredible obtuseness when he speaks about the novels. He can say, for example, 'Peacock is bourgeois in every paragraph'.[10] Does he mean by this that Peacock's houses and the characters they contain represent a middle-class ideal: the pot of aspidistra writ large? So that Gryll's estate might be anticipatory of the suburban house, his banquets the Sunday dinners after Sunday papers? Whatever charge is intended, it is of dubious application. For in one sense or another all the important nineteenth-century writers – and probably most of the eighteenth-century writers – are *bourgeois*: of, for, and about the middle class. Jane Austen presumably is. So is Dickens; so is George Eliot. The Marxist critic Georg Lukács calls Walter Scott great largely because he could depict historical periods in terms of *bourgeois* ideals. To label a writer *bourgeois* is, without careful definition, to misuse an already overused word, to avoid the issue. The term is poor censure because it is inaccurate description.

If, however, Mr. Praz intends by the term the loose associations of easy optimism or faith in progress or the smugness consequent on newly-acquired wealth, then one can say categorically that he could not be more wrong. As much as Arnold, Newman, Thackeray, and George Eliot, Peacock censured the philistinism of his time. He hated the Bounderbys, the Podsnaps, the Pumblechooks, and the Pecksniffs as much as Dickens did. And if, like Dickens, his conception of economic forces left much to be desired, that makes him no less a responsible observer of how men thought and lived. One has only to compare him with Trollope to see how critical, how iconoclastic he was. In short, the implications of Peacock's isolated comic dialogues do not have to be negative at all. Peacock *chose* a particular art form, or, rather, created one to suit his needs. He was not necessarily

incapable of feeling, callous to suffering, insensitive to tragedy –
or hopelessly middle-class. But even if Peacock had these and
other limitations as a man; even if his novels reflect a certain
temperament, the statement made in the novels is of a different
order entirely. Peacock, like many great comic novelists, illustrates
that fiction takes the form of self-criticism and self-parody almost
as easily as it does self-apology.

There may indeed be escapism in his novels. No doubt Peacock would have applauded Matthew Arnold's comment in
*Popular Education in France* (published a little more than a
year later than *Gryll Grange*): 'For anyone but a pedant . . . a
handful of Athenians of two thousand years ago are more interesting than the mills of most nations of our contemporaries.' But as
'Aristophanes in London' makes clear, an interest in Greece had
implications for Peacock comparable with those it had for Arnold.
'Now', Arnold writes, 'all the liberty and industry in the world
will not ensure these two things: a high reason and a fine culture.'[11] For Peacock as for Arnold, culture itself was not only
the end, it was also a means to a further end, for 'culture begets
a dissatisfaction, which is of the highest possible value in stem-
ming the common tide of men's thoughts in a wealthy and industrial community.'[12] Arnold's use of culture in this passage
from *Culture and Anarchy* has not quite the same meaning as
in the lines from *Education in France*. What is important, however, is not the definition but the overwhelming concern with
quality of life or civilization in Crystal Palace England.

It is worth repeating that Peacock's characteristic mode of
criticism was not Arnold's and that the medium itself inevitably
modifies the terms of criticism. Nonetheless, Peacock's fictional
worlds do two things that Arnold is calling for. They offer
critical debate, and they offer an alternative vision, based upon
'the spectacle of ancient Athens'. His appeal is for intelligent
scrutiny, for order, beauty, art. He does not defend the *status
quo*, nor is he an easy reactionary. Like Arnold, he concerns himself with a whole state of mind, which he rightfully associates
with the state of literature and the state of politics.[13] Arnold
spoke of Peacock, appropriately, as 'a man of keen and culti-
vated mind'.[14]

Peacock's houses are the setting for a singular type of comedy, full of exuberant intellectual gaiety and, whatever the satiric or critical basis, full of music, dance, and the ritual ingredients of older comedy. Where Arnold points soberly towards an ideal, Peacock brings his to life. Like Walter Landor, he creates in his imaginary conversations glimpses of the best that has been thought and said. In a setting where dialogue is as much a staple as the dinners and the port, he lets his characters talk their way to a kind of absurd rationality. At the least he lets them pass judgment on the 'crazy fabric' of the world outside. His worlds are not Biedemeier worlds, not the stuffy retreats of an abject middle class. Their ideals are as old as Plato's.

S O U R C E : extract from *His Fine Wit: A Study of Thomas Love Peacock* (London, 1970) pp. 273–86.

### NOTES

1. Buchanan, *A Poet's Sketchbook* (London, 1883) p. 105.

2. *A Collection of Letters of W. M. Thackeray,* ed. Brookfield (London, 1887) p. 100. Quoted in Halliford, I clxxviii.

3. *Saturday Review*, XL (16 March 1861) 222. Of all Peacock's stories, *Gryll Grange* contains the most classical references and quotations, but, as the *Saturday Review* suggests, they do not intrude. The response of the magazine was evidently typical, for *Gryll Grange* seems to have been well received. Tennyson, e.g., whose portrait of Cleopatra is likened to the 'Queen of Bambo', is supposed to have ranked himself among Peacock's 'most devoted admirers'. Cited in I, cci.

4. In a lengthy footnote Peacock alludes to the dialogue in Plutarch where 'Gryllus maintained against Ulysses', as well as to Book II of the *Faerie Queene*, in which there is the 'hog' 'hight Grylle by name'.

5. Part of Peacock's brief introductory note to *Gryll Grange* casts light on both the *tensons* – the formalized, spontaneous debates – and the form of the chapters themselves. 'The mottoes', he writes, 'are sometimes specially apposite to the chapters to which they are prefixed; but more frequently to the general scope, or to borrow a musical term, the *motivo* of the *operetta*.'

6. Carl Van Doren, *The Life of Thomas Love Peacock*, p. 233.

7. 'Cotswold Chace.' Peacock's last published work was a partial translation of the Italian play *Gl' Ingannati* (1862), which 'with numerous verbal changes is reprinted in the Appendix to Furness's "New Variorum" edition of *Twelfth Night*' (Halliford, 1 cciii).

8. According to one account, Disraeli 'was much delighted with Peacock, and surprised to find in him the author of *Headlong Hall*, and calling him [*sic*] his "master"; but, says Peacock to me, "I did not know he was my pupil."' Hobhouse, *Recollections of a Long Life*, quoted in Halliford, 1 clxxvii. Disraeli was not the only statesman to enjoy Peacock. Gladstone, too, owned and read the Cole Edition. See J. L. Madden, 'Gladstone's Reading of Thomas Love Peacock', *Notes and Queries*, N.S., xiv 10 (October 1967) 384.

9. 'The Argument of Comedy', in *Theories of Comedy*, ed. Paul Lauter (Garden City, 1964) p. 454.

10. Mario Praz, *The Hero in Eclipse in Victorian Fiction* (London, 1956, repr. 1969) p. 100.

11. In Trilling, *The Portable Matthew Arnold*, p. 462.

12. Trilling, Ibid., p. 477.

13. Compare F. R. Leavis's remarks on Peacock, included . . . as a footnote to Jane Austen in *The Great Tradition*, p. 19: 'In his [Peacock's] ironical treatment of contemporary society and civilization he is seriously applying serious standards, so that his books, which are obviously not novels in the same sense as Jane Austen's, have a permanent life as light reading – indefinitely rereadable for minds with mature interests.' One would not have expected Mr. Leavis to subscribe to this estimate of Peacock, and of course he cannot do so without a certain twisting of the word 'serious' and an appeal to that dubious category of 'light reading'. Implicitly Mr. Leavis suggests that a 'great tradition' can and should be more incorporative than his own rhetoric would lead one to believe.

14. Arnold, *Essays in Criticism*, Second Series, p. 224.

# SELECT BIBLIOGRAPHY

RECOMMENDED TEXTS

*The Novels of Thomas Love Peacock*, ed. David Garnett, 2 vols
(1948; repr. London : Rupert Hart-Davis, 1963). This edition
contains biographical material, and an individual introduction
for each novel.
*Novels of Thomas Love Peacock* with an introduction by J. B.
Priestley and notes by Barbara Lloyd Evans (London : Pan
Books, 1967). This contains three of the satirical novels
(*Headlong Hall, Nightmare Abbey* and *Crotchet Castle*) plus
*The Misfortunes of Elphin* (1829).


Apart from those represented in this collection, the following books
and articles are relevant and useful :


BOOKS

A. H. Able, *George Meredith and Thomas Love Peacock: A Study
in Literary Influence* (Philadelphia : University of Pennsylvania,
1933).
H. F. B. Brett-Smith and C. E. Jones (eds), *Works of Thomas Love
Peacock*, 10 vols (London and New York, 1924–34; repr.
1968). Vol. 1 contains a very valuable biographical introduction noting contemporary opinion of Peacock, and a bibliography, pp. 167–86.
K. N. Cameron (ed.), *Shelley and his Circle, 1773–1822*, 2 vols
(Cambridge, Mass., 1961). Vol. 1 contains useful biographical
and critical information.
O. W. Campbell, *Shelley and the Unromantics* (London : Methuen,
1923; 2nd ed. 1924; repr. New York, 1966).
H. N. Fairchild, *The Noble Savage: A Study in Romantic Natura-
lism* (New York : Columbia University Press, 1928).
Ian Jack, *English Literature, 1815–1832* (Oxford University Press,
1963). Sets Peacock in the context of traditional literary
history.

Diane Johnson, *The True History of the First Mrs. Meredith &*
*Other Lesser Lives* (London : Heinemann, 1973). Exploratory,
part-fictional biography of Mary Ann, Peacock's daughter and
Meredith's wife; good on Peacock's attitudes to women (and
his interest in cookery).

J. B. Priestley, *English Comic Characters* (London : John Lane,
1925; repr. The Bodley Head, 1963).

J. I. M. Stewart, *Thomas Love Peacock* (Writers & Their Work
No. 156, London : Longmans, Green & Co., 1963).


ARTICLES


R. W. Chapman, 'Thomas Love Peacock', *Saturday Review of*
*Literature*, I (1925) 685–6.

Humphry House, 'The Works of Peacock', the *Listener*, XLII
(8 December 1949) 997–8.

G. D. Klingopulos, 'The Spirit of the Age in Prose', in *From*
*Blake to Byron*, vol. v of *A Guide to English Literature*, ed.
Boris Ford (Harmondsworth : Penguin, 1957).

Walter Raleigh, 'Lecture Notes on Thomas Love Peacock', in *On*
*Writing and Writers* (London : Edward Arnold, 1926) pp.
151–4.

Bill Read, 'Thomas Love Peacock : An Enumerative Bibliography,
Part II', *Bulletin of Bibliography*, XXIV 3 (1964) 70–2; 4
(1964) 88–91. An indispensable checklist of works about
Peacock.

Pauline Salz, 'Peacock's Use of Music in his Novels', *Journal of*
*English and Germanic Philology*, LIV (1955) 370–9.

# NOTES ON CONTRIBUTORS

OLWEN W. CAMPBELL: Author of *Shelley and the Unromantics* (1923; 2nd ed. 1924; rep. New York, 1966) and of *Thomas Love Peacock* (1953).

CARL DAWSON: Assistant Professor of English Literature, University of California at Berkeley. His publications include *Thomas Love Peacock* (1968) and *His Fine Wit: A Study of Thomas Love Peacock* (1970); and he has edited the 'Critical Heritage' volume on *Matthew Arnold: The Poetry* (1973).

JOHN W. DRAPER: Emeritus Professor of English Literature, University of West Virginia. His publications include *Funeral Elegy and the Rise of English Romanticism* (1929; rep. 1967), *Eighteenth-Century English Aesthetics* (1931; repr. 1967) and studies on Shakespeare.

A. E. DYSON: Senior Lecturer in English Studies, University of East Anglia; in 1976 Visiting Professor at the University of Connecticut. Co-editor of the *Critical Quarterly* and general editor of the Casebook series, his publications include *The Crazy Fabric: Essays in Irony* (1965) and (with Julian Lovelock) *Masterful Images: English Poetry from Metaphysicals to Romantics* (1976).

A. MARTIN FREEMAN: Author of *Thomas Love Peacock: A Critical Study* (1911) and editor of *Vanessa and Her Correspondence with Jonathan Swift* (1921).

NORTHROP FRYE: Professor of English, University of Toronto. His publications include *The Anatomy of Criticism* (1957), books and essays on Shakespeare, Milton and Blake, and studies of romanticism and the social context of literature.

L. CONRAD HARTLEY (died 1941): A Manchester businessman with literary interests, his publications included essays in the *Manchester Quarterly* on Peacock, Francis Thompson and Alexander Smith.

ALDOUS HUXLEY (1894–1963) : Novelist and essayist.

LIONEL MADDEN : Senior Lecturer, College of Librarianship, Aberystwyth. His publications include *Thomas Love Peacock* (1967), *How to Find Out About the Victorian Period* (1971) and edited collections on Robert Southey (1972) and Sir Charles Tennyson (1973).

JEAN-JACQUES MAYOUX : French writer on literature and the arts. His studies in English literature include *Melville, par lui-même* and *Vivants Piliers: Le roman anglo-saxon et les symboles.*

HOWARD W. MILLS : Senior Lecturer in English and American Literature, University of Kent at Canterbury. His publications include *Peacock, His Circle and His Age* (1968), and he has edited Peacock's *Memoirs of Shelley, and Other Essays and Reviews* (1970).

MARIO PRAZ : Italian critic and literary historian. His publications include *The Romantic Agony* (English trans. 1951), *The Hero in Eclipse in Victorian Fiction* (English trans. 1956) and *Studies in Seventeenth-Century Imagery* (1964).

J. B. PRIESTLEY : Novelist and essayist. His critical studies include *Literature and Western Man* (1962), *English Comic Characters* (1963) and *Art of the Dramatist* (1973).

CARL VAN DOREN (1885–1950) : American man of letters, author of several literary and historical biographies.

VIRGINIA WOOLF (died 1941) : Novelist and critic, author of the two volumes of *The Common Reader.*

# INDEX

*Note.* References to Peacock are not included, nor are the titles of novels and the names of characters when they are simply mentioned in passing and not made the subject of comment.

**BIR**

If